THE LANCASTER PLAYS

In memory of my son, Gareth,
who was with me when these plays came to pass.

David Pownall

THE LANCASTER PLAYS

GAUNT
LILE JIMMY WILLIAMSON
BUCK RUXTON
A TALE OF TWO TOWN HALLS

OBERON BOOKS
LONDON

First published in 2006 by Oberon Books Ltd

521 Caledonian Road, London N7 9RH

Tel: 020 7607 3637 / Fax: 020 7607 3629

e-mail: info@oberonbooks.com

www.oberonbooks.com

A catalogue record for this book is available from the British Library.

ISBN: 1 84002 644 8

Cover design: Andrzej Klimowski

Typography: Jeff Willis

Contents

Introduction

THE FOUR PLAYS in this book were written thirty years ago. From 1971 to 1976 I was resident playwright at the Duke's Playhouse in Lancaster. At the time I was a newcomer to the English stage, relatively unknown outside the north, except as an author of fiction and radio plays. Returning from Africa in 1969 to write for a living on the strength of a handful of early short pieces and one Cowardian comedy seen only on the Zambian Copperbelt, by the beginning of this period I had only one professional stage comedy to my credit, produced, on tour in the north-west – *How To Grow A Guerrilla,* template for all highly improbable dramas about large-scale clandestine cultivation of marijuana. Local councils threatened to cut off funding. *The News of the World* reported it was impossible to get a ticket. As a result, an impresario drove all the way up from London to check out its commercial viability. As the play was being performed in a mobile theatre in a municipal car park in Preston, his Rolls-Royce had to be slowly edged through a narrow entrance guarded by an automatic barrier. The car was so long, the chauffeur so careful, the pole descended on the vehicle before it got through. The impresario didn't enjoy the show either.

The 330-seat Duke's Playhouse, Lancaster's new repertory theatre, included a studio. The building was a conversion from an eighteenth-century church in the town centre. It opened in November 1971, brain-child of the Town Clerk and the general manager of the Century touring mobile theatre. Since the demise of Lancaster's repertory stage in the 1950s, the mobile had provided the only live theatre for the town, a three-week run of 3/4 plays. The old Century vehicles and machinery were on their last legs (though lovingly kept alive by amateur enthusiasts elsewhere for another decade), and the Arts Council had become impatient with the heavy repair costs. The town did have a fine, commodious nineteenth-century playhouse, the Grand, which belonged to an amateur group. The University of Lancaster Theatre Department also possessed a very good stage. That meant Lancaster, a town of 50,000, now had four theatres.

At a time when the Labour government was determined to revive professional theatre in the regions as part of its culture policy, Lancaster seemed a good prospect. It had been in the economic doldrums but there were signs it was waking up. An extensive audience watershed from mid-Lancashire in the south to Cumbria and far west Yorkshire in the north was in place. There were plenty of theatreless towns within easy striking distance. In the summer there were plenty of tourists seeking entertainment.

The problem was the people of Lancaster. As the first publicity officer as well as resident writer of the new building, one who spent much time asking residents, shopkeepers and publicans to put up posters, I had to report to the management that the preferred option of the population was life without a resurrected repertory. We don't need one, they said. We've got the telly. We've got the amateurs for the pantomime. We've got shows galore in Morecambe and Blackpool on the doorstep. Besides, we don't like what you're doing.

The first Artistic Director was a Yorkshire-born Australian, Peter Oyston. His declared credo was never to give the English what they want because it's bad for them. The new theatre opened with *Moby Dick Rehearsed,* by Orson Welles, followed by *Under the Sycamore Tree* by Samuel Spewack (a play about ants).

The audience figures were disastrous. At a management crisis meeting with Andrew Leigh, the administrator, someone said it was fortunate we were on the run-up to Christmas. Punters would come to a traditional pantomime. True to his beliefs, Peter quashed the idea without a second thought. He already knew what he wanted to do – a new kind of nativity play, minus God, that I'd recently outlined to him. Down at the quayside Wagon and Horses, sitting on the grass watching the shrimp boats come up the tidal Lune, we had recently chatted about religion – quite idly, so I'd thought.

I accepted the commission with thanks, although certain it would make our predicament worse. Andrew Leigh resolved my quandary by firing me as publicity officer the same afternoon. I had failed to fill the theatre – always the fault of that unfortunate minion. I sat down to write the play with a mixture of pleasure and foreboding. That it was a blasphemous use of consecrated ground was one of the common criticisms of the new theatre.

Originally I had titled it simply *Lo!* This was scoffed at by the management and I was sent away to find a new one. The replacement must rank as the most off-putting title ever attached to any dramatic work. The opening verse of chapter two of St Luke's gospel reads: 'And it came to pass in those days, that there went out a decree from Caesar Augustus, that *all the world should be taxed.*' My italics give the title used. The box-office figure for the run was nineteen per cent.

The play was condemned from the pulpit by the Roman Catholic bishop. He told the faithful to give the show a miss, but we assumed, out of fairness, he must have been amongst the few who caught it. If he did, he didn't wear his outfit or make himself known.

It was two years before I was let loose again. By this time we had all learnt a few things. After the initial mauling, the choice of plays for the main house tended to be on the conservative side, but I had written a lot of work to get behind the guard of the same audience: late-night variety shows for the studio, street theatre, pub theatre, shopping-precinct theatre, plays for the theatre-in-education team, any kind of theatre anywhere. Peter Oyston threw everything at his disposal into this assault on Lancaster's indifference to our existence. To settle the vexed question of what to do for Christmas that was not the thin end of a Pom-appeasing wedge, I adapted *Beauty and the Beast* into an audience-participation fest (the roaring monster, foully fronded in green plastic, spent a lot of time tearing round the auditorium), and I was able to fulfil an ambition by transforming him into a handsome prince using Pfeffer's Ghost, the classic stage illusion.

What had emerged during this period was a hard-won realisation: what people want and what people are don't have much to do with each other. We are more interested in ourselves than our tastes. In fact, taste is an obstacle to be surmounted, not appeased. If the public can identify with the subject of a play, there are freedoms to be found within.

The many-pronged approach using every available form of theatre to get under the skin of Lancaster also taught us something: people enjoy being approached by theatre rather than having to approach it themselves.

But the search for new main stage audiences ends up with the same faces – those who like to see live actors being put to the test, talking dialogue on a stage, creating a character, making a play work. No matter how wide you open the door, how loudly the welcomes are shouted, how much press publicity is drummed up, it is these *aficionados* who will do the trick. Referral, passing on the good word to the non theatre-goer, a play comes from within what they know, touches their history, creates a viable chance newcomers will cross the threshold.

Lancaster is dominated by a castle, a grim pile built and maintained by the dukes of Lancaster, still used as a Grade B prison. The Crown court was held in its environs. John of Gaunt was someone known to all. A pub with his name was a well known hang-out. After writing two comic novels set in Africa peopled by mad autocrats, sycophants and unwilling revolutionaries, medieval history was natural territory; a time when order and the operation of hierarchy could be seen clear as clockwork through disorder. Behind the fourteenth-century originator of England's blood line of monarchs and his racketeering world stood Shakespeare. Yes, the Lancastrian knew his Shakespeare. There was also a pub called after him.

Peter Oyston had a gift for bringing life and energy out of a young company – and they were a multi-talented lot, a dozen actors who were also singers, instrumentalists and dancers. Everything I had seen them do in the outreach work had to be in *Gaunt,* somehow. The script was enormously over-written, the issues underlined several times. Going over it a generation later, an old man revising a young man's work, I see how hard I must have pressed to keep the undoable alive, the excess in place.

For anyone who remembers these plays and notices the reshaping, I'm sorry historical authenticity has been traduced. I just couldn't let the embarrassment ride.

I remember wondering after one dispute (the actors were probably pleading as well as arguing) whether I should cut through all the interference and demand to direct it myself. Mercifully, and surprisingly, I found enough good sense not to make the suggestion. Writers can only direct their own work successfully if they and the script are faultless, which can never be the case, except in a sycophantasy.

With a company of lively actors and composer Stephen Boxer's Middle-Ages melodiousness, driven forward by the director's wholehearted passion, *Gaunt* the republican polemical musical mystery play worked as well as the other standard pieces we had been producing, running in at about fifty per cent. We were heartened to learn the Lancaster audience would come to see a new piece on the main stage, and laugh at the bull-baiting of a legend.

When we discussed the commission for the play, Peter asked for a strong musical element. He had directed *How To Grow A Guerrilla* in the mobile on tour in 1971 and harked back to the way a particular scene worked. The play was not written for the company and had four less characters than the number of actors in the group. Peter asked me to write an extra scene especially for the surplus. He detailed John Adams, his associate director, fresh from the Traverse, Edinburgh, to direct it. We instinctively saw eye to eye, recognising we shared a similar sense of humour (with interesting variations). And he breathed music.

The plot of *How To Grow A Guerrilla* was tortuous. To think about altering it so the four characters could be properly incorporated was a nightmare. I took the easy way out and created what was effectively an entr'acte musical show. The Smoke-Cats, way-out hipsters on the road, arrive at a market garden looking for grass. In the double-entendre confusion, the felonious, pot-growing owner is terrified, thinking they may be police spies. There is much extended word-play, exchanges of mutual misunderstanding, then the four punning potheads break into a totally unrelated song: *I'm The Bread-Man For My Baby,* and shuffle off in four-part harmony.

It was the high point of the show. The renegade nun living in the attic didn't get a look in. The screaming psychotic in his jungle den amongst the marijuana plants was forgotten. Even if we were playing to an audience of forty sheepmen in a field in West Cumbria, there was a round of applause as the Smoke-Cats sashayed off singing their anthem. Peter was looking for the same impact in *Gaunt.* I pointed out that although medieval market gardens must have existed in some form, we were in very different territory. This play was set in Purgatory and a special theatre dimension where Time was compressed. And where would we find enough rebecs, shawms and portable organs? His reply was an Oznian simplicitude. Dave, just go for it.

The *Gaunt* cartoon blend of drama, song and dance and musical accompaniment performed by actors rather than singers and instrumentalists interested me, and them. First, they loved to be called upon to do this kind of work, for which they had been trained at drama school; second, the audience approved the live performance of music, preferring it to fake-playing, which is as unconvincing as on-stage as sex. *Gaunt* was the beginning of my attachment to music as part of playwrighting, both in practice and as a subject. Since 1973, when the play was performed, of the 26 stage plays I have written, more than half have had a musical element either in performance content or subject matter.

It was a year and a half before the main stage was mine again. In this time I settled deeper into the town and got to know quite a few local people – some of them important networkers: Hedric Tyson, second-hand bookseller and coffee-bar owner (drugs in the cappuccino in the Sixties 'Where would I get the money to do that?'), Les Fisher, the publican at the Wagon and Horses (décor unchanged since 1918) and Arthur Thompson, the photographer who seemed to have taken pictures at everyone's baptism over the last hundred years. Because they were so well-known, and people knew their connections, through them came audience feedback. It arrived in imperative spurts, which is very northern, usually on the theme: what those buggers want to do is knock together a play about...

While writing a novel, I listened to a lapping shorewash of suggestions. Two names kept coming up. From the frequency with which they were mentioned, I could judge both were lodged deep in local folklore, both still capable of provoking opposed opinions about the fundamental character of the town itself. As might be expected, these opinions divided on roughly political lines, but the actual mix was much more complex. Lancaster was a mill town with a royal name and tradition – both these elements profoundly conservative. In addition, it was a place of incarceration (the prison), and mental healing (two enormous county mental hospitals), a market town, a new university town, and linked directly to the sea and Morecambe (with its own peculiar resonances) by the river estuary. Out of this conservative, liberal, socialist amalgam (it had occasionally fielded a Labour M.P.), two stories had enough muscle to push themselves forward, elbowing the rest aside.

Lile Jimmy Williamson was a powerful ghost in Lancaster. The reason why the tobacco-stained décor of the Wagon and Horses was stuck in the Twenties was this man. The colour of the whippet-room ceiling was his hey-day complexion. Ancient Sniggy Bill with his enormous flat cap who sat in the corner and put four pints into his eight-stone frame every night claimed time stopped when Lile Jimmy, the lino king, died. All meaning went with him to the grave. Since then, the look of the town had hardly changed. It was still as he had left it – which was only right because he had owned Lancaster, lock, stock and barrel.

Industry was something I understood and had some feeling for, having worked for ten years in between car manufacture at Ford and copper mining in Africa. From the initial sketchy research I did in the afternoons while finishing my novel, I soon discovered the truth behind the claim he had owned the town. There were those still alive who loved him, and those who hated him – both for the same reason, his power.

From the room where I wrote I could see the white dome of the Ashton Memorial (Lile Jimmy's ennoblement name was Baron Ashton) the hugely pretentious building he had erected in 1906 on the town's highest point in order to outdo the castle. Inside it contained nothing but a model of itself. Locally, it was still known as *the structure*, as if the amazement of the lower classes at the egomaniacal squandering of so much money on a folly had restricted their vocabulary *in perpetuum*.

The old stone farmhouse I had bought with Peter Oyston for our two families was on the eastern edge of the town, beside the prison farm, next to the abattoir, near enough to the M6 to hear the hum. We had bought it at auction during the rehearsals for *Gaunt*. The defunct owner was Doctor Walsh, a psychiatrist at the nearby Moor Hospital, a colossal mental institution half a mile away. Walsh had been a noted eccentric, definitely on the side of the insane. From the stories I collected about him the protagonist was constructed to play opposite the lino king – Doctor Loco.

He is of the mad, for the mad, there to represent, articulate, diagnose and set out to cure the mad – an impossible task as anyone mad with success, money or power is, to quote David Mamet, as irredeemably crazy as a shit-house rat.

The structural device employed in *Lile Jimmy Williamson* was a development of what had worked in *Gaunt*. The main character is attended by his foil, or fool – someone in a privileged and protected relationship with the subject, sharing the madness of his power-consciousness first hand. In the case of Gaunt in Purgatory it was his third fool, Heron. He broke his neck doing a somersault when he heard Gaunt was dead, joining him in the afterworld where he guides him through the agony of primogenital infinity. In *Lile Jimmy Williamson* it is Doctor Loco, psychiatrist at the Moor mental hospital, who serves a similar purpose. He has the lino king as his one private patient, guiding him through the suffering of greed, meanness, paranoia and megalomania.

Playwrights mark off their existence by premieres not years. At the end there will be a book-balance between disaster and triumph, if you're lucky. A lot of murk will lie under the mixed reviews in the middle. I knew the play *Lile Jimmy Williamson* would upset some people. I had already received anonymous telephone calls prompted by newspaper interviews. Being condemned from the pulpit and having my first two novels banned in South Africa and Rhodesia had not upset me unduly – but this was different. I would be coming face to face with the people I antagonised. I knew it mattered to them, for and against, because that was how the play originated – in their feelings and memories.

The play was written with two Lile Jimmy characters – one the tight-fisted, lunatic despot of 1928 challenging Lloyd George, the other, a good man, a model liberal employer being progressively corrupted over forty years from within the flaws of his nature. Verses of a ballad sung by a worker marked the in and out of the time scheme. Instead of having two actors to make this work, Peter Oyston gave both parts to Robert McIntosh, a clever actor with a flair for comic timing. I saw the advantage in keeping potential confusion to a minimum but honestly did not believe any performer could be that flexible without the show collapsing into a hat-dance.

With Peter's ozoptimism firmly pushed aside I watched the first set of scene time exchanges work in front of an audience. Robert McIntosh was in complete control of the audience, as Lile Jimmy had been in complete control of the town. This left me with one major anxiety – the end. Lloyd George comes to Lancaster to destroy Lile Jimmy's power, which he does in a single speech. In the tradition of the House of Commons, he is to dine with his victim, who, in his bitter wheelchaired loneliness, in spite of his annihilation, is looking forward to talking over old times. Lloyd George cries off and goes back to London. To keep his patient happy, Doctor Loco rustles up a replacement dinner guest. He brings on a skeleton in an identical wheelchair and leaves them staring at each other.

I will never forget my fear as the lights faded to blackout at the end of the play. There was a long silence in the complete darkness. Typically, you've overdone it, said an inner voice. Then the applause started. It was not polite, or restrained. There was a full sense of release – a feeling the drama was worth the audience. The play sold out for the entire run.

The second story, a notorious double murder, was brought to me with a rigorous extension of the northern imperative, *what you want to do,* into *what you <u>must</u> do.* Where *Lile Jimmy Williamson* ended in period, this legend began. Buck Ruxton, a Parsi Indian, was a very popular GP amongst the working people in Lancaster in the early Thirties when there was no Asian community. Ambitious to be accepted in the ranks of the middle-class professionals, he found himself a victim of his wife's infidelity with men of that class, who held him in contempt. He killed her and the children's maid, cut them into small pieces and scattered them over a hillside on the road to Edinburgh. He was tried and executed at Strangeways, Manchester, in 1936.

Once again, the feelings aroused by the story were polarised. Buck Ruxton was hated and loved. There were those who would cheerfully have operated the gallows and those who considered his execution a national disgrace. After reading a detailed physical account of what he had done – an astonishingly barbaric and terrible crime, and there was no doubt of his guilt *at all* – I was at a loss to understand where all the sympathy had come from. But the voices in my ear saying 'write this play' were on his side. The other side had already been given their satisfaction by Albert Pierrepoint, the public hangman.

For an Indian to attract such affection in a tough northern town in the middle of the Great Depression with Gandhi actively trying to bring down the Raj was no mean achievement. For this Bombay doctor's cause to be still alive forty years later on, not because he was innocent, but because he had such reason to kill he was virtually guiltless, was a bizarre concept. But I needed facts, research material beyond the trial, which was dominated by his Not Guilty plea, which was as sad as it was outlandish.

I was contacted by a woman in Preston who had been a secretary for one of the solicitors on the case. She had gathered together all the newspaper clippings of the time. Unreliable and erroneous as the Press consistently is over emotional issues containing great drama such as capital punishment, the huge national scope of the case was all there, plus scores of comments and interviews from Lancaster residents. The town was more the focus of attention then than at any other time. The burning of the Lancashire witches on the moor was a sideshow compared to this.

People contacted me privately. It was eerie to listen to forty-year old gossip. A retired policeman showed me a dossier of statements he had purloined for a memento when a sub-police station was closed down. Before he would let me read the documents he said I must promise not to use the information. I knew there was no point in asking what the purpose was in showing them to me. It was to assuage his own guilt as part of the collective guilt. He hoped something would creep into the play, without attribution. A balance might be restored. Day by day I was being dragged back into 1936. If you have a Tardis, this is not a period to visit for pleasure.

We judge other times too harshly, taking a moral attitude because a discernible pattern of right and wrong has been established. People have been capable of greater humanity than ours – often mysteriously. As I uncovered the cause of the profound disquiet and resentment over Buck Ruxton's death, I kept harking back to a visit I'd made to the hospice of John of God to see a very, very old man – Doctor Dixon, the

Roman Catholic organist and choirmaster who had played at the reception when Lile Jimmy's new town hall was opened in 1910. In his high-heels, women's clothes, rings through his nose, ears, nipples, navel and, it was rumoured, foreskin, he was known to everyone, a living transvestite legend lodged close to the heart of the gritty Protestant north. In a very light whisper he told me how so many glasses of port were sent up to the organ loft during the town hall reception he decided to play a composition of his own called *The Storm* at full blast, and had to be forcibly removed.

Buck Ruxton, Doctor Dixon, and all the others whose stories supersede our latent prejudices, have the effect of reducing pessimism. Although the play I wrote about the murders gave me the only depression of my life so far, the gains were considerable. Following on the premiere of *Lile Jimmy Williamson* in February, *Buck Ruxton* opened in November the same year. By this time Peter Oyston had returned to Australia – to everyone's regret – and John Blackmore had become Artistic Director. He took over the new play with real confidence and imagination, for which I was grateful. In the final week of rehearsals my anxieties lessened. The casting worked. Stephen Boxer and Fiona Victory were in firm control of the unhappy couple. There had been no anonymous calls. People seemed to know what the play was for – to let something out into the air. In that year, 1975, the theatre had become a part of the town's psyche.

Buck Ruxton had children who were taken into care then adopted after his execution. From family photographs one could see he was a good-looking man and his daughter an attractive little girl. On the opening night a tall, beautiful, big-eyed woman in her fifties wearing a sari, entered the foyer alone. She picked up her ticket at the box office and stood by herself, very straight, waiting for the auditorium doors to open. Everyone in the foyer noticed her.

Whether she was Buck Ruxton's daughter or not, I don't know, but she might just as well have been for the effect it had on me. In a full house she was an audience of one, unpleasable. How could I ever get the story right for her? If Buck was her father and this travesty (all plays are travesties of the literal truth) was claiming to be his life, and she knew who she was, then her experience in the theatre that night was beyond my control or understanding. However, at the end of the play, the moment of release came. The folklore was replaced by the catharsis. Buck Ruxton came out of his quicklime grave, guilty and not guilty, sane then insane with jealousy and religious righteousness. Life supervened law and madness. The show sold out.

In the nine months between *Lile Jimmy Williamson* and *Buck Ruxton* other forces began to make themselves felt in my writing life. I knew the intense relationship with Lancaster had only a little time left to run. There was pressure to expand and extend. In four years I had worked with a number of actors. One of them, Christopher Crooks, who had played Herod in the godless nativity play and stole the show – even the goat deciding to ravish the donkey in the stable scene couldn't upstage him – rang me up. He was out of work. 'If you think I'm such a good actor,' he said, 'why don't you do something about it? Write me a play.' The upshot was a solo piece, *Crates On Barrels,* premiered at the Edinburgh Festival that year, the first Paines Plough play of many, directed by John Adams of *Smoke Cats* fame.

This period is a blur of work in remembrance. I was writing *Music to Murder By* for Paines Plough while I was writing my last play for Lancaster, as well as a novel. *A Tale of Two Town Halls* did not emerge from any psychic reservoir. People had suggested municipal small-time corruption as a subject but it was better served by soaps. The new play was written as a satire on the mix of municipal politics. Its targets included Freemasonry, Britain's economic desperation at the time of the IMF crisis, EEC bland cultural winsomeness and the takeover of the conscience of subsidised theatre by the naive Left. This final target was attacked by means of smoke and mirrors. It had to be because the satire was against the hold the Workers Revolutionary Party had over Duke's Playhouse acting company. The subjects of the satire – the activists, new arrivals – had to appear in the play in roles presenting a comic interpretation of secret-cell revolution. Because the theatre and the town had got so close I didn't feel it was an in-house piece. Had I posted the target up, the powers of political correctness would have snuffed the play out before it even got started.

I was lucky in having John Blackmore to direct this piece. He was politically alert, but no dogmatist. He concentrated hard on the entertainment, leaving the polemical arena to sort itself out. He knew what the play was designed to do. A powerful, pugnacious actor can make a meal of an idea as well as a part. (He also does very well as an evangelist. Christopher Crooks, my Herod and Crates the Cynic, became dean of a bible college on top of a mountain in Australia. He was venerated by students from all over the world. When I visited him, he stood up at dinner and warned everyone not to listen to anything I said.) As rehearsals for *A Tale of Two Town Halls* progressed, the WRP men began to get annoyed, in concert. They insisted the political message in the play was to undermine the whole programme of socialism – a cynical misuse of theatre by an essentially Tory mind. If revolution was to be on the stage it should be the classic model. We were perverting Marx for reactionary purposes.

There were magnificent stand-up rows on the rehearsal floor. John Blackmore was caught between the two factions, if a writer constitutes a faction (he probably does). As a man with a show to get on, there was nowhere for the director to go. He couldn't take sides. My case was simple – it's only a play, and a comic one at that. Marx need not turn in his grave, the Grand Masters of the Lodge are safe in their mystery. We won't change or damage anything with a mere play. I suppose I was waiting for the strike. I would have enjoyed the experience, having been through many in the car and mining industry. But the showdown never came. All that mattered was the dialectic, the exchange.

The WRP activists were the stars of the show. The play came and went, as all plays do. In spite of my malfeasance, revolution kept both its classic and comic lines. I look back upon the production with affection. My favourite memory is of the lead – a genial, knotty left-winger struggling to stay on the fringe of the row – losing his cool in a very creative way. Impatient with yet another ding-dong on theory, he broke a rehearsal block by taking down his trousers and singing a Wagnerian aria. At the time it was intended as an insult to the looseness of the scene, and the writing, but the effect was to make it all work. The actor, the man, and his character could sing. If it works, keep it in. As for insults, theatre is an insult to reality but a compliment to life.

The mid-Seventies was a golden age – with a dark lining. For ten years it had been the will of the elected government that live theatre should thrive *everywhere*. The thinking was: the stage is a right, an altar and a platform, a connection with a powerful past, an antidote to blandness, pap and adverts. We need it as much as we need television, probably more. Look at the CVs of writers, directors and actors at this time. It was not uncommon for people in the profession – against the advice of their London agents – to gladly spend three years with a regional company.

From the vantage-point of 2005 this naivety is embarrassing. When Margaret Thatcher turned on the subsidised theatre and set about punishing it for becoming socialism's cut-throat razor, we all felt the brutal effect. Our culture can be controlled by those in power, if they choose to be bothered. In general, politicians know that people don't vote because of what they see on the stage. Only extreme, oppressive governments demand complete authority. Good intentions were at the bottom of the revitalisation of live theatre. But there was a price to pay for the 1970s *mésalliance* between the subsidised stage and socialism, journalism and tertiary education. The misshapen dwarf, Right On Baby was born. It kicked imagination out of the pram.

However, a time of hope is not to be put aside so easily. If governments can have such powerful effects on theatre, a future one might decide to revive the working model of the Seventies. There is no reason why not. The organisational forms theatre can take are very limited. The wheel may be coming round to the same point where this introduction started. There are signs the residential company ideal is breaking out in the regions again. History is behind it.

David Pownall, 2005

GAUNT

Characters

In Purgatory, the place of eyes

JOHN OF GAUNT, Duke of Lancaster

HERON, his third fool

In historical time

The House of Lancaster

HENRY 4, Gaunt's son

HENRY 5, Gaunt's grandson

HENRY 6, Gaunt's great-grandson

HENRY 7, Gaunt's great-great-grandson

GLOUCESTER, Protector of Henry 6

BEAUFORT, a cardinal

SUFFOLK

The House of York

EDWARD 4

RICHARD 3

Richard, Duke of YORK

QUEEN, wife of all the kings

The Church

SCROOP, Archbishop of York

PRIEST

Commoners

HEADS, an executioner

LOLLARD, a follower of Wycliffe

PENY, a speechwriter

DAUNSE, a macabre man

FLY-AWAY, an old soldier

SUNSHINE, a whore

Set in England, France and Purgatory 1399–1485

Gaunt was first performed at the Duke's Playhouse, Lancaster on 28 February 1973, with the following cast:

GAUNT, Michael David

HERON, William Zappa

HENRY 4, RICHARD 3 & BEAUFORT, Ben Cross

HENRY 5, EDWARD 4 & SUFFOLK, Michael Melia

HENRY 6 & 7, Stephen Boxer

GLOUCESTER, SCROOP & PRIEST, Alan Collins

QUEEN, Celia Gregory

HEADS, John Cording

PENY, Stephen McKenna

DAUNSE, John Golder

FLY-AWAY & LOLLARD, Charles Haggith

SUNSHINE, Christine Noonan

Director, Peter Oyston

Designer, Russell Craig

Music, Stephen Boxer

ACT ONE

Blackout and silence. After five seconds, clank of gigantic bolt, scream of stiff hinges. Unintelligible muttering, whispers and sighs.

GAUNT: Hello? Hello?
> (*A scuffle followed by a loud shout of fear. A snarl of indignation, a giggle, a whoop. Hinges scream again and massive door crashes shut. Bolt clanks as it is shot home.*
> *Pause.*)

Here! Don't go away!
> (*Shaking of many tiny bells.*
> *Thudding of soft clad feet.*
> *Into the first patch of misty light bounds HERON, the fool, in motley, jacket hung with bells.*
> *He is shaking with excitement.*)
> (*Still unseen.*) Don't leave me!

HERON: What a ride that was! Whoosh, and you're gone!
> (*GAUNT enters in a white shroud. He stands uncertainly on the edge of the light, shielding his eyes.*)

GAUNT: Don't go running off and leaving me behind.

HERON: You and I are still in touch. That has to be.

GAUNT: The light hurts my eyes.

HERON: We still have our eyes. Did you expect that?

GAUNT: You were trying to desert me.

HERON: (*Taking off his jacket of bells.*) It's warm here. What's a long journey but short? The one we've just taken.

GAUNT: You are bound to me!

HERON: Bound? You do no binding now.
> (*HERON puts his coat down and goes over to GAUNT, pulling him further into the growing light.*)

GAUNT: Take your hands off me!

HERON: Don't hang on to the world. Bondage ends in Purgatory. I feel free – in command.

GAUNT: You babble, as always.

HERON: Death wasn't so bad. Not at all what I'd been led to expect.

GAUNT: Can't remember much. There was a road. I was behind you in the crowd. You were the only one I thought I knew. Then you'd gone!

HERON: Take your time. No need to absorb the changes all at once. When you die you should relax.

GAUNT: No one spoke to me. Why was that?

HERON: They've done something to you. In your prime, you are. They've ironed forty years out of your face.

GAUNT: You may see it but I don't feel it.

HERON: How about me? Have I improved?

GAUNT: I only had a vague idea what you looked like.

HERON: Yes, after all, I was only your third fool. Look! (*Does a cartwheel.*) A long time since I could do that!

GAUNT: So that was death.

HERON: Yes, dear old death. What would we do without it? There'd be nothing to talk about, would there?

GAUNT: I can't get over the way I've been treated.

HERON: Don't worry about it. Probably a mistake.

GAUNT: They spoke to you, but they ignored me.

HERON: Everyone loves a chatterer. Maybe they were in awe of you, a little intimidated.

GAUNT: I looked to be counselled. I offered my ear.

HERON: Who can understand that kind of behaviour? They strike up conversations with a fool…maybe even supply him with inside information and a little useful advice…but a great man, they ignore.

GAUNT: I'm appalled. Someone will pay for this insult.

HERON: (*Leaping in the air.*) Eyes! Eyes! I thought it was bits of quartz or something…a wall.

GAUNT: A deliberate affront! It will not be forgotten.

HERON: (*Looking at the audience and edging frontstage.*) Look at all the eyes!

GAUNT: To be shunned like a leper!

HERON: Borrow my bells? Come and see the eyes!

GAUNT: (*Going back into the darkness upstage.*) John of Gaunt is known everywhere! I'm not staying here. Open up! I demand to be released!

(*HERON runs back for GAUNT and pulls him towards the audience.*)

HERON: You can see yourself in them. Look out there.

GAUNT: (*Resisting.*) What's the matter with these people?
They're disobeying my order! Don't they know who I am?
What they're dealing with?

HERON: You must look at the eyes and be humble. Forget
your power. Accept what has been given you.

GAUNT: They'll hang for this!

HERON: Eyes with necks?

GAUNT: Dragged here, imposed upon! No courtesy, no
manners!

HERON: Be quiet.

GAUNT: What? Don't you dare talk to me like that or I'll
have you flogged. (*Pause.*) You know it's wrong. Why do
you do it? (*Weakly.*) We'll forget it this time but don't do it
again.

HERON: Feel your eyes, man. (*Runs his fingertips over his own
eyes.*) Jellies…more sensitive than any other part, even
your prize genitals – but we'll come to those awe-inspiring
appendages later… Purgatory is a place of eyes – eyes that
know no fear. They cannot be gouged out or burned with
irons in your torture chamber, great John, because this is
THE torture chamber – for the mighty.

GAUNT: You're babbling, fool. I can't be punished by being
made to stand in front of eyes. That's how my life was
lived – in full view. I'm accustomed to it. But where is the
peace that was promised?

HERON: The priests must have got that wrong.

GAUNT: After all that bustle, I end up here with my third
fool! That's what I call unjust.

HERON: Demeaning for the fourth son of a king! (*Laughs and
circles GAUNT.*) Let's get down to business. That death-bed
speech…we can't let you get away with it.

GAUNT: You weren't there. It was a good speech…a very
good speech.

HERON: The eyes see all, remember? Be careful. They know
you had that speech ready to hand in your bedside cabinet
for ages.

GAUNT: I was advised to be prepared in case I became
incoherent. There was a lot I wanted to get off my chest

at exactly the time people would be paying maximum attention. England! Sceptred isle…seat of Mars…this precious stone set in a silver sea…other Eden, demi-paradise.

HERON: You never meant a word of it.

GAUNT: I did.

HERON: We know the background.

GAUNT: It was heartfelt.

HERON: You remember when you had that first bad stroke and they put you by the open window all the summer, and the priests came to remind you of death and we, your fools, to remind you of life?

GAUNT: I remember some of your jokes. They were as old as the hills.

HERON: You sent for that man. He sat with you for a week scribbling, eating and drinking everything he could, pestering the chambermaids. He was a charlatan. He said he could see into the future.

GAUNT: There are always plenty of those around.

HERON: The two of you were putting together that speech. He did such a good job they say it will be the model for all death-bed speeches for centuries to come.

GAUNT: Those were my personal thoughts passed through a professional. I wanted to help King Richard before I went, effete wretch that he is, and show him the error of his ways. I wanted to teach him to love England as she deserves – with manly passion.

HERON: Eyes, our task is hard. Prepare for much embarrassment.

GAUNT: He said there was only one writer threaded through time and he always said the same sort of thing – keep the natural order, do as you're told, don't rock the boat.

HERON: What did you honestly care for this *England?* What is it, anyway?

GAUNT: Ask the English. They looked up to me. They would have died for me.

HERON: As a commander you made them do that often enough. And what a petty autocrat! You destroyed the Good Parliament – the only good parliament anyone ever recalls – you blasted democracy when it was young and tender.

GAUNT: An unworkable heresy.

HERON: D'you remember the night the London mob came after you, screaming for blood? If you hadn't got out the back door, they'd have torn you to pieces. They burned your house down.

GAUNT: And you? Who loved you?

HERON: God has a soft spot for fools.

GAUNT: A monkey could have done your job. How did you get here with me anyway?

HERON: I broke my neck doing a somersault of sheer joy when I heard you were dead.

GAUNT: Envy.

HERON: Is that what it was?

GAUNT: The envy of nothing for something.

HERON: It takes more than that to make an old fool attempt what's out of his range.

GAUNT: I want nothing more to do with you. Leave me alone. I must pray. (*Kneels down, head lowered as HERON skips round him.*)

HERON: Not sure prayers work in Purgatory. All that phase is over. The sentence has been passed. (*Pause.*) Here we have the reduction – power on its knees. Diplomat disasterous, scourge of bishops and heretics alike, rabble-rouser, adulterer, whoremaster, archetype of the grasping, rack-renting, tenant screwing, droit-de-seigneur demanding, absentee landlord of a thousand manors. He had more castles than fingers. Enjoyer of countless church benefices, this pillar of Satan's empire appointed priests and took their income. His orders to his pet prayer-boys were: keep the congregation always helpless on its knees – where we find him now.

GAUNT: Silence! Have you no respect for a man making his peace with God?

HERON: Give God some peace. (*Pause, then to the audience.*) At the age of two he was made Earl of Richmond.

GAUNT: Advanced for my age.

HERON: As a spotty teenager, appointed Lieutenant of Provence.

GAUNT: Beautiful country.

HERON: Which he lost.

GAUNT: That wasn't my fault. Duplicitous French. Irritating Italians.

HERON: Lieutenant of the Scottish Border – that got severely dented.

GAUNT: Impossible people. Rapacious, rancid-minded wild cattle.

HERON: Duke of Acquitaine – lost that.

GAUNT: Everything was made difficult. Reason was unheard of.

HERON: Duke of Gascony – lost again.

GAUNT: Circumstances beyond my control.

HERON: But, putting all this failure and squandering aside, he did manage, by dint of at least one of his weapons that worked, the father of the queens of Spain and Portugal.

GAUNT: A unified Europe was a dream of mine.

HERON: With him ruler of it all. What he couldn't achieve by force of arms – something he wasn't much good at…

GAUNT: (*Jumping to his feet.*) What d'you mean? What about my victories at Najera, Orenna, Pontenedra, Vigo, Bayonne, Ribadare, Brest?

HERON: Skirmishes. (*To the audience.*) He lost all the wars. Leave it to Gaunt. He was a marvellous loser.

GAUNT: He's distorting my record. I had quite a reputation!

HERON: And the money for the campaigns – where did that go?

GAUNT: It was understood we should make a reasonable profit. That's the business of war…how war is run. My expenses were enormous. Imagine running my lands and estates – possessions as big as Wales.

HERON: But never a king.

GAUNT: I was! I was King of Castile!

HERON: No, you weren't. You only said you were.

GAUNT: The Pope said I was! By my marriage to Costanza, daughter of Pedro the Cruel – and was she like her father! – I was the King of Castile.

HERON: Eyes, have pity on this poor man. The nearly-made-it, the on-the-verge-of, trembling-on-the-brink-of, unconsummated king!

GAUNT: (*Stamping his foot.*) I don't care what you say, I was a king! I was! I was!

(*Burst of light. Crash of drums.*
HENRY 4 enters wearing a crown attended by PENY, DAUNSE, SUNSHINE and FLY-AWAY.)
That's Henry, my son! What's he doing wearing the crown?

HERON: He's usurped the throne.

GAUNT: I don't believe it. Henry would never do such a thing.

HERON: Richard, the rightful king is in prison.

GAUNT: (*Horrified, retreating upstage.*) A son of mine to imprison an anointed king? Unthinkable!

HERON: (*Dragging Gaunt back.*) You're not allowed to run away.

GAUNT: I reject this! It's not happening!

HENRY 4: God has changed his agent.

(*The COMMONERS dance around HENRY and sing:*)

COMMONERS: The motion of your limbs
is accompanied by music,
and in your lying down
is the reclining of the mighty sun,
death, I must remind you,
comes even to the monarchy,
but don't let it worry you.
The closing of your eyes
is the shutting of a dungeon door,
the odours of your body
are scents of the nightshade flower,
bankruptcy, I must remind you,
is part of a regal destiny,
but don't let it worry you.
No mouse can build its secret nest
without some hair from your head,
many will lie dead for need of you,
there will be blood on your hands

as flour covers the baker
and wax fills the nails of the candle-stick maker,
but don't let it worry you.
No swallow will leave a chapel roof
without your blessing in its wings,
no virgin marry out of youth
without you handling her ring,
when men say love within your hearing,
they won't mean you but office-bearing,
there'll be a wall, you in the pulpit, us in the stall,
but don't let it worry you.
(*HENRY 4 falls asleep.*
SUNSHINE takes off the crown and puts it at his feet, kisses his forehead.)

SUNSHINE: The king sleeps.

COMMONERS: God save the king...from himself.
(*The COMMONERS exit.*)

HERON: You created your second generation kingdom in bed.

GAUNT: (*Shaken.*) I never taught him this!

HERON: He observed the way you worked. All your eleven children were influenced by dad. Even your bastards are madly ambitious.

GAUNT: No usurper is a son of mine.

HERON: Time is God's theatre, John. He can shorten a scene or give someone a speech a thousand years long. This could last, this drama of your blood.

GAUNT: Let me out of here!

HERON: We've had all our exits. There are only entrances within entrances from now on. Why has your son committed this crime?

GAUNT: He was wronged by King Richard...but this, no, no...he would never go so far.

HERON: You must believe your eyes.

GAUNT: I will never be convinced. It's an hallucination. I've been through a lot lately. (*Pause.*) Oh, this is too much.
I didn't expect to keep my state. That would have been unreasonable. But to be forced to watch this?

HERON: What were they thinking about when your
punishment was designed? How can they get things so
cruelly wrong? (*Stands by HENRY 4, a hand on his head.*)
He did it for you, you realise that? For your thwarted
ambitions.

GAUNT: This is my reward for a life of devoted public
service?

HERON: They've obviously got an odd way of repaying
debts. You kept the afterlife well-supplied with souls during
your time. Without you, they might have had to close the
place down. (*Picks up the crown.*) Now's your chance. Try it
for size.

GAUNT: Never!

HERON: Go on, indulge yourself while I tell you what you've
got to know. Because after that there'll be no interruptions,
and certainly no charity.

GAUNT: I could have been king many times but I chose
to stay loyal...to do my duty...(*Takes the crown and tries it
on.*) See? It's nothing. A mere symbol. What's all the fuss
about? Here, take it away. (*Hands the crown back to HERON.*)

HERON: It's a hard thing for you to be so small.

(*HERON puts the crown back beside HENRY 4. Half asleep,
he gropes around for it, finds it, holds it to his chest, kisses it,
puts it on his head. He claps his hands and the COMMONERS
enter.*)

HENRY 4: If only my dear old dad could see me now.

GAUNT: Evil rogue, I'm ashamed of you!

HENRY 4: I have the crown by right of blood through my
father, John, son of Edward the Third. I'm easy about that.

HERON: He is a simple, graceless, ordinary liar. His untruth
completes your diminishment. John of Gaunt, Duke of
Lancaster, for crimes, sins and wrongs, for bloodiness,
avarice, ambition, for inhumanity, for offences against the
God you claimed as friend and guide, you are doomed to
watch as your descendants rule and ruin your native land.
(*GAUNT cries out as he scrambles away to the rear but HERON
collars him and brings him back. GAUNT stuffs his hands in
his eyes and ears, moaning.*)

GAUNT: Don't do this to me, Jesu. I crusaded for you in the far north! I slew infidel Poles with this hand. Heretics I burned wherever I found them.

HENRY 4: Anyone wish to question my right to the throne?

GAUNT: Yes, by God, I do!

HENRY 4: No protests from the Pope?

PENY: Not a word, sire.

HENRY 4: How about Parliament?

FLY-AWAY: Very quiet, sire.

HENRY 4: Foreign princes? They might feel I've encouraged rebellion, undermined established authority. Anything from them?

DAUNSE: Sire, they really didn't like the boy-kissing, man-sucking, lady-lord, Richard. He was an insult to the very idea of majesty.

HENRY 4: Glad to be rid of him. Is that what you think, Sunshine?

SUNSHINE: He wasn't a real man, sire. Not like you and your father.

(*GAUNT groans.*)

HENRY 4: But I suppose I'll have to do penance. But not too much. Dear Dicky...such a waste of time. Can't imagine who'll miss him.

GAUNT: Well, I suppose it's a fait accompli.

HERON: You didn't have the balls to do what he did.

GAUNT: I had the experience to be a monarch...the know-how.

HERON: The ambition...the vanity...but not the balls.

GAUNT: There was a time when you would never have dared say that to me.

HERON: That time has gone, Johnny.

GAUNT: Johnny? Am I down to Johnny?

HENRY 4: Let me drink! Wine! Wine! We will celebrate the building of the House of Lancaster.

(*DAUNSE flits off and returns with a cup and gives it him.*)

DAUNSE: I heard in the hall, sire, that your rival, King Richard...

HENRY 4: Before you go any further, get it right. He isn't a rival and he isn't a king. He's just, well, what he is.

DAUNSE: Sorry, sire. What I meant to say is the ex-king in prison in Pomfret Castle, has met with an accident.

HENRY 4: Oh, dear. How sad.

DAUNSE: Dead, sire.

HENRY4: Can't be old age. Poisoned? There's a thought. Here, take a sip. (*Makes DAUNSE take a drink of the wine.*) How d'you feel?

DAUNSE: Better than poor Dick. Cold steel did for him, sire. A man called Exton. You've never heard of him.

FLY-AWAY: You've certainly never seen him, or had a word on the side, given him orders.

HENRY 4: Exton? Can't say I can bring him to mind.

DAUNSE: His motive for the murder was some sort of personal frustration with the way things are.

SUNSHINE: He got past the gaolers…somehow. Then got into the cell…it's amazing how he did it… He must be the invisible man.

HENRY 4: Well, no point in going on about it. Dicky was never a very good king. My father cushioned him. In fact my father was the de facto king of England.

COMMONERS: De facto, eh? Hmmmmm.

HENRY: All I've done is given real political substance to a pre-existing but unconfirmed situation.

COMMONERS: Hmmmmmm. Pre-existing and unconfirmed!

HENRY 4: My father did all the fighting and administrative work, the law, the Church, the tax system. In relative terms they'd changed places.

COMMONERS: Relative terms? Hmmmmm. All that stuff.

HENRY 4: The conferences, the diplomacy – my dad did all the work. He was, effectively, the king. Queer Dick, was a parasite on the host body of my pater. Without him, he was nothing.

HERON: Over the door of the seraphims' rest-room we passed on the way here was a sign: Bullshit Baffles Brains. Are you taking all this in?

GAUNT: Don't…don't…my son a regicide…a thief…a liar…

HENRY 4: It would have been nice to have the old man here to see his dream fulfilled. We'll drink to him. To John of Gaunt, founder of a dynasty!
(*HENRY 4 drinks and passes the cup to the COMMONERS.*)

HERON: By having Richard murdered, he showed there was nothing sacred in the person of a king. Now he's got the problem of claiming an exception in his own case.

GAUNT: The king is a man. I always said that. Nothing but a man. It's the idea of kingship that's sacred.

HERON: Back to the seraphims, John.

FLY-AWAY: (*Drinking, then passing the cup round.*) To the destruction of your enemies, sire!

HENRY 4: I'll go along with that.

PENY: To a teeming treasury and a sycophantic Parliament! To the guile of your tax-collectors and the sleight-of-hand of your accountants!

HENRY 4: With you all the way.

DAUNSE: Plague and pestilence pass you by. May you live a long life!

HENRY 4: Amen to that.

SUNSHINE: May you know the love of a good woman and know its worth.

HENRY 4: That I will, sweetheart.
(*Enter the QUEEN in mourning.*)

SUNSHINE: Here's the queen's queen. How sad she looks.

QUEEN: Tidy up after yourself, Henry. You killed my Richard, now kill me.

HENRY 4: Give the poor bitch a king-size pension and lock her up somewhere so she can't spend it.
(*The QUEEN curtsies and exits. DAUNSE follows her, imitating her walk.*)
You shall be my man.

DAUNSE: I am your man already, sire.

HENRY 4: If anyone speaks against me, be my ears.

DAUNSE: They call you Accursed Mole, others call you the Fox. As yet, the people dare not love you.

HENRY 4: Why is that?

DAUNSE: There is an archbishop who says behind his hands that no Christian should love a murdering usurper.

HENRY: Which archbishop? I've only got two.

DAUNSE: Scroop of York.

HENRY 4: (*Calling off.*) Heads!

FLY-AWAY: Trouble coming.

(*Enter HEADS bloody in a leather apron carrying a bucket and a towel. He puts the bucket down, slips the straps of his apron off his shoulders.*)

HEADS: Give me a rub-down, Sunshine.

HENRY 4: Whose blood is that, Heads?

HEADS: God knows. I don't keep track. (*SUNSHINE washes him.*) Gay, gay, gay, gay, think on dreadful doomsday. Don't forget under me arms.

SUNSHINE: Ever done an archbishop before?

HEADS: Nothing's new in this business. Once they're on their knees they're all the same. Gay, gay, gay, gay, think on dreadful doomsday.

SUNSHINE: There's a rebellion. They don't like the new king.

HEADS: What happened to the old one?

(*SUNSHINE draws a finger across her throat.*)

I didn't hear about that. Sounds as if someone's pinching my business. Where's this rebellion then?

SUNSHINE: Up north.

HEADS: There's always a bloody rebellion up north. I spend half my life running up and down the Great North Road. Haven't had a holiday for years.

SUNSHINE: (*Drying him with the towel.*) The archbishop's name is Scroop and he's incredibly old.

HEAD: Then he'll hardly notice, will he?

SUNSHINE: If you dawdle on the way he might die before you get there.

(*HEADS picks up the bucket and towel and wanders over to HENRY 4.*)

HEADS: I charge extra for clergymen. It puts me eternal soul in jeopardy. (*Wanders off and exits.*) Gay, gay, gay, gay, think on dreadful doomsday.

GAUNT: Henry musn't do this. Executing old Scroop will turn the whole of Yorkshire against him.

HERON: Politically inadvisable?

GAUNT: Suicide. (*Goes over to HENRY 4.*) Henry, think again.

HERON: He can't hear you. You're not allowed to interfere. He must make his own mistakes. Isn't this the way you taught him to silence critics?

GAUNT: I would never have considered killing a prince of the Church. Go for the middle orders, perhaps, but not the top.

HERON: Yes, that was always your technique. Remember the lame-brained Irish priest, John Latimer?

GAUNT: Should I?

HERON: He accused you of treason. He was murdered on your orders.

GAUNT: Why should I waste time arguing with every imbecile who raised his voice against me? Get them out of the way.

HERON: Is it any wonder your son uses your methods? Latimer is only one name I've used from a roll-call of hundreds you had assassinated.

GAUNT: Henry! Don't do it. Scroop is a doddery old lunatic. He's not in his right mind and everyone knows it.

HERON: So ancient he's close to the Almighty, and already touched by the divine – so the people believe. I'll tell you what, for the time it takes a lame-brained priest to count his rosary, you may counsel your boy without him knowing it. Enter his mind as a moment of fatherly advice in disguise. (*The thudding of a drum.*

HEADS enters and claps his hands, then exits.

DAUNSE exits and returns with a big Bible.

A pike is thrown to FLY-AWAY. A block is pushed out to PENY.

The scene is set for an execution.

Wringing his hands, GAUNT stands by HENRY 4.)

GAUNT: Henry, this isn't the way to get what you want…

HERON: Quiet! When I'm ready.

(*Axe in hand, HEADS drags on a dummy by the hair, lays it on the block.*

DAUNSE opens the Bible and mumbles. HEADS raises the axe.)

Hold it.

(HEADS is poised with the axe in the air.)

Go ahead. But you haven't got long.

(GAUNT pleads soundlessly in HENRY 4's ear.
HENRY 4 stands as if in deep thought, a finger on his lip.
When GAUNT has finished, HENRY 4 smiles reflectively as if
in a sentimental moment, then shivers.)

HENRY 4: Brrrr. There's a draught. Close all the windows.

HEADS: I'm still stood here waiting.

HENRY 4: Oh, go on. He wants to get to heaven anyway.

(HEADS decapitates the dummy.)

GAUNT: You didn't listen to a word I said! Scroop was a saint to the general public! There'll be miracles at his tomb… tomb? What am I talking about? Shrine!

HERON: Your lad didn't take much notice, did he?

GAUNT: Old Scroop won't be coming here, will he?

HERON: After a lifetime of Christian duty, and a martyrdom, d'you think he'd end up here with you? That's arrogance if you like.

(HEADS and the COMMONERS sing as they clear up after the execution:)

HEADS / COMMONERS:
When nettles in winter bear roses red
and thorns carry figs naturally,
when whitings hunt harts in the nobleman's park
and herrings blow horns for the kill,
when sparrows build churches and raise steeples high
and wrens carry sacks to the mill,
when curlews drape hedges with linen and silk
and sea-mews bring butter to market for sale,
when mice mow the corn with a wave of their tails
and the cock on the dunghill crows Christian mass,
on that day a father is wise to his son.

GAUNT: He'll never get away with it – never be popular. Not that he's got any right to be there at all, but since he is he might as well try to make a success of it.

HERON: The Pope isn't amused.

GAUNT: He should try and keep in with the Pope.

HERON: Especially if needs any bastards legitimizing. If Pope Boniface hadn't given a helping hand, those Beaufort boys of yours would have been out in the cold. Cost you a bit, though.

GAUNT: Parliament declared them legitimate.

HERON: If I'd had a bastard the woman would have been condemned as a whore and the child scorned as an outcast for the rest of its days.

GAUNT: I loved Katherine for twenty-five years.

HERON: Pity you were married to someone else at the time.

GAUNT: That was an arranged marriage. You can't expect politics and love to coincide.

HERON: Who can't?

GAUNT: Not at my level.

HENRY 4: (*To the audience.*) I'm really very sorry for the crimes I've committed. A lot of it can be blamed on my advisers.

DAUNSE: Sire, you have been the best of kings.

HENRY 4: I've written to the Pope to ask for absolution for murdering Dicky and Scroop. I might as well ask him to include usurping the throne and knock that on the head while I'm at it.

(*The QUEEN enters.*)

QUEEN: You're far too impetuous, just like your father.

HENRY 4: Sit with us, wife. (*She sits on his knee.*) My conscience is troubling me.

QUEEN: Your what?

HENRY 4: I keep hearing my father's voice in my head. He could be such an old bore when he wanted to.

GAUNT: Ungrateful, insolent boy!

(*Music. The COMMONERS dance erotically.
During the dance FLY-AWAY slips off.*)

HENRY 4: Your breath is sweeter than balm, sugar or liquorice, true as a turtle or a tree without treason.

DAUNSE: Her fair hair hanging down to her knee. Those rolling eyes which are as glasses clear.

SUNSHINE: Her strawberry lips as sweet as honey. Her soft cheek as comfortable as blossom.

PENYS: Like lavender seeds in a coffer is the perfume of her neck, white as the great whale's bone.

HENRY 4: Mmmm...I was thinking of going on a pilgrimage to Jerusalem.

QUEEN: That's a long way. It's at least a thousand miles.

HENRY 4: I don't think I'll bother.

(*FLY-AWAY enters at the run.*)

FLY-AWAY: Treason! Listen to an old campaigner!

HENRY 4: What is it, soldier?

FLY-AWAY: Old friends make the worst enemies. They know too much.

HENRY 4: Any names?

FLY-AWAY: Even those who helped put you on the throne: Hotspur, Northumberland, Worcester, and the Welsh wizard, Glendower.

HENRY 4: Heads! Heads!

HEADS: (*On entry.*) Whassamarer now?

HENRY 4: To the north!

HEADS: I only just got back!

(*The COMMONERS march and sing with HEADS, HENRY 4 and the QUEEN, HERON behind them copying HENRY's gait.*)

HEADS / COMMONERS:
Thirty-two teeth all sharp and clean
have England's royal king and queen,
bones two hundred and ninety-five
prop up the house till death arrive,
two hundred sixty and seven veins
hold Henry upright while he reigns.

(*Five dummies are thrown on stage. HENRY 4, HEADS, PENY, FLY-AWAY and DAUNSE wrestle with them while the QUEEN and SUNSHINE yell encouragement.*)

HERON: The battle of Shrewsbury!

(*The dummies are dismembered.*
HEADS goes off and returns with a huge brush and sweeps the pieces away.)

HENRY 4: Peace again. How pleasant.

(*SUNSHINE and the QUEEN sing:*)

QUEEN / SUNSHINE: Peace is man's richest possession
and helps him home to heaven,
peace of soul, peace of mind,
peace from plague, peace from war,
my liege lord, hear what I say,
if old wars can be forgotten,
make peace your friend
and God will give you a kingly end.

DAUNSE: War is the mother of all wrongs. It slays the priest
at mass.

FLY-AWAY: War makes cities fall. It overpasses law. Your law,
my lord, the law that is the king's peace.

GAUNT: Listen to him, Henry. That's a good point. When
there's war, law goes out of the window. Settle down…
settle down – consolidate. Take your time.

HENRY 4: From now on we shall be a canny king. Let us all
go home and forget war. Let us brood. Let us rebuild our
consciences. And on our march home let us think of the
people for they are the road on which we travel.

(*They sing a route-march song.*)

HERON: In January, what do we do?

ALL: By this fire I warm my hands.

HERON: In February, whadowedo?

ALL: With my spade I dig my land.

HERON: In March, whadowedo?

ALL: Here I set my trap to spring.

HERON: In April, whadowedo?

ALL: I'm as blithe as bird on bough.

HERON: In May, whadowedo?

ALL: Here I make my chicken-run.

HERON: In June, whadwedo?

ALL: Weed my corn with rake and hoe.

HERON: In July, whadowedo?

ALL: Shear my corn down to the ground.

HERON: In August, whadowedo?

ALL: With my scythe the grass I mow.

HERON: In September, whadowedo?

ALL: With my flail I earn my bread.

HERON: In October, whadowedo?

ALL: Sow my wheat so we'll be fed.

HERON: In November, so whadowedo?

ALL: At Martinmas I kill my swine.

HERON: In December, whadowedo?

ALL: It's Christmas time! I drink red wine.

> (*HENRY 4 sits down, tired. He puts his head in his hands and
> shakes it. He is an older man. During the scene he falls asleep.
> The QUEEN exits with HEADS.
> HERON goes back to GAUNT.*)

HERON: You probably don't remember that natural order of
things.

GAUNT: Don't preach at me. I knew the way people lived. I
shared the same rhythms.

HERON: Are you waking up to your predicament?

GAUNT: It needn't be so bad. Henry is learning.

HERON: I had few sins. All I ever did was make people
laugh. They asked what reward I thought I deserved for
a fairly blameless life. I asked for this – my own back for
having to live under your thumb.

GAUNT: Still the fantasist. Still the joker. You're out of your
depth.

HERON: Don't believe me if you don't want to.

GAUNT: My son has brought stability. People can get on with
their ordinary lives, bring up their families, go to church.

HERON: Ah, church. You cared little for the clergy. But you
had more than a nodding acquaintance with a religious
rebel called Wycliffe. Not that you agreed with his attack
on corruption in the Church – what did you care about
corruption? – but he was useful in disgracing enemies.

GAUNT: Wycliffe made some good points. I went along with
him a little way. (*Pause.*) Now this Henry, this sadder, wiser
man, is a better king than Richard ever was.

HERON: Would Richard not have got sadder and wiser in
his own way? Why should his education in life have been
by-passed? (*Pause.*) Your son is getting old. He's had a few
years of peace but it will be religion that torments him at

the end – your friend Wycliffe on the one side, the Pope on the other.

(*HENRY 4 is woken by FLY-AWAY.*

DAUNSE turns his collar to show a clerical one.

PENY gets the Bible. They stand opposite sides of the stage.)

HENRY 4: What is it?

FLY-AWAY: The disputation, sire. We have two learned men to argue over Christian truths.

HENRY 4: I think I'll go to bed.

FLY-AWAY: The people need your guidance, sire. It's Heresy versus Corruption. Priest-murder and religious riot are getting too frequent.

HENRY 4: God help me, is there no peace?

FLY-AWAY: You did make an appointment with them, sire. The head of state should have these issues at his finger-tips.

HENRY 4: Oh, alright. Carry on, but not too loud. If you see my eyes close I won't be asleep, merely pondering the great questions naturally arising from the discussion. (*Goes back to sleep.*)

(*During the disputation between the PRIEST (Daunse) and the Wycliffian LOLLARD (Peny), HENRY 4 dies.*

FLY-AWAY and SUNSHINE remove him without disturbing the scene.)

PRIEST: The sun is eclipsed in all his twelve points, disfigured by heresy that is ruining our churches.

LOLLARD: You'd be much better off greasing a sheep under the tail and buggering it than putting a strain on your brain with subtle syllogisms.

PRIEST: At the mass Christ's actual flesh is eaten.

LOLLARD: Disdaining cannibalism, Wycliffe says the bread is only symbolic of the divine body.

PRIEST: This is consummate heresy, to be destroyed by fire!

LOLLARD: Cruel, stupid, unlettered priest – when you get a penny for saying mass, are you selling God's flesh for a penny?

PRIEST: If you were merely impertinent, I would forgive you – but your heresy is another matter. It is beyond my power to forgive it.

LOLLARD: Fuck your forgiveness.

PRIEST: You say that, but remember, forgiveness can only be given by a priest, lawfully ordained, a man whose soul has been pricked by the thorn of Christ.

LOLLARD: We know priests are pricks and prick each other as well as perforating little boys.

PRIEST: If Lollardy, your cursed heresy, is allowed to grow, the king will not be pleased. He loves order as God loves order, and it is the Church that controls men's souls while the King has charge of their bodies.

LOLLARD: You talk about bodies a lot, you shameless corrupter of congregations. Is Man not better than a brute beast? Will sheep accept a shepherd no better than the dung they drop?

PRIEST: Priests are chosen for their learning, their Latin and their blameless lives.

LOLLARD: The people have even less Latin than you have, parrot. God lives in England as well as Rome. With us, he speaks our tongue. Or don't you think Almighty God has enough brain to manage that?

PRIEST: The Father, Son and Holy Ghost have no conversation with commoners.

LOLLARD: What makes you believe, shit-ignorant as you are, that a psalm sung by you in a flat key, plus ten shillings, brings a soul out of Hell?

PRIEST: As an ordained priest I have the keys to the Infernal Regions. It is within my competence to rescue the damned.

LOLLARD: For ten shillings? Cheap at the price! You don't give the money to God, or even the Devil. You go off and spend it on whores and ale.

PRIEST: I refuse to debauch the dignity of the Church by talking with you further. We will roast this heresy out of you.

LOLLARD: Tell me, depraved one, why do priests spend all their time kissing the arses of the nobility while the common people are neglected?

(*FLY-AWAY and SUNSHINE return with HENRY 5 in coronation regalia and sit him down. The disputation continues over.*)

PRIEST: God's Church has survived for fourteen hundred years. If Our Lord returned today he would be able to recognise what He made on earth.

LOLLARD: The Pope is anti-Christ, bishops his members, friars his tail.

PRIEST: Lord king Henry, fifth of that name, I appeal to you. Defend the Church!

HENRY 5: Pray for each other, you two, while I ponder about all this.

(*HENRY 5 thinks.*
The PRIEST and the LOLLARD kneel on either side of him and pray.)

HERON: Your grandson. How serious he looks. Anything of yourself there? He was a considerable piss-artist while Prince of Wales, kept bad company as a point of honour, trying to prove that he could be all things to all men. But now he's in the saddle, he's grown up fast. His dad has left him not badly off for money. All he has to do is settle this religious bickering and he could be off to a flying start.

GAUNT: Well, no one can say he's a usurper.

HERON: The sins of the father don't apply?

GAUNT: There's a strong, centralised monarchy in place, thanks to my son.

HERON: Would you like me to whisper some advice from the heart of his people?

GAUNT: Bear in mind, he still has to rule.

HERON: I'll remember.

(*HERON weaves in and out of the spaces between HENRY 5 and the PRIEST and LOLLARD.*)

Noble prince, please God as if He were your people. Sustain right, magnify truth, defer vengeance, give no decisions until you hear both parties, do not encourage favourites. treat reason affectionately…

PRIEST: Your majesty should persecute the Lollard heretics. That way you will be thought religious.

HERON: Be faithful, true and stable.

LOLLARD: Restrict the powers of the Church.

HERON: Be brave, unchangeably honourable, love north and south alike, prefer peace, hate war.

FLY-AWAY: But be good at it, like your father.

(*HENRY 5 fingers the blade of his sword.*)

HERON: Be merciful except to those who pursue their own interests at the expense of the commons. Lightly forgive when you can afford it. Keep your promises. Be generous. Keep the realm intact. Put aside flattery. Treat adulation with scorn. Bring folk together, don't push them apart. Love your kingdom last, your people first. They have to endure as well as love you.

(*HENRY 5 marches off with the COMMONERS, leaving GAUNT and HERON on their level of Purgatory.*)

HENRY 5: Left-right-left-right. Whadowedo? We pick a fight.

HERON: Religion obviously isn't his strong point. The boy's a soldier. Prepare for the worst.

GAUNT: Not necessarily. After ten years of peace, a foreign war works wonders with the people. Get them excited about those lost French provinces. Label all your critics at home traitors. Take credit for the victories. Blame defeats on your commanders. Yes, he's on the right track. This is the king we've been waiting for since my father, great Edward the Third, and my brother the Black Prince, hammered the French into the ground fifty years ago.

HERON: Steady now. Have you forgotten where you are?

GAUNT: Why shouldn't I want him to succeed? He's my blood, my grandson. Isn't that natural? Crecy? Can you take that away from us? Poitiers? The power has returned. We will be fulfilled in this boy.

HERON: You look forward to conquests?

GAUNT: Is any joy greater than victory? If there is, I never knew it.

HERON: You never fought for a foot of the ground you owned. And what you were given, you lost. Your first wife, Blanche of Lancaster brought you the duchy, and died. Costanza brought you Castile.

GAUNT: O, envy, envy, envy – what a poison you are!

HERON: Even your mistress, Katherine Swineford, brought you a lot of country in her womb.

GAUNT: Leave Kate out of this.

HERON: She suffered enough bringing up four little bastards.

GAUNT: She was happy with me. I made her happy for twenty-five years.

HERON: She was a prisoner.

GAUNT: She was not!

HERON: You were the bars on her window and the lock on her door. She was shut up in you and your progeny.

GAUNT: If Kate was my prisoner, we shared a cell. We looked on the world from the same window. What woman would have so many children by a man she didn't love?

HERON: Romance won't save you from my revenge. Here's your grandson again – in top form.

(*HENRY 5 enters armed with HEADS and the COMMONERS.*)

HENRY 5: O Lord, bless our ships, bless our beams, bless our ballast and bless our bulwarks!

ALL: Amen to that.

HENRY 5: Bless our sheets and sails, bless our knots and navigation!

ALL: Amen to that.

HENRY5: Bless our bills and blades, our helms and hauberks, our shafts and string!

ALL: Amen to that.

HENRY 5: Bless our enterprise, bless our empire!

ALL: Amen to that.

GAUNT: This is the man we've been waiting for!

HENRY 5: The breeze has come. We face a long, expensive foreign war. My manpower reserves are very low. I need more soldiers. Women of England, I appeal to you. Do it for me. A foetus for France!

FLY-AWAY: Infants for infantry!

DAUNSE: A one-night stand for the fatherland!

SUNSHINE: For such a star, it's nothing.

(*Music – SUNSHINE is lifted onto the shoulders of the COMMONERS for a patriotic hymn:*)

Women of England, England's ladies,
patriots don't go to Hades,
put chastity and vows aside,
our Henry would through Paris ride.
Women of England, England's treasure,
time to give love its fullest measure,
if husbands fail let others come
so boys can march behind the drum.
Women of England, England's flower,
blossom into your finest hour,
breed men for us to do or die
and we will get back Normandy.
(*SUNSHINE is borne off in triumph.
Lights fade on GAUNT and HERON.*)

End of Act One.

ACT TWO

Lights up on GAUNT and HERON on their level looking down on HEADS and the COMMONERS rolled up in blankets asleep. Weapons are stacked in a pile. It is night. HENRY 5 in armour, reading a document, sits with PENY.

HENRY 5: This is your draft?

PENY: My first attempt, sire. I think you'll like it.

HENRY 5: I'll be the judge of that.

PENYS: What I meant to say was – I hope you'll like it.

HENRY 5: Let's go through the text together. I thought the one you did for me at Harfleur was a bit far-fetched.

PENY: We took the town, sire.

HENRY 5: Strangely enough, I don't think that was entirely due to your rhetoric.

PENY: If my poor work helped to gain one inch of ground…

HENRY 5: Soldiers are simple. One minute you had me telling them to imitate the action of a tiger – a creature none of them has ever clapped eyes on – the next they were supposed to be greyhounds in the slips. You got them confused.

PENY: It's animal imagery, sire. Speech-writers use it all the time – crocodile tears…bear-hug…cat-nap…pig-sick…

HENRY 5: As if you hadn't mixed them up enough, you then had me ordering the poor wretches to be jutty rocks hanging over the sea, brass cannon, and Alexander the Great!

PENYS: Historical allusions underpin authority no end, sire.

HENRY 5: Then I had to tell the men not to dishonour their mothers. In their worst moments, they'd never have contemplated such a thing.

PENY: Perhaps that wasn't clear enough, sire. What I was trying to get over was they shouldn't shame their mothers by being cowards. This is my first experience of writing speeches for war. Up until I now I've been a death-bed man. But this one for tomorrow at Agincourt, sire, is much better. I've learnt from my mistakes.

HENRY 5: It may need a touch of apology. I've seriously under-estimated the French and frankly we haven't got much of a chance. My supply-lines are overstretched. We're outnumbered three to one. We've got hardly any heavy armoured cavalry. Most of my manpower is in archers and you know what they're like.

PENY: Most of them are only here for the wine, sire.

HENRY 5: If they do get an arrow into the air it's as likely to fell a friend as a foe. Ah, well. That's what comes of being in too much of a hurry. If you take the sweepings of knocking-shops and alehouses, what d'you expect? Read me the speech. I'll stop you if there's a point I want explained. Do it with some gestures so I can get an idea how to put it over.

PENY: As you must already be aware, majesty, I write with considerable flair and nuance. Look out for the subtleties.

HENRY 5: Get on with it.

PENY: (*Striking a pose.*) Proclaim it throughout my host that he who hath no stomach for the fight let him depart...

HENRY 5: Are you mad? If they take that seriously I'll be facing the French on my own tomorrow.

PENY: You don't mean it, sire.

HENRY 5: The archers will run all the way back to Calais taking five-barred gates in their stride.

PENY: No sire, they won't. I beg you to hear out this section of the speech then you'll see how the whole thing works.

HENRY: Carry on.

PENY: Let him depart, his passport shall be made and crowns put into his purse...

HENRY: What? Give them money as well? With an offer like that I'd be bankrupted and deserted in five minutes.

PENY: (*Forcefully.*) We would not die in that man's company. (*Pause.*)

HENRY 5: Ahaaa! I catch your drift.

PENY: You have it, sire.

HENRY 5: Could there be a *nuance* to make them understand that anyone shameless enough to accept my insane offer would never get home in one piece?

PENY: I'll see what I can do, sire.

HENRY 5: Go on. Let's have more.

PENY: This day is called the feast of Crispian.

HENRY 5: Who's he?

PENY: Some obscure saint I found in my calendar, sire. He's the patron saint of cobblers.

HENRY 5: Always learning, aren't we?

PENY: He that outlives this day and comes safe home will stand tip-toe when this day is named and rouse him at the name of Crispian...

HENRY 5: A day to remember. Go on.

PENY: He that shall live this day and see old age will yearly on the vigil feast his neighbours and say, 'Tomorrow is Saint Crispian,' then he will strip his sleeve and show his scars and say, 'These wounds I had on Crispin's Day.'

HENRY 5: Hold on, hold on. What is this saint's name? Crispian or Crispin? Make your mind up.

PENY: Actually, sire, it's two people we're dealing with here. The story is they were wandering Roman cobblers who emigrated to France and preached the gospel as a kind of double-act in Soissons.

HENRY 5: I didn't intend to release a torrent of useless information.

PENY: I like to get the background sorted. It's important to me.

HENRY 5: Don't get it. Great-grandfather, King Edward the Third, made a Turkish squaddy called George our patron saint. No complaints from the people. No one asked why. Plenty of local-grown English saints we could have had. Saint Cuthbert, Ethelwold. Now here we go again, taking a couple of Frenchified Italian cobblers on board. Ah, well, you've done your research, I suppose. In the unlikely event of a victory I can get the Church to bump up this Feast of St Crisp and Crackling to be a major festival like Christmas.

PENY: Every year you can get the whole country behind you, sire. On the feast there'll be thousands waiting in droves for your command. They'll fight whoever and whatever you want.

HENRY 5: And that is wherein I sometimes feel guilty.

PENY: Guilty, sire? I don't understand.

HENRY 5: I am their end and their beginning. Creating and destroying are my right and left hands. Why is this so? Because the people are credulous, fearful and idle of mind. They let me rule. Am I worthy? Am I essential? What am I doing to them? Isn't there an alternative system?

GAUNT: Be careful! This speechwriter might seem an ageless genius – he did a good job for me, but he's leading Henry into danger. Bleeding together can't become *being* together. He must keep some distance.

HERON: If he sheds his blood with the common herd the distinguishing line might be lost? We can't have mingling. When a cold stream and a warm ocean meet, the distinction is there in spume on the surface, one side blue, one side grey. For the sake of respect we must keep it that way.

HENRY 5: Why should we be governed at all? Whose idea was it we should suffer this way? What's all this about obedience? Who needs it?

GAUNT: Henry, my boy, shut out such thoughts. Someone must lead.

PENY: Sire, these thoughts are interesting, but not for this time.

HENRY 5: What? Doesn't Sir Nuance know any other way? I thought writers were all about alternatives?

PENY: Will you hear the rest of my speech, sire?

HENRY 5: I can guess the rest. (*Looks at the sleeping COMMONERS.*) I am the end of their world. They must give up the one thing they have for me. Life itself. Why should they? Because I will not run and be sensible? What is it makes me demand this payment? I see no further than my need, and they see no further than the end of my nose.

PENY: You have lost me, sire.

HENRY 5: Then that was well done for you are worth losing. Let's finish your subtle serpent of a speech. (*Takes the paper from PENY and reads.*) This story shall the good man teach his son and Crispin Crispian shall ne'er go by from this day to the ending of the world but we in it shall be remembered...

PENY: Remember*ed*, sire. Put a final stress on the *ed* for the sake of the pentameter.

HENRY 5: On the *ed*. What a mind you have. Let's get this over with before I 'it you on the 'ed! We few, we happy few, we band of brothers, for he today that sheds his blood with me shall be my brother...

PENY: At this point you should weep, sire.

HENRY 5: In front of them?

PENY: Yes, sire. It's important to the orchestration of the build-up.

HENRY 5: If I commit to this treacherous, suicidal sentiment, I'll have to be completely in control. For me to cry would be dangerous.

PENY: You could hold an onion, sire.

HENRY: I'm not standing up in front of my troops holding an onion.

PENY: We need the crescendo, sire. I want you to really let go at the end, give them no option but to be with you one hundred per cent. They should be begging for battle.

HENRY 5: How about this for a crescendo? (*He boxes PENY's ear.*) How much did we agree for this masterpiece?

PENY: Er...ouch, that hurt...let me consult my notebook...

HENRY 5: How about this? (*HENRY 5 kicks PENY all round the stage.*) One for God, one for Harry, one for England, one for St George, one for Crispin, one for Crispian, and one for luck! (*Kicks him off.*) Bring on the Frenchman! (*Drums. Trumpets.*
HEADS and the COMMONERS wake up, grab weapons and run around as if under attack.
PENY wheels on a cartoon of the Devil as a Frenchman, cock in hand, frogs legs sticking out of his mouth, holding a sword with a baby spitted on it.)
Hate him!

SUNSHINE: Murderer! Rapist! Blasphemer! Fiend!

DAUNSE: From the sulphurous anus of Hell he crept!

COMMONERS: Kill! Kill!

HENRY 5: He's all kinds of corruption and foulness!

COMMONERS: Kill! Kill!

HENRY 5: Evil, malice and lies!

COMMONERS: Kill! Kill!

DAUNSE: Deceit, dishonesty, death and damnation!

COMMONERS: Kill! Kill!

HENRY 5: Archers, stand ready.

(*The COMMONERS mime drawing bows.*)

SUNSHINE: God speed our arrows to his filthy heart!

HENRY 5: Shoot!

(*A big twang. Screams, drums, trumpets and the sound of battle as the heart of the cartoon sprouts a bunch of arrows.*)

Bull's eye!

(*Blackout.*

Silence.

A beam of light in Purgatory. HERON sits, arms round his knees.

GAUNT paces angrily up and down.)

GAUNT: You take away the glory. War brings out the best in people. Where else do our heroes come from? Give me the names of our greatest men? Every one is a soldier. Who saves the tribe? Who saves the race? The fighting man. Without him we are nothing. We have no personality, no strength, no self-respect without the warrior's example.

HERON: If death is virtue, life is vice. Your grandson Henry the Fifth wins his French wars and marries the daughter of the King of France. The standing of the house of Lancaster is at its height.

GAUNT: You could see he had promise. There's a glint in his eye, the Plantagenet flame. He reminds me of my father.

HERON: And, like your father, as he lay dead he was robbed of the very rings on his fingers by the mistress he loved.

GAUNT: Alice Perrers, that greedy, thieving bitch! She took a diamond that was promised to me.

HERON: The fifth Henry was robbed by his mistress Death and her accomplice Dysentry when he had France and fame in the palm of his hand.

(*The COMMONERS enter with a coffin, DAUNSE beating a drum, followed by the QUEEN.*)

GAUNT: Oh, how tragic! Imagine the conquests he might have made had he lived.

HERON: The soldier who never ran from a fight died of the runs. But his military achievements were colossal, it has to be said. This warrior-king laid waste some of the fairest land in Europe, emptied the Exchequer his father had accumulated, sent thousands to their deaths…

GAUNT: France is a rightful part of the English king's dominion.

HERON: So is Ireland, Wales, Scotland, Castile…wherever his desires are made manifest. Let's claim the North Pole. But first we must bury the captain king

GAUNT: Did he have a son? Will the line continue?

HERON: You still care about that, even as you suffer. In fact, that's all you care about, isn't it?

GAUNT: Did he?

HERON: Tell me, is *for England* tattooed along the length of your cock?

GAUNT: Did he have a son? I beg you, tell me yes or no.

HERON: The Commons cannot quite forgive your grandson for dying on them while yet another Henry of your blood, your great grandson, is still a small, rather weak boy – in his minority.

(*The boy HENRY 6 enters and runs to the QUEEN.*)

GAUNT: Thank God!

HERON: That organ of yours has the longest hard-on in history.

GAUNT: His father's victories have cemented his right to the kingship. No one can deny his claim to the throne.

HENRY 6: Open the coffin for me. I'd like to see him.

QUEEN: That wouldn't be a good idea. He is much changed.

HENRY 6: That can't be for I never saw him.

QUEEN: You're right. You never saw your father.

HENRY 6: Did you ever see him?

QUEEN: Of course I did! (*Pause.*) Now and again.

HENRY 6: I'm going to play.

(*HENRY 6 runs out.*
The QUEEN sits on the coffin and sings.
The COMMONERS accompany her on triangles.)

QUEEN: As I myself lay the other night
alone without fear or friend,

I dreamed of you, my absent love,
not knowing you had met your end
in a far country, in a stranger's bed,
but in my dream we had our way
and in my mind we were in bliss,
when I awoke the dream was gone
but not the love I have, ywis.
(*The QUEEN gets off the coffin, lifts the lid, looks in, closes it.*)
Who was that? Someone I used to know. I'm still young...
I'm still young.
(*She exits whistling the tune of the song.*)

HERON: Remember this merry French widow, Queen
Catherine. She forms a liaison with a Welsh squire named
Owen Tudor and starts another family in what might be
thought a wilderness.
(*The COMMONERS take off the coffin, DAUNSE dancing in front.*
HEADS enters with a shovel and mimes digging a grave bawling the mass for the dead.)

HEADS: Deliver me, O lord, from eternal death in that awful
day when the heavens and the earth shall be shaken; when
Thou shalt come to judge the world by fire...gay, gay, gay,
gay, think on dreadful doomsday!
(*As HEADS and DAUNSE dig, HENRY 6 as an adult enters with GLOUCESTER and CARDINAL BEAUFORT, their arms held out in a mime of hawking.*
PENY and SUNSHINE enter and watch.)

HERON: Here's your grown-up great-grandson, a peace-
loving man and a pious – where did he get that from? – out
hawking with two powerful lords, his uncle the Duke of
Gloucester, the Protector appointed by Parliament, and his
uncle Cardinal Beaufort, both of the Gaunt blood.
(*Birdsong.*)

GLOUCESTER: I feel a wind.

BEAUFORT: What a calm day.

GLOUCESTER: There's a skylark.

BEAUFORT: It's a goldfinch.

(*They walk around with HENRY 6 crooning, stroking and chucking their imaginary hawks.*)

HENRY 6: That's a beautiful falcon you have there, Protector. What kind is it?

GLOUCESTER: A peregrine, sire. Strikes like lightning.

HENRY 6: Mine is too peaceful. She only eats if she is hungry and she has already breakfasted on stale bread.

BEAUFORT: Mine is a Sahara Arab's hawk, sire. His eye covers great tracts of country. (*A lark's song rises very close.*) Kill!

(*He launches the hawk. They all watch.*
The lark's song ends abruptly and a shower of feathers descends.)

What a point he made! Wham! Wonderful! Home, boy, home!

(*The hawk returns to BEAUFORT. He mimes taking the lark out of its claws.*)

The devil doesn't want to let go. But he must, eh, lord Protector?

GLOUCESTER: The cardinal is fond of climbing high.

HENRY 6: Show us your peregrine, uncle Gloucester. It must have a pitch as high as Beaufort's.

GLOUCESTER: Oh, higher, majesty. Much higher.

(*GLOUCESTER launches his falcon.*)

HERON: Great sport. The Cardinal is one of the lateborn bastard boys your mistress gave you. He's climbed up the ladder of Holy Mother Church. I wonder if his blood drives him forward to be pope, or the first priest-king?

GLOUCESTER: She stoops!

PENYS: Like an arrow she goes!

GLOUCESTER: A hit! A hit! Halloo! Come back, madam! Come back! (*The peregrine returns and is divested of the kill and tied.*) Did you see that, sire? She struck a foot from the ground. What courage.

DAUNSE: Will our king now try his bird? The sky is full of doves.

PENY: Show us your skill, sire.

SUNSHINE: I bet it climbs higher than the Protector's and hits closer to the ground. From your gentle hand, sire, I wouldn't wonder if it ascended to the Elysian Fields.

HENRY 6: He may fly, for that is his nature. As for the killing part, I give no encouragement.

(*HENRY 6 sends off his hawk.*

As he does so FLY-AWAY runs in on crutches in bloody tatters.)

FLY-AWAY: News from France! News from France!

(*He is ignored as they watch the king's hawk fly upwards.*)

Bad news from France! Bad news from France!

HENRY 6: What is it, old soldier?

FLY-AWAY: The French have risen against your rule, sire. The Dauphin Charles is crowned king in Rheims. The Dukes of Anjou and Alencon have sworn him homage. Burgundy has gone over to him as well. And our Talbot is dead. Salisbury is dead. Guienne is lost. Champagne is lost. Orleans is lost. Guysors is lost. Poitiers is lost. Paris is lost.

(*HENRY 6 bursts into tears.*)

DAUNSE: The king's oiseau stoops!

(*They follow the hawk as it falls. It hits the ground with a thud. Blackout.*

Light up on HERON and GAUNT looking over an empty stage.)

HERON: Well, all that hard work for nothing. The Frenchman is back on his feet again.

GAUNT: What's the matter with this lad? Why isn't he over there at the head of his troops?

HERON: By some freak of heredity, your great-grandson is more of a chicken than a fighting cock. But he might have inherited your fancy for being at the rear in a punch-up.

GAUNT: It's the best place to keep an eye on things. No, the trouble is he's weak - hasn't got it in him!

HERON: How can that be? He's of the blood.

GAUNT: Nature has dealt him a poor hand. He's more of a monk than a monarch.

HERON: Monk or not, he must be put to the female.

(*The QUEEN enters.*)

GLOUCESTER: This woman, Margaret of Anjou, is a
disaster in the making. Niece of the French king, she is
wicked, wilful, variable, false, fickle, fell, frivolous, spiteful,
deceitful, unkind, cruel, cursed, covetous, outlandish,
lecherous, disloyal, faithless, felonious, refractory, stand-
offish...

PENY: Unmeek.

GLOUCESTER: Unmeek? Alright...unmeek, malicious,
angry, austere...

PENY: Scatheful.

GLOUCESTER: Scatheful?

PENY: Full of scathe. It's a word.

GLOUCESTER: If you say so. Scatheful, slanderous, grim,
ungracious, ungentle...disgentle...non-gentle?

PENY: Ungentle will do.

GLOUCESTER: Ungentle, scalding, vile, vexatious, without
virtue...I have to say, I don't like her at all.

HENRY 6: Uncle Gloucester, our new queen! Isn't she
lovely?

(PENY slips GLOUCESTER a note.)

GLOUCESTER: Oh, yes she is, she is! *(Reads.)* Her sight
doth ravish and her beauteous grace astounds the eye.
Contemplating your happiness, my liege, I fall to weeping
joys. *(Snivels.)* Such is the fulness of my heart's content, I
can hardly talk. Lady, with a cheerful voice I say: welcome
to England.

(Everyone bows and scrapes to the QUEEN, except for DAUNSE
who dances and sings, collecting and leading everyone into the
daunse macabre:)

DAUNSE: Sir, emperor, lord of all the ground,
high prince, son of a noble house,
you must give up your golden sceptre,
your treasure-trove, and with all dance my way;
holding hands with Adam's children as they go,
some going quick, some going slow.
People look on this shell,
the gestures in an antic dance;
see what you are and where your nature leads,
food for worms, uninstated trash,

with only words and blood and sons
for remembrance.
Here he stands who is a king,
alive but dead, a doomed inanimated thing.
I have never learnt to dance with hope,
but only at the mass with savage steps;
who is the humblest is the most wise,
the king would be better with the dancer's eyes.
(*SUFFOLK enters and watches the QUEEN.*
She sees him and smiles.
He crooks a finger.
She disengages from HENRY 6 and leaves him dancing in little
circles, eyes upraised, hands together in prayer.
The QUEEN goes to SUFFOLK. They kiss passionately.
Cardinal BEAUFORT enters with a cup.
GLOUCESTER enters looking worried.)

DAUNSE: What have you there, Cardinal? Christ's blood for
the mass?

BEAUFORT: We all want the Protector out of the way. He's
redundant. The king has grown up. He's married a woman
with backbone. If the king doesn't respond with something
unbendable of his own, his grace the Duke of Suffolk will.

HERON: Suffolk is another one of yours. You spread like
mushroom spores, John.

BEAUFORT: Enjoying the party? Have a drink, Gloucester.

GLOUCESTER: Very good of you, cousin. (*Accepts the cup.*)

HERON: The poisoner is yours, Gaunt. The victim is yours.
The blood prepares to turn upon itself.

SUFFOLK: Margaret, mon amour...

QUEEN: Sweet Billy de la Pole.

SUFFOLK: To possess you I would even go so far as to accept
the burden of kingship.

HENRY 6: Praise the Lord, O my soul. I will praise the Lord
in my life. I will sing to my God whilst I have any being!

QUEEN: Pole's the right name for you, Billy.

SUFFOLK: Because I'd pollinate you?

QUEEN: Another reason.

SUFFOLK: Because our affair is so politically dangerous?

QUEEN: Because you use me as a vaulting-pole to the throne.

SUFFOLK: That's hardly a polite remark, dear heart.

QUEEN: We must stay poles apart.

(*They giggle and smooch.*
GLOUCESTER stands beside them, the poisoned cup in his hand.)

GLOUCESTER: My king has married disasterously. As Protector, I must accept the blame. I arranged the marriage. When the country discovers the price to be paid for the French whore, it will all backfire on me. The truth is, the woman will be the real ruler. She has tripes of iron, her womb is steel. From the way she looks at me I know I'm not long for this world. I might as well give old Beaufort a better chance of Hell by murdering me than provide any satisfaction to the Gallic harlot. So goodbye England, goodbye the heat of my noble blood. Gloucester is going.

(*He drinks the poison and dies while the QUEEN and SUFFOLK stand over him, intertwined.*
Pause.)

HERON: Gaunt!

GAUNT: I hear you.

HERON: They do have some mercy, those who have ignored you and put your punishment in my hands. I've been given permission to administer a pain-killer before the final stage begins. You won't sleep but it will reduce your anguish.

GAUNT: These are merely arguments within the family, internecine disputes, easily settled. If only the king would wake up to his responsibilities!

(*FLY-AWAY enters in bloody tatters with a broken pike followed by the COMMONERS in a state.*)

FLY-AWAY: Even worse news from France, sire. The French are breaking the truce declared at your marriage. My lord Somerset…

HERON: Another of the blood, John. They're everywhere.

FLY-AWAY: …asks you to remember the nigh infinite costs and effusions of goods and blood that England has born and suffered for Normandy's sake, and begs for reinforcements.

DAUNSE: You can't let the French have Normandy! Your dad will turn in his grave!

QUEEN: What a fool the French make of you! The whole of Europe is laughing!

SUFFOLK: The people won't stand for it. They're ashamed of your pusillanimous ways. They want strong and virile government and a positive, outgoing foreign policy.

PENY: Relieve Somerset!

SUNSHINE: Protect Normandy!

DAUNSE: Break the truce like the French did!

FLY-AWAY: To hell with France and all things French!

(*HEADS enters with a big pot.*)

HEADS: Normandy is lost.

(*Pause, then everyone turns on HENRY 6 and beats him up.*)

QUEEN: You useless spoilt priest! Half-man! Imbecile! *Espèce de cretin!*

(*They draw back.*

HENRY 6 gets to his feet, dusting himself down.)

HENRY 6: (*Looking into the pot.*) What have you got there, Heads?

HEADS: The ashes of Joan of Arc.

HENRY 6: God save her. Remember the girl, Cardinal? She was the one who kept having visions.

BEAUFORT: She was a witch and we did well to burn her. What have you kept her ashes for?

HEADS: The French, having driven us out altogether, are now saying she was a saint. I reckon her ashes will be worth quite a bit.

BEAUFORT: You have an eye to the main chance, Heads. You're not as stupid as you look.

HEADS: No, sir, I'm not. I've got a good head for business. If the Pope says she's a saint then you'll have to agree, being a cardinal, and our lord king, being a very religious man, he'll go along with it. Since we were the ones who burnt her, and us having such strong French connections through the new queen, I wouldn't be surprised if Joan got bumped up to be female patron saint of England. She'll match up nicely with George, the Turk, and Crispy Crispian the wandering Italian cobblers.

BEAUFORT: Heads, don't overtax your mind old fellow. Take a rest while you can. You're going to have your work cut out.

(*HEADS exits with the pot followed by everyone but GAUNT and HERON.*)

HEADS: (*As he goes.*) I can sell her by the handful. Gay, gay, gay, gay, think on dreadful doomsday.

HERON: Well, Gaunt – England is breaking up. After a mere thirty years and three of your blood successively on the throne, we're in a hell of a state. Government is hapless. Taxation, crippling. Money, worthless. Law, non-existent. Now the weather gets worse. Harvests fail. People look back on the French wars and say – look where it's all got us.

GAUNT: It need never have happened. If I'd been allowed my say…

HERON: But you had you say. Your own son wouldn't listen. None of them listen. Even this one. He appears to be listening but actually he only listens to God – who's not saying much.

GAUNT: This queen will help him. She looks strong.

HERON: The house of Lancaster is in danger of becoming a slaughter-house.

GAUNT: Henry can still save himself. Blame Somerset for losing Normandy and Gloucester for the state of the economy.

HERON: That keeps it in the family. Is this a variation on the hereditary principle?

GAUNT: That pain-killer you mentioned…

HERON: Wait a while. I might have to join you. I've been told self-criticism is healthy in Purgatory. It's all very well me standing on the side-lines being sardonic but whose fault is this, really? Who let this happen? (*Sings and dances.*)
The people are naturally servile
and never move faster
than when they're deferring

to their privileged masters.
Eyes, come view this tragedy,
the ruin of pomp and heraldry,
our civil wars, blue blood, dead men,
roses rotting on the stem.
(*The COMMONERS enter with HEADS. They carry ripped
and tattered armorial banners, singing.*)
COMMONERS: The eagle's down, the lion has gone,
the fiery cresset torn from light,
portcullis worn, the fortress breached,
lords now stumble through sour night.
devices torn, emblems decayed,
the baron's bloodstained case, unmade.
HERON: The English sentimentally
indulge their aristocracy,
endure their taunts, relish their scorn,
and mourn when noble houses mourn.
COMMONERS: The white hart is out of mind,
the boar is far into the west,
the falcon's gone, the lion sleeps,
on shield and helm the angels weep.
HERON: Although vicarious joys they find
in dukes and earls and fawning blind,
a moment comes of cold inspection –
result: a peasant insurrection!
(*Cacophony.*
*Dummies are thrown onto the stage with pitchforks, scythes,
sticks and spades.*
*The COMMONERS batter the dummies in a swirling red light
then run off.*
HEADS enters with a huge broom.)
HEADS: (*Sweeping up.*) And the king's gone mad!
HERON: Jack Cade's rebellion. You'll remember Jack Straw's
in your own time. It was crushed, mercilessly.
GAUNT: How else do you deal with the mob? You can't have
chaos.
(*YORK enters, gorgeously dressed.*)
HERON: Here's its spawn. This is Richard, Duke of York.

GAUNT: Is he related to me?

HERON: Aren't we all?

YORK: Here we stand and here's my case. I claim the throne. You'll have to listen carefully. Edward the Third had seven sons. The firstborn was Edward, known as the Black Prince because of the condition he left any country he passed over. The second was William of Hatfield. The third Lionel, Duke of Clarence. The fourth, John of Gaunt. The fifth, Edmund Langley, Duke of York. The sixth, Thomas, Duke of Gloucester. And last, William of Windsor. But only two of these sons outlived him: Edmund and John.

HERON: Concentrate hard.

YORK: The Black Prince died before his father. This meant that by the law of primogeniture, Richard, the Black Prince's son, was heir to the throne. When Edward the Third died, his grandson Richard became the second king of that name.

HERON: Follow closely. This is a crucial juncture, John.

YORK: Henry, the son of John of Gaunt, then usurped the throne and had King Richard murdered, upsetting the apple-cart.

HERON: What an intellectual challenge this is. Thomas Aquinas would have a job keeping up.

YORK: To no one's surprise, King Richard the Second left no heir. After the murder, the legitimate right to the throne could not devolve on Henry because he'd already usurped it. So the rightful claim dropped to the second son's son, Lionel of Clarence, and he had no son…

HERON: Listen carefully.

YORK: But Lionel did have a daughter (*Speeding up.*) who married Edmund Mortimer, Earl of March, you needn't know much about him, and they had a son called Roger and he had a son called Edmund who died without issue in captivity but there was a daughter called Anne who married Richard, Earl of Cambridge, and they had ME! (*Pause.*) And I'll have what's mine.

GAUNT: This is no claim at all! How can he put the whole country to such a trial?

YORK: And I have four bonny, bouncing sons, Edward, George, Richard and little Rutland! The future will be secure.

GAUNT: The man's mad.

HERON: But you see how your son Henry might have inherited the throne legitimately if he'd only waited for Richard to die instead of killing him? Then none of this tragedy need have happened.

GAUNT: He couldn't afford to wait. The kingdom was collapsing into ruin under Richard.

HERON: As it is now under your great-grandson. Your bastard, Cardinal Beaufort, believe it or not, dies of the conscience for poisoning his cousin, Gloucester...there's some decency in the Gaunt strain, somewhere, perhaps... Somerset, the defeated commander in lost Normandy is murdered by this fast-talking York lad, and Suffolk, Billy de la Pole-Vault, the leg-over king, is banished for his shinnanikins inside the *mésalliance* of the monk-boy King Henry the Sixth to the French bitch-on-heat, Margaret of Anjou. I'll leave Heads to describe to you what happened to Billy, the Lancaster lover when Fate finally caught up with him.

HEADS: He was taken out of the ship bearing him into exile and put in a boat and rowed to the shore. An axe and a block were standing by, plus one of the lewdest of the crew, possibly a relative of mine. He addressed the Duke and bade him lay down his head on the block so he could be fared with. The Duke said he was of noble Lancaster blood and preferred to die by the sword like a gentleman. So the fellow took a rusty old blunt-edged hacker and cut off his head with half-a-dozen strokes and laid the body on the sands of Dover.

HERON: I'll get the pain-killer, John. Will brandy do?

GAUNT: What's the matter with these people? Why are they doing this to each other? They're supposed to be family, family!

(*HERON runs off and returns with a flagon and two cups. As he returns, HENRY 6 enters in a nightshirt, holding a red rose.*)

HENRY 6: Here, I am, mad – let out for a little while to walk. In my room where they give me rest but do not rest me, there is a jug waiting for the red rose of returning sanity. Then the bees will make me their feeding-trough. Then the women will put me between their breasts. Then will I return to glory, stock and stamen restored. God help any greenfly I find upon my inner soul. Goodnight. (*Throws the rose aside.*) Blow out the candle before you go to bed. (*Exits.*)

(*YORK enters armed, in armour decorated with white roses. He takes up a position R and takes off his helmet.*)

YORK: Me again. We can't have a mentally defective altarboy on the throne. Something has to be done.

(*The QUEEN enters, armed, in armour decorated with red roses. She takes up a position L and takes off her helmet.*)

QUEEN: Margaret, second she-wolf of France to descend upon England. The first was married to the homosexual layabout, Edward the Second. A hundred years ago she had to kill him for the sake of the country. In the fix England finds itself, history might have to be repeated with my god-crazed, useless husband. Meanwhile I must do his fighting for him.

(*The COMMONERS enter to the beating of drums – PENY, FLY-AWAY with red roses join the QUEEN; DAUNSE and SUNSHINE with white roses join YORK.*

HEADS, in evening dress as a Master of Ceremonies, lugs on his basket, block, axe and broom and stands centre.)

HERON: Have a good swig of brandy, John. You're going to need it.

HEADS: My lords and ladies, the first dance is a slow fox-trot – the First Battle of Saint Albans.

(*Music. Red and white formally dance with each other, humming slow-slow-quick-quick-slow, then break into wrestling. The red faction is thrown to the ground. Dummies are thrown to HEADS who beheads and sweeps them off stage.*

YORK sits on a bench and FLY-AWAY crowns him.)

YORK: I won. I'm king. Anyone want to argue?

HEADS: Take your partners for a quickstep: the Battle of Sandal Castle.

(Music. The dancers hum quick-quick-slow, quick-quick slow.
This time red wins.
The QUEEN drags YORK to HEADS who executes him.
Then the dummies are thrown on.
The QUEEN goes off and returns leading HENRY 6 by the ear.
She makes him sit on a bench and crowns him.)

QUEEN: Richard of York was king, or thought he was king,
for such a short time we never gave him a number. He was
Richard the Nothing. This is your rightful king, Henry the
Sixth.

(YORK enters in his white rose armour.)

YORK: They cut my dad's head off after the battle of Sandal
Castle. I'm very like him, they say. I inherited all his
naturally regal qualities. My name is Edward. So I'm
Edward the fourth of that name.

HEADS: Ladies and gentlemen, let's be having you for an
old-fashioned waltz! The Second Battle of Saint Albans!
(Music.
The white faction is defeated.
HEADS does his work.
HENRY 6 prays through it all.)
Now who's for a dose of the Dashing White Sergeant? The
Battle of Taunton!
(The red faction is defeated.
HEADS does his work.
YORK sits on the bench and is crowned by SUNSHINE.
HENRY 6 is led to one side by DAUNSE and chained. He
stands in the wings mumbling over a rosary.)
Everybody's favourite. Stand by to make new friends in a
general Excuse Me. The Battle Of Warwick.
(The dancers excuse each other and exchange roses until there is
complete confusion.
GAUNT is drinking heavily. He groans in torment.)

GAUNT: This is horrible, horrible! No more, no more! I can't
bear it! Get them to stop!

HERON: People are changing sides a lot. They just want to
survive the chaos if they can.
(HEADS takes a breather, leaning on his axe.)

HEADS: I don't know who's who any more. I'll just have to keep getting on with the job. Come on, no slacking now. (*Resumes work.*) Bloody Battle of Barnet, bloody Battle of Tewkesbury. Christ, my arm is nearly dropping off!
(HEADS decapitates the dummies.
HENRY 6 is led back to the bench, still in chains, and crowned by the QUEEN.
EDWARD 4 comes up behind HENRY 6 accompanied by RICHARD, who has a humpback covered in white roses. They put a noose round HENRY 6's neck and garrot him.
The COMMONERS exit.)

RICHARD: There, brother Edward. All over. York has won. Lancaster has lost. Peace at last.
(HEADS is sweeping up.
RICHARD goes over and tips him.)
Well done. You deserve a holiday. But don't go too far.
(HEADS drags HENRY 6 off and exits.
PENY enters and slips RICHARD a piece of paper.)

PENY: If you're looking for a speechwriter, you might give me a try, sir. I've had a lot of experience.

RICHARD: What's this – an advertisement?

PENY: Something appropriate. Why not give it a whirl?

RICHARD: (*Reading.*) Now is the winter of our discontent made glorious summer by this sun of York...oh, yes...I like that...sun with a u and son with an o.

PENY: Glad you picked up on that, your grace. Nice to be appreciated.

RICHARD: I like puns.

PENY: There's good stuff to come.

RICHARD: I admire your modesty. And all the clouds that lour'd upon our house in the deep bosom of the ocean buried...

PENY: You'll find it works better if you put a stress on the final syllable of buried for the sake of the pentameter.

RICHARD: Really? Buri*ed* sounds odd. Are you sure?

PENY: That's the way I wrote it, your lordship. Those are the cadences I heard in my mind.

RICHARD: You're very particular.

PENY: Caring for details comes naturally to a true artist, your grace.

(*RICHARD smiles and puts an arm round PENY's shoulder. PENY tries to recipricate but the hump gets in the way.*)

RICHARD: Let's be friends.

(*They exit.*)

GAUNT: (*Drunk.*) Is it all over?

HERON: You'd better ask the English.

GAUNT: May I go?

HERON: There are plenty of Lancaster loose ends still running round.

GAUNT: I feel ill.

HERON: Inherited power and inherited wealth are never quite yours. They belong to the dead.

GAUNT: It needn't have turned out like this.

HERON: All that matters is it did.

GAUNT: It's only a fool's joke!

HERON: There's more.

GAUNT: Oh, no…no…please… Let me go…send me to the lowest pit of Hell! Burn me to cinders three times a day! Anything would be better than this.

HERON: You're so close to being cured, John – purged clean. Stick with it. Take your punishment like a man.

GAUNT: Perhaps this is a dream? I didn't die after all. I saw this fool in my window during my sickness and he took over my mind. He made wisecracks that rocked my soul.

HERON: When will you wake from this dream then?

GAUNT: When I hear the bell, I will wake in my bed. None of this will have happened.

(*The tolling of a funeral bell.*)

HERON: Edward the Fourth dies. His son, Edward the Fifth, a mere lad, and his little brother are murdered in the Tower by Dick, the hunchback. This usurpers' usurper becomes Richard the Third.

(*RICHARD enters in armour and white roses and stands R.*)

GAUNT: He's York…York…nothing to do with me. The expiation of my sins is over!

(*HENRY TUDOR enters in armour and red roses and stands L.*)

Who the hell is this? Get off the stage!

HERON: The Wars of the Roses aren't over. Remember the widow of your famous grandson, Henry the Fifth? She went off with a Welsh squire called Owen Tudor and they had a son who had a son. We come to this one, another Henry, eyeing the throne.

GAUNT: What, a claim through a widow's toy-boy? Where's the Lancaster blood in him?

HERON: I'm afraid his mother was a Beaufort from your line of bastards, John. And his father's father was that Owen Tudor who went where the great warrior king Henry the Fifth had been. He lay on the same breast. His right arose from touching the same flesh as a legend. Succesful warriors make things sacred.

GAUNT: Take him away. It's a farce.

HERON: The Gaunt seed still blows, the royal blood still flows. If he does win, it will be just like old times – another usurper in the family. Heads!

(*HEADS enters wearily, still as Master of Cermonies.*)

HEADS: I'm so knackered. I need to take it easy for a while. Where to this time?

HERON: North again.

HEADS: Take your partners for the last dance. The Battle of Bosworth.

(*Music.*

The COMMONERS enter in white and red roses as before and dance in slow-motion.

HENRY TUDOR dances with RICHARD and gnaws out his throat.

GAUNT subsides to the ground, sobbing.

HEADS sweeps up and drags RICHARD off by the heels.

HENRY sits on the bench and is crowned by DAUNSE.)

HERON: Get up, John. Here's Henry the Seventh, a new Lancaster – well, that's what he says he is – on the throne. There could be better times ahead. He marries a Yorkist bride, hoping to settle the issue.

GAUNT: I'm dead. Haven't I got any rights?

HERON: That's an interesting concept.

GAUNT: That Welsh rogue will die childless. Say it will end
with him. Please!

HERON: Well, John, you were a better gardener than
that. You were a famous sower of seed, ghost seed, seed
of legend, the soul and idea of seed. This Henry will
have another Henry who'll have an Edward, a Mary
and an Elizabeth – she might bring a smile to your face
– and while they reign, others of your dandelion breed
will sprout in other countries. There'll be a James, two
Charleses, another James, a William, an Anne, a set of
German Georges, a William, a Victoria, another couple of
Edwards, more Georges, another Elizabeth, and another
Charles who waits. That is God's mercy on your soul. I've
finished my job, my joke, and had my reward. Now I must
leave you with the eyes.

GAUNT: Leave me? No, don't do that…

HERON: Until the English cure themselves of the disease
of deference, this will go on and on. We could be talking
about eternity.

GAUNT: Stay, please!

HERON: You must be alone from now on. I'm going to do
stand-up comedy ad infinitum for angels and archangels.
Not an easy task, I have to say. They're not known for their
sense of humour.

(*HERON picks up his jacket of bells.*)

GAUNT: In charity…for the times we've had together…stay
with me. I'll be more patient. I've learned my lesson. From
now on I'm a convinced republican.

(*HERON laughs.*)

I am, honestly.

HERON: There was a time-limit put on my reward. Beyond
this point they say I'd just be gloating, which is bad for my
eternal soul. In the old days, when you were bored with
me you'd say, hey, you, what's-your-name, I'm fed up with
your shaggy-dog stories and puerile clowning, fuck off. If
you can go back to that attitude, it might help.

GAUNT: Oh, I'm too much changed for that. But we could
watch together, from a distance, not getting too involved,
talking through the finer political points. Come on, stay

with me. Please. (*Pause.*) If you could choose to stay out of fellowship, would you?

HERON: Would I be such a fool?

(*GAUNT lowers his head.*
HERON drapes his jacket of bells over GAUNT'S shoulders
and runs off.
Light dwindles on GAUNT.
Blackout.)

The End.

LILE JIMMY WILLIAMSON

Characters

LILE JIMMY,
James Williamson, Lord Ashton, lino king of Lancaster

DR LOCO, his medical adviser

JESSE, his second wife

MAUD, his third wife

JAMES WILLIAMSON, Snr, his father, a ghost

GLADSTONE, a prime minister

HODKINSON, a Labour leader

WALL, a Labour agitator

SHED, a works manager

THE KAISER

REVEREND MELVILLE, a minister

THOMAS STOREY, an industrialist

MRS STOREY, his wife

LLOYD GEORGE, a prime minister

EDITORS
of The Lancaster Guardian, The Lancaster Times,
The Lancaster Observer, The Lancaster Gazette

COLONEL MARTON, a Tory candidate

COLONEL WHALLEY, Maud's first husband

RAMSBOTTOM, a Tory candidate

TRIBUNAL OFFICER

CABINET MINISTER

TELEGRAM DELIVERY BOY

PRESS OPERATOR

WORKERS

Set in Lancaster and London between 1886 and 1928

Lile Jimmy Williamson was first performed on 30 January 1975 at the Duke's Playhouse, Lancaster, with the following cast:

LILE JIMMY, Robert Mackintosh

DR LOCO, Will Tacey

JESSE & TELEGRAM DELIVERY BOY, Harriet Walter

MAUD & EDITOR, Fiona Victory

REV MELVILLE, SHED & EDITOR, Charles Haggith

GLADSTONE, MARTON & KAISER, Leader Hawkins

HODKINSON & LLOYD GEORGE, Trevor Griffiths

WALL, MELVILLE & CABINET MINISTER,
Stephen Boxer

STOREY, RAMSBOTTOM & TRIBUNAL OFFICER,
Bob Eaton

MRS STOREY & EDITOR, Elizabeth Revill

PRESS OPERATOR & EDITOR, Noreen Kershaw

WORKERS, the company

Director, Peter Oyston

Music, Stephen Boxer

ACT ONE

1928. A walled garden L with a pagoda and a weeping willow tree. R of the wall are the fronts of terraced houses. In the background the Lancaster skyline minus the Ashton Memorial.

Enter LILE JIMMY at eighty-six, being pushed into the walled garden in a wheelchair by DR LOCO from L.

DR LOCO: And you never wanted to be a writer? When your letters can destroy a statesman like Lloyd George? James, consider a change of career.

LILE JIMMY: I wrote to him direct.

DR LOCO: That was very English of you, James. Having shot off a dozen indignant tirades against the man to both friends and enemies alike, there was no moral requirement for you to tell him about it.

LILE JIMMY: I told him what I thought. He won't win now.

DR LOCO: Poor fellow. I truly pity him. He must shake all over when he hears the postman.

LILE JIMMY: I don't like you standing up when I'm sitting down. Get a chair.

DR LOCO: (*Going to the pagoda and getting a deck-chair.*) When are you going to grow up, James? You're leaving it very late.

LILE JIMMY: I never trust the Welsh. Very poor sales in Wales.

DR LOCO: Very poor sales in Wales?

LILE JIMMY: Can you hear them over the wall? (*Pause.*) What are they saying about me?

DR LOCO: Oh, what I'd give for one glimpse of greatness.

LILE JIMMY: Why do they never stop spying on me?

DR LOCO: Because you're so interesting.

LILE JIMMY: I'm cold.

DR LOCO: Don't let them see you're cold.

LILE JIMMY: Who?

DR LOCO: James, your weeping willow is about to collapse under the weight of several hundred trade union observers.

LILE JIMMY: I showed old Lloyd George. Even when we were in the Commons together, I distrusted him. He was always too fluid for me.

DR LOCO: Yes, I'd say you certainly showed Lloyd George.

LILE JIMMY: He betrayed me!

DR LOCO: Lloyd George is the best politician in Europe because he betrays everyone so beautifully.

LILE JIMMY: The Shanghai Defence Force should have been sent out right away!

DR LOCO: Chop-chop!

LILE JIMMY: Did you know the peaks of Chinese gaolers' caps are made from a fabric manufactured at my works?

DR LOCO: Strangely enough, I did.

LILE JIMMY: The Chinese have betrayed me, Doctor. They were in league with Lloyd George.

DR LOCO: James, don't feel you're being picked on. We're all betrayed on a daily basis.

LILE JIMMY: Who by?

DR LOCO: The economy, James, the economy. What cure is there for the Great Depression?

LILE JIMMY: Is Maud in her room?

DR LOCO: Curtains drawn.

LILE JIMMY: She's plotting something up there. D'you know what she keeps asking me to do?

DR LOCO: James, I can only guess.

LILE JIMMY: She wants me to make a will. What the devil do I want to make a will for?

DR LOCO: Preposterous.

LILE JIMMY: I've got nothing and I'm in perfect health.

DR LOCO: James, this is the first time I've heard you confess to good health. What's brought this on?

LILE JIMMY: It's got nothing to do with your therapies.

DR LOCO: You've always wanted my second opinion, James – never my first. All these years I've neglected my patients in the asylum for you – my one private patient. But you've never actually admitted to having any condition whatsoever.

LILE JIMMY: I believe in preventive medicine.

DR LOCO: Look at you, my best advertisement. I kept him sane.

LILE JIMMY: It was a good letter I wrote to Lloyd George.

DR LOCO: Very good.

LILE JIMMY: I reminded him of his treachery to me during the General Strike. He wouldn't send the Army down the mines. We ran out of coal.

DR LOCO: It was only because he knew the officers were too corpulent to get down the shafts.

LILE JIMMY: My letter has probably turned the tide against the Liberals.

DR LOCO: Ah, the Liberals. How we cling on to our political dinosaurs. Look at you, James – the last of the armour-plated monsters – the great carnivorous lizard – Tyrannosaurus Rex Lancastrium.

LILE JIMMY: I don't care what you say, it was a damn good letter.

(*Blackout.*)

1886. A brass band plays 'See the Conquering Hero Come'. Lights up on the street. Enter WORKERS carrying LILE JIMMY (44) on their shoulders. They put him down and the music stops.

LILE JIMMY: Working men of England!

WORKERS: That's our Lile Jimmy!

LILE JIMMY: Thank you! Thank you!

WORKERS: Nay, thank thee!

LILE JIMMY: Well, the long night is over for us. The power is now in your hands.

WORKERS: Our hands, Lile Jimmy! You're one of us!

LILE JIMMY: And always will be. At last, long overdue, you have the vote. (*A great cheer goes up.*) Reform has done its job. The government is upon your shoulders. Power now sits where it should, with the people! (*Another great cheer.*) The grip of the landowners, the City men and the military has been wrested from the tiller. The Tories no longer captain our country. First class passengers they may be, but for how long, eh?

WORKERS: Chuck the buggers overboard!

LILE JIMMY: I, and my father before, always believed it to
be the natural sense of justice and sympathy found in the
hearts of the working folk of England that has made her
great. Her wealth is her people! (*Huge cheers.*) Any man
who turns his back upon them deserves what he gets. He
should be doomed to beggary! No leader should be able to
survive without the affection of the people. If he can, then
there's something wrong with the system we live under!

WORKERS: Well said! That's telling 'em!

LILE JIMMY: All I have to offer is myself, and little
that is.

WORKERS: Th'art lile but great!

LILE JIMMY: Some of my friends in high places tell me I'm a
fool because I consistently side with the people.

WORKERS: Do without such pals, Jimmy!

LILE JIMMY: For myself, I hope to remain the friend of the
working men of this town all my life.

WORKERS: Tha' wilt!

LILE JIMMY: I am nobody, but my cause is as good as
mortal man can be engaged in. I have nothing to gain. All
I want is the happiness of the people.

WORKERS: We're thy men, Jimmy! Go where thou wilt,
we'll follow thee!

LILE JIMMY: I see amongst you many a familiar face – men
who work for me, and who worked for my father, that
inventive genius who put linoleum onto the markets of
the world! It is always good to be among friends. But that
in no way makes you beholden to me. If I thought your
vote would merely follow your employment, willy-nilly, I
would withdraw from this election. Believe me, I want to
represent a town of free men in the next parliament, not
a huddle of obedient serfs! (*Takes a paper from his pocket.*) I
have written to every man who earns his living from me
and my manufactures, stressing this point. Please believe
me. A vote from a free conscience is a pledge of faith
– from a wage-slave it is nothing but a hollow sham. Thank
you and God bless you all.
(*Tremendous cheer.*

The WORKERS crowd around LILE JIMMY as he leaves,
shaking his hand, patting him on the back.
General exit R to the brass band.
DR LOCO enters the walled garden with a newspaper.
JESSE enters from R.)

JESSE: Well, Doctor, what did you think of that?

DR LOCO: Extraordinary scenes of jubilation, Mrs
Williamson, quite extraordinary.

JESSE: I think the men were splendid. They're loyalty is so
touching.

DR LOCO: They really look up to him. There's something
in my paper here I must keep. (*Tears out an item.*) You
wouldn't think it was possible in 1886. The eccentric and
sybaritic King Louis the Second of Bavaria has ordered
the manager of the Royal Theatre, Munich, to produce
Mr Sanders' play *Theodora,* at a cost of twenty thousand
pounds. (*Folds the item and puts it in a notebook.*) There will
be only one performance and one person in the audience
– his majesty. We can take comfort this could never happen
in Lancaster.

JESSE: James is the only man who could afford it and he's not
all that enthusiastic about the theatre.

DR LOCO: The longer he retains his grip on reality, the
better the town will like it.

JESSE: And he was so doubtful about being put up for
election. Can you imagine it? He's the obvious choice.
I tell you, Doctor, he goes on about the people and
democracy to the point where I have to stop myself getting
a little exhausted by it all.

DR LOCO: (*Making notes.*) Oh, whatever happens, one must
avoid that.
(*LILE JIMMY enters.*
DR LOCO withdraws to the pagoda.)

JESSE: What a day you've had. I've never seen anything like
it. They love you, James. They really do. Fancy taking
the horses from your carriage and pulling you all the way
home. It was wonderful. I can see why you think so much
of them. What fine people they are.

LILE JIMMY: I can't get over it.

JESSE: They worship you, James. They'd do anything for you.

LILE JIMMY: You think so? Honestly? What worries me is – am I up to it? Am I good enough? They expect so much.

JESSE: Of course you're good enough. The Tories don't stand a chance against you.

LILE JIMMY: This is a conservative town, Jesse. The prison, courts, hospitals, the garrison, shopkeepers…you won't find many Liberals in that lot.

JESSE: But you're the biggest employer, James. Without you the town would be moribund. You have your workers – the ordinary people. You're exactly what they need – a born leader. A new man. An alternative to those dreadful old Tory types. The rule of the colonels is over, James. I'm so proud of you. (*Kisses him.*)

LILE JIMMY: Yes, I believe you are.

(*LILE JIMMY and JESSE exit R arm in arm.*
DR LOCO walks around the garden scribbling in his notebook.
The PRESS OPERATOR enters downstage L and sings:)

PRESS OPERATOR: Lile Jimmy Williamson
how I look up to you,
I'd never shake that feller's hand
who won't give you your due,
you're keeping me and mine alive
and that is all to me,
I won't stand by while Tories cry
your name to infamy. (*Exits L.*)

Back in 1928, LILE JIMMY propels himself into the walled garden in the wheelchair.

DR LOCO: D'you remember Jesse? She laid out this garden.

LILE JIMMY: Jesse?

DR LOCO: Your second wife. You bought this house for her.

LILE JIMMY: She deserted me, just like the first one did.

DR LOCO: She died, James, they both died. At a pinch, one
could call that a kind of desertion, I suppose.

LILE JIMMY: When Lloyd George writes back, don't let
Maud see the letter. She'll make a note of his address.

DR LOCO: It was a wise buy, this house. Right in the middle
of it all. No mansion out in the country in those days, no
vast estate and private golf-course, oh no. Here you were
right at the heart of your community.

LILE JIMMY: Maud would write off to him, offering herself.
And he'd take her up on it. He's got the morals of a ferret.

DR LOCO: Has Maud agreed to be locked up in her room
yet?

LILE JIMMY: No. She's being as unreasonable as ever. Oh…
(*Falls back in the wheelchair.*) I feel strange… Ouch! What
was that pain? Get me inside! It's happening, Doctor! It's
happening!
(*DR LOCO pushes the wheelchair off R.*
The PRESS OPERATOR enters from L and sings:)

PRESS OPERATOR: Lile Jimmy Williamson
my man will vote for thee,
he'd rather throw the thing away
than follow the Tory,
we know you'll stand up in the House
and speak up for us folk,
telling those London whites of egg
that Lancaster's the yolk. (*Exits L.*)
(*Enter LILE JIMMY from R, taking off his jacket.*
DR LOCO enters with him, feels his pulse, listens to his heart
with a stethoscope.)

LILE JIMMY: They drain me, Doctor. What a business.

DR LOCO: Love does drain, James.

LILE JIMMY: Are you using that word correctly?

DR LOCO: They have faith you'll change their lives by caring
about them. In my book that's a fair definition. No doubt
there are others.

LILE JIMMY: But they always want something from me. Isn't
that selfishness of a kind? If only I didn't get so tired. Will I
have the energy, Doctor, the energy?

DR LOCO: Electioneering is an unnatural pastime. You're tired because you're sincere. You put your heart into it.

LILE JIMMY: I feel so out of sorts all the time.

DR LOCO: How can any man distil a lifetime of serious political thought and genuine concern into a handclasp and a smile? It must be very wearing.

LILE JIMMY: They deserve only my best. How can I possibly give them that if I'm always under the weather?

DR LOCO: Delegate.

LILE JIMMY: Delegate what?

DR LOCO: Get yourself a manager for the works. Let someone else do the worrying for you while you're down in London attending Parliament.

LILE JIMMY: Oh, I don't know about that. My business is at a crucial stage at the moment. Who could I trust with it?

DR LOCO: Find a lieutenant.
(*LILE JIMMY puts his jacket back on, deep in thought.*
COLONEL MARTON enters to a spot R.)

MARTON: (*To audience.*) This is my political swan-song, so I'll keep it short and snappy. Marton, colonel, England, old England before they gave every idiot not on the parish the vote. This election was fought through the minds of working men struggling with the Irish Question – a combination of mud and bloody lunacy.

DR LOCO: (*To LILE JIMMY.*) Conserve your energy for what's important. Live frugally. Avoid all-night sittings. Keep off oysters and champagne if you have to.

LILE JIMMY: I'm going to Westminster to work, Doctor, not to socialise. Are you going to give me something?

DR LOCO: You're a healthy man, James. You've got a marvellous constitution.

LILE JIMMY: A tonic! Give me a tonic!

MARTON: Williamson bought votes with his blasted enormous breakfast. One morning, he fed the entire town! The whole damn town! It must have cost him a fortune.
(*GLADSTONE enters to the spot L with MARTON.*)
Gladstone, you jumped-up Liverpool docker, just because your birthplace is heaving with Irish malcontents it don't

mean we all have to be obsessed with the slovenly whores!
Why are we fighting elections over Paddies? Ireland's
nothing but a potato patch. Give it back to the bastards,
I don't care. As for Williamson, he doesn't know the
difference between Dublin and Doncaster!

GLADSTONE: Colonel Marton, it is no loss to the House
of Commons that you will not be joining us again. If I
remember correctly, you only attended fifteen per cent of
the divisions in the last parliament, and on two of those
occasions managed to vote against an act forbidding the
sale of liquor to children under thirteen, and to obstruct
an act granting allotments to impoverished farm labourers
in order they should be able to grow staple food. I suggest
you go home and sleep off your political past.

(*GLADSTON exits R.*)

MARTON: Bet that sanctimonious bastard is a member of the
Irish Republican Brotherhood and an undercover Catholic
to boot. (*Exits L.*)

(*Spot out.*

JESSE enters the walled garden.)

JESSE: Well, Doctor, is our magnificent MP fit for work?

DR LOCO: Five thousand votes say he is. Good luck, James.
(*Shakes his hand.*) I'll be thinking about you.

LILE JIMMY: And you won't give me anything?

DR LOCO: If I did, I'd be admitting I don't know a healthy
man when I see one. (*Exits through the pagoda.*)

JESSE: There you are, James. I told you nothing was the
matter. It's only the excitement.

LILE JIMMY: He doesn't know what he's talking about.

JESSE: You won't go slipping off to Harley Street, I hope.

LILE JIMMY: I must accept his diagnosis. Once I get stuck in
down there in London, I won't have time to worry about
my health. I have a master to serve and his health comes
first.

JESSE: James, I think you must be the best man in the world.
(*LILE JIMMY and JESSE exit R as the PRESS OPERATOR
enters L and sings:*)

PRESS OPERATOR: Lile Jimmy Williamson,
the river flows your way,

to me you are the difference
between dark night and day,
if it wasn't for your factory
I'd be out on the road,
my children fading like the flowers
before the winter cold.
(*DR LOCO enters with a telephone with a cut cord, pushing LILE JIMMY in the wheelchair.*)

DR LOCO: What dreams are you dreaming now?

LILE JIMMY: Lloyd George hasn't telephoned?

DR LOCO: No, James, he hasn't.

LILE JIMMY: Perhaps they've lost my letter, or deliberately mislaid it. A lot of Socialists work in the Post Office these days. They open my mail, you know.

DR LOCO: All Welshmen, so I've heard.

LILE JIMMY: There you are then!
(*Magpies chatter off.*)
Morning, Mr Magpie. Morning, Mr Magpie. Morning, Mr Magpie.

DR LOCO: Magpies are prehistoric, you know, James. They lived on ticks and fleas between the scales of the dinosaurs. Great power, little feeling and pea-sized brains always supported the magpie.

LILE JIMMY: You've disconnected the telephone!

DR LOCO: This is not your telephone, James. It is a telephone without a home, without a function, cut off from everything. I am studying the telephone as an instrument of acute isolation. Lloyd George will probably choose to send you a telegram. One can be so curt in a telegram.

LILE JIMMY: When that telegram is delivered, I don't want the boy seeking me out, looking me in the eye. Keep him away, d'you hear?

DR LOCO: Why can't you face a young working lad, James – a son of the town that made you rich?

LILE JIMMY: You must accept Lloyd George's telegram on my behalf! That's the kind of thing I pay you for!

DR LOCO: Oh? That kind of thing, is it?

LILE JIMMY: You must prevent me getting upset. It's not good for me. And if it's not good for me, it's no good for anyone in this town.

(In a temper, LILE JIMMY propels himself off in the wheelchair.

DR LOCO sits by the pagoda.

The PRESS OPERATOR enters and sings:)

Lile Jimmy Williamson
Ireland wants liberty,
you'll have to spell the problem out
for numbskulls such as me,
I can't keep up with what goes on
when I must struggle hard,
to see beyond my husband's wage
and the wall of our back yard. *(Exits L.)*

(GLADSTONE enters R with LILE JIMMY. They shake hands frontstage.)

GLADSTONE Welcome to Westminster, Mr O'Williamson.

LILE JIMMY: There's no O, sir.

GLADSTONE: Not a hundred and fifty miles from your own constituency is a nation held in the vilest subjection.

LILE JIMMY: I was turning that over in my mind while coming down from the north. How can so many men of Liberal principles be blind to the oppression and exploitation of their cousins, the Irish?

GLADSTONE: Land and money. Always look for the Tory twins. But, I'm sad to say, there are many wealthy Liberals who vote for us but secretly hope the Tories will win.

LILE JIMMY: Faced by that kind of dishonesty, sir, I wonder you haven't given up.

GLADSTONE: Once a week, at least. But all it takes is a chat with an honest, down-to-earth fellow like yourself and I find the strength to soldier on. *(A division bell sounds off.)* Ah, the call of battle. We have votes to cast, my friend.

(GLADSTONE puts an arm round LILE JIMMY's shoulders and they exit R.

The PRESS OPERATOR enters and sings:)

PRESS OPERATOR: Lile Jimmy Williamson
you stick up for the poor,

you'd never turn a hungry man
away from your back door,
if we fall sick and cannot work
you keep us in your pay,
if you should die, God help this town,
it would just fade away.
(*LILE JIMMY enters unsteadily with the aid of two walking-sticks, DR LOCO following behind him with the wheelchair. LILE JIMMY totters and falls backwards into it.*)

LILE JIMMY: I told you it was hopeless. I've lost the use of my legs. What's next? I ask myself. Not my mind. I couldn't bear that.

DR LOCO: Nature is merciful, James. When we do lose our minds we seldom realise something's missing.

LILE JIMMY: I wrote to Ramsbottom as well as Lloyd George – a very long letter.

DR LOCO: The Conservative candidate? Why?

LILE JIMMY: I'm going to support him.

DR LOCO: Hold on, hold on. (*Takes out his notebook.*) What's the time? (*Looks at his watch, then writes.*) At four-thirty, June tenth, 1928, you finally went overboard.

LILE JIMMY: Lloyd George betrayed me so I'm going to betray him. I'll write to every one of my workers and strongly advise them to vote for Ramsbottom.

DR LOCO: Or else?

LILE JIMMY: Doctor, when Shed comes up with the Red Book, he'll start talking about the flywheel.

DR LOCO: Will he now?

LILE JIMMY: I don't want to talk about the flywheel.

DR LOCO: I've always had the job of making you talk about unpleasant things. Tell me about this flywheel.

LILE JIMMY: It's cracked. It'll cost me a fortune to replace. Shed will say the crack is growing day by day but it's not. The crack has stopped. In fact it's repairing itself.

DR LOCO: The world has got a crack in it, James. The system is falling apart. But, like your flywheel, it continues going round and round. (*Pause.*) How many cures have we tried?

LILE JIMMY: Hundreds.

DR LOCO: All came to nothing. You've stayed healthy but you can't believe it. That makes you a sick man, James. I doubt if you'll live to be a hundred.

LILE JIMMY: I daren't go to sleep.

DR LOCO: If you take a nap right now, I guarantee you'll wake up.

LILE JIMMY: If I don't, it'll be your fault.

(DR LOCO touches LILE JIMMY'S forehead.

A blackbird sings.

LILE JIMMY falls asleep.

DR LOCO wheels him off R.

The PRESS OPERATOR enters and sings:)

PRESS OPERATOR: Lile Jimmy Williamson,

what sickness ails thee now?

It's all imagination,

come surely tha' must know,

just think on lads stuck in thy mills

for hours and hours and hours,

and thy great heart will right itself

and bring back all thy powers. (*Exits.*)

(LILE JIMMY enters L, very agitated. He turns and beckons impatiently.

DR LOCO strolls on in a straw hat, licking an ice-cream cone.)

LILE JIMMY: Hurry up, man! I haven't got all day. I've got a committee meeting in ten minutes.

DR LOCO: Calm down, James. I can't keep coming to London when you get in one of your panics.

LILE JIMMY: I can't go on. I'm doing my best but it's not enough. Have you heard about the lies Tom Storey is spreading about me?

DR LOCO: Terrible, isn't it?

LILE JIMMY: I'm being forced time after time into confrontations. Tom Storey wants my business. So he slanders me...says I'm mean. I tell you, I'm dreading this next election.

DR LOCO: Look into my eyes.

LILE JIMMY: Oh, stop fooling.

DR LOCO: I'm going to mesmerise you.

LILE JIMMY: (*Covering his face.*) No!

DR LOCO: Come on. Don't be shy. It might help.

LILE JIMMY: Alright, I'll take a chance. I'm trusting you, mind. Don't take advantage.

(*LILE JIMMY looks into DR LOCO's eyes. He sinks to the ground. Pause.*

DR LOCO waves a hand in front of LILE JIMMY's face.)

DR LOCO: You're beside the sea. You can hear the sound of the waves.

(*LILE JIMMY sits up, looks out into the audience.*)

Can you smell the ozone?

(*LILE JIMMY nods.*)

Beneath you is mud and shifting sand. Can you feel it.

(*LILE JIMMY nods again.*)

Say after me: I am an oyster.

LILE JIMMY: I am an oyster.

DR LOCO: Storms, wars and famine pass you by. You can feel the seismic tremors of far-off earthquakes and volcanic eruptions. (*Shakes him.*) There! That was a big one!

(*LILE JIMMY trembles.*)

DR LOCO: In your fear, what gives you comfort? What's all around you in your oyster-bed? Other oysters, James, other oysters.

LILE JIMMY: I'm in my shell. (*He covers his face and peers through his fingers.*)

DR LOCO: Where's your pearl?

(*LILE JIMMY clutches his stomach and looks frantically around him.*)

LILE JIMMY: (*Whimpering.*) Keep them away!

DR LOCO: Are you the only one with a pearl, James?

LILE JIMMY: (*Nodding.*) I've got it safe. They'll never get it off me. Oh, the light's getting brighter. I can hear sounds from the surface. It's the tide! I hate the tide! (*Rolls into a ball.*)

DR LOCO: Striding across the sands in his great boots comes the fisherman. What is he looking for, James? What does he want?

LILE JIMMY: My pearl!

DR LOCO: Shall he ever have it, James?

LILE JIMMY: Never!

DR LOCO: He stands looking at the thousands of barnacled shells, at the mess of weed and mud and sand, then he spots you. He starts to work out how to penetrate your shell for that pearl.

LILE JIMMY: I'm not here! I'm not here!

DR LOCO: He takes a few giant steps towards you but…it's too late. The tide is already returning. (*Snaps his fingers.*) Wake up, James.

LILE JIMMY: What am I doing on the floor?

DR LOCO: We've been fishing, James. Only fishing.

(*The PRESS OPERATOR enters and sings:*)

PRESS OPERATOR: Lile Jimmy Williamson

our town was sinking fast

when thy old dad got down to work

and built it up to last,

if he'd not left his homeland hills

to fill our working need,

this town would likely turned and died

for lack of strength and seed. (*Exits.*)

(*Birdsong.*

DR LOCO pushes LILE JIMMY, who is dozing, on in his wheelchair. DR LOCO looks up and puts his finger to his lips. The birdsong stops.)

DR LOCO: Sweet dreams.

(*DR LOCO exits R.*

A clap of thunder and blackout.

Spot on the pagoda.

LILE JIMMY's heavily bearded FATHER comes out in a white robe.

LILE JIMMY wakes and cries out in terror.)

LILE JIMMY: No, no, Father! Not you, please!

FATHER: (*In a strong north Cumbrian accent.*) Lya noo Jimmy lad! Purrup t'wages, tu baddun tu. Aa see thee stripped nakitt to the sarke. You've a heed as sad as a bull's liver. Ya's brakin ma heart.

LILE JIMMY: Don't keep haunting me, Dad. I can't work properly wi' thee allus breathin' doon ma neck.

FATHER: Wisht, ya scrimpy! Ya spend your life scrowmally after pennies, mon. Ya scroby merrybegot, aam ashamed o' thee! Ya gi' work tae a raft o' fwok but ya wonna gi' 'em a proper wage.

LILE JIMMY: I do, Dad, I do… It's all I can afford.…

FATHER: Doant gi' me that. Aa ken thy profits, lad! Purrup t'wages. Be a menseful swort o'captain. Ya've got men doon at the quay there like mice in a meal kist, but norra decent wage for them tae feed their bairns. Ya mak me rap an' tear, so ye do!

LILE JIMMY: Times are hard, Dad. There's a recession on the way…

FATHER: There's allus wun o' those on the way! Life's up an' doon, man, up an' doon, but that' disnae mean ye can starve thy men. Wun day ya'll hear frae thy works thy fwok rowtin laak a thoosand cattle, cursin' ya! Rub thy work fwok up the wrong way an' ye'll ruinate thysaelf. Dinna ryve all thy profits for thyself. Gi' sum out in t'wages. Share oot, mon! It'll be a boon to thee later. If ye doan't, it's sarten they'll come to hate thee.

LILE JIMMY: It's not as easy as that, Dad…economics often dictates…

FATHER: Shurrup, tha miserly man! Ye dumfounder me wi' ya economics. Ye'll drabble ma guid name in t'mud, an still gi' me cheek! When aa think how thy mudder an' me padded the hoof frae Keswick to Lancaster fifty year agoa. We were skint. Aa know what it feels like.

LILE JIMMY: Father, times have changed. I've expanded the business. You wouldn't know the factory now. To stay competitive in world markets I have to keep wages down.

FATHER: Och, Jimmy, gang thy ways. Aa'm takin tae a stoon. Ye mawk midge wages an' ya duzzent mind. Aam ashamed o' thee! In torment! Purrup t'wages, aa tell thee! Purremup!

LILE JIMMY: If I do they'll think I'm scared of the Socialists. I can't let them think that. Anarchy would follow.

FATHER: Jimmy, aa'm wastin' ma time. Ya scrattin' on
    ma headstrane an aa'm sick o' thee. D'ya want a factory
    crammed wi' lickplates or honest fwok? They'll turn
    against ye if ye stay nar-gangan. Och, aa'm doin' nae guid
    here beatin' ma gums. Aa'm off.

LILE JIMMY: Father, wait a moment.

FATHER: What d'ya wan't, ya scroby num-thoom?

LILE JIMMY: I've been thinking about buying a factory in
    Antwerp to better open up the European market. From
    your very special vantage point, d'you think it would be a
    good long-term investment?

FATHER: (*As he exits through the pagoda with a dismissive gesture
    of despair.*) Ach, Jimmy, aa scarcely knew ya.
    (*R Spot out.*
    L spot for the PRESS OPERATOR who enters and sings:)

PRESS OPERATOR: Lile Jimmy Williamson
    no other bosses care,
    they think the world is theirs to pluck
    and they don't treat us fair,
    if men complain they get thrown out,
    ignore us when we grieve,
    so we must turn to our good Jim
    in whom we still believe.
    (*Chairs and table set for dinner frontstage centre.*
    THOMAS and MRS STOREY enter from R with LILE JIMMY
    – all in evening dress.)

LILE JIMMY: Thank you for coming, Tom.

STOREY: We might as well sort it out sociably rather than on
    the hustings.
    (*JESSE enters with a drinks tray.*)

JESSE: Sherry?

MRS STOREY: Oh, yes, please.
    (*JESSE hands sherry round.*)

LILE JIMMY: Tom, twelve years ago when you stood as
    Liberal candidate for Lancaster I gave you five hundred
    pounds.

STOREY: You contributed to my election expenses. Not that
    it did much good in the end.

LILE JIMMY: And now you're getting ready to stand against me.

MRS STOREY: Lovely sherry.

JESSE: Amontillado.

LILE JIMMY: It's Liberal against Liberal. Where's the sense in that?

STOREY: You know why.

JESSE: We have a London shipper.

LILE JIMMY: Tom, we've managed to see eye to eye for a long time. We agree about so many things. I can't imagine fighting an election with you – especially when I know the central issue is of no real interest to you.

STOREY: Every Englishman has to care about the Irish Question.

LILE JIMMY: Tom, I'll be frank with you. We're both factory owners. Between us we employ more people than all the other businesses put together. It's ridiculous for the two of us to spar up in front of the whole town. It can only weaken our position.

STOREY: I know too much about the way you do business.

LILE JIMMY: It takes two to make a deal.

STOREY: Aye, one to have his throat cut, the other to cut it.
(*Pause. The women eye each other uncomfortably.*)

MRS STOREY: Do come and look around our Institute some time, Jesse. Mechanics can be fascinating. And education is so important.

JESSE: I'm very busy rehearsing for my platform appearances once the campaign gets under way. Why does the Liberal Party have to have yellow as its colour. It doesn't suit me at all.

MRS STOREY: Well, if I've got to wear it, I suit creamy rather than buttery.

LILE JIMMY: (*Curtly.*) We'll have dinner now.
(*They sit at the table with a flourish of napkins.*
JESSE rings a little bell. The first course is served. They eat.
WALL enters frontstage in working clothes and addresses the audience.)

WALL: I'll let you in on a few home truths about Williamson
– our Member of Parliament. He hardly ever attends
debates, being so busy flogging lino. That's what he uses
the House of Commons for – business contacts, home and
abroad. Back here, he runs his works with a rod of iron.
If a valued man wants to leave the company to better
himself, Williamson tells that man he'll be blackballed with
all other employers, no references, so he'd best change
his mind. Each year he shuts down his works for a month.
There's no holiday pay. That knocks a big hole in a pound
a week spread over a year, doesn't it? Five thousand men
who can't afford a holiday have to hang around the streets
with nothing to do. And d'you know what they talk about,
these mugs? What a wonderful man he is.

LILE JIMMY: I hear you've actually done a deal with the
Tories, Tom. They're not putting up a candidate and
advising their supporters to vote for you. So, that makes
you a Tory in my book.

STOREY: That's fair enough. You're the workers' friend, so
you say. Does that make you a Socialist?

LILE JIMMY: That'll be the day. I'll have no truck with
Socialism, at any price.

STOREY: I'll beat you, Jimmy, and I'll dictate wages in this
town, and the price of lino leaving the factory. Meanwhile,
you – the man of the masses – will be left whistling at the
gates.

WALL: What's the difference between Satan and Lucifer.
They're both mean, they're both tyrannical, they're both
greedy. But the people must have work to live. (*Exits L.*)

LILE JIMMY: I believe in equality, that's true enough. I'll
admit no barriers of class or background in my life, but I'll
manage my own works in my own way.

STOREY: And mine, and Colonel Sly's, and Helme's, and the
Wagon Works, and Waring and Gillows, and the Council,
the lot! That's why I'm standing against you, Jimmy!
You're too powerful in this town.

LILE JIMMY: You'll lose. I'll see to that.

STOREY: If I do, where does that leave me? No worse off. I
could break you in London if I wanted to…

LILE JIMMY: Pshaw!

STOREY: But it's not worth it. I don't want your boots, Jimmy
– just to cut you down to size a little.

MRS STOREY: Is this turbot?

JESSE: That's what it started out as. I must tell cook to tone
down the sauce in future.

LILE JIMMY: I strongly advise you to withdraw, Tom.

STOREY: If you agree to us manufacturing lino in real
competition at our own prices, no undercutting, no
tampering with our credit, no bullying our buyers or
flooding our markets, you can have the parliamentary seat.
I won't even try.

LILE JIMMY: We have an agreement on wages, working
conditions, prices, everything Tom. I'm holding you to
that.

STOREY: You've used it to create an oppressive monopoly.
You're trying to corner the cork market, the linseed
market, and cut off my supplies. You'd put me out of
business if you could.

LILE JIMMY: Well, after this display I'll have to think about
it, Tom. Damn it, man, I haven't got your advantages! I've
got no coal mines to supplement my income, just a couple
of floor-covering items I do well…

STOREY: Jimmy, it's not lino you're printing these days, it's
pound notes. You're a millionaire for God's sake!

(*Pause.*)

JESSE: Are you really, James?

LILE JIMMY: Ring the bell.

(*JESSE rings the bell.*
The fish course is cleared away.
HODKINSON enters L and addresses the audience.)

HODKINSON: Brothers, fellow-workers, the last person
our union would criticise is Mr Williamson. He's got
the biggest heart in Lancaster. Helps the sick and needy.
Paid for all the kids to go to Manchester to see the Great
Exhibition. Got us cheap fares on the railway on market
day. Saw to it the postal services were improved. Bought
up all the market tolls – fifteen hundred pounds of good

money that cost him! – and has never collected them since. I know of children from poor families whose education he's paid for right through, never stinted. The church, orphanages, hospitals, anywhere you look you see what a generous fellow he is. But we're here to talk about the low wages he pays. He can be as charitable as he likes, but he mustn't save money on us. If he wants our support in this election, he'll have to do something about the money we're getting. It's not enough. In fact, it's a bloody disgrace.

(*Exits L.*

A huge pie is brought to the table.)

LILE JIMMY: Let's move on to more congenial subjects. How was the Riviera, Tom? I assume you were getting healthy for the fray.

STOREY: That's some pie you've got there.

(*A long knife is handed to LILE JIMMY.*)

LILE JIMMY: How much d'you want?

STOREY: Half.

LILE JIMMY: That's too big.

STOREY: Then be damned to you. Come.

(*STOREY stalks out followed by MRS STOREY.*)

LILE JIMMY: Well, my dear, it's just you and me.

JESSE: (*Upset.*) I'm not really hungry. I think I'll go to bed.

LILE JIMMY: (*Tucking his napkin under his chin.*) Suit yourself.

(*He pulls the whole pie over, picks up his knife and fork and...blackout.*

The PRESS OPERATOR enters to a spot L and sings:)

PRESS OPERATOR: Lile Jimmy Williamson

the promises you made

had all the best intentions

but trade is nobbut trade,

out there it's every dog eat dog,

a jungle cruel and harsh

keep hold thy wolfhound courage,

a spaniel's heart is marsh. (*Exits.*)

(*Spot out.*

Lights up on the walled garden.

*LILE JIMMY is in the wheelchair, whimpering and twitching
in his sleep
MAUD enters and stands behind him, flapping the end of a
feather boa in his face.)*

LILE JIMMY: (*In his sleep.*) Oh, no, Father! Don't tell me tha's
got wings noo!

MAUD: Oh, do snap out of it, James. I'm off to lunch. See you
later.

(DR LOCO enters L.)

DR LOCO: How is he, Maud?

MAUD: Raving.

(LILE JIMMY wakes.)

Would you like to come out to lunch, Doctor? My treat.

DR LOCO: I'd love to, but my patient here has asked to see
me.

MAUD: Don't get too bored. (*Exits.*)

LILE JIMMY: Oh, Doctor, I've been dreaming about my
father again and again. Is there a cure for that?

DR LOCO: Only by having no father in the first place.

LILE JIMMY: We should be able to control our dreams.

DR LOCO: Can't help you there. James, you need cheering
up. I prescribe a little music. The new minister has asked
me for help with the choir at the Mission.

LILE JIMMY: I didn't know you were a musical man.

DR LOCO: Harmonics fascinate me, James.

LILE JIMMY: I'd rather be left in peace.

DR LOCO: I've arranged an impromptu concert for you,
here, in your garden. These are your own employees come
to serenade you.

LILE JIMMY: I don't want a concert. Crash bang wallop!

DR LOCO: We're due to start any minute. Just sit back and
relax.

*(DR LOCO brings a stepladder out of the pagoda and props it
against the wall of the garden.)*

LILE JIMMY: What are you doing?

DR LOCO: (*Climbing up the ladder.*) I have to conduct a
particularly difficult piece of polyphony.

LILE JIMMY: I don't want any damn polyphony! I want to
be left alone, in private!

DR LOCO: Nothing to get upset about, James. They can't see
    you. You'll just hear their voices.

LILE JIMMY: Come down off that ladder!

DR LOCO: Ready, choir? Oh, I should mention, James – the
    piece was written especially for you.

LILE JIMMY: Oh, that's kind. But don't let them climb over!

DR LOCO: It's called: 'Lament for the Declining Pound.'
    One-two-three!
    (*Over the wall, the choir of WORKERS sings in parts:*)

WORKERS: Hellfire, doom, the hangman's knot,
    prison, birch, and getting shot,
    these are nowt, no perturbation,
    compared to this devaluation.
    We ask those men whom we elect:
    Be sure thou always will protect
    us from the worst affliction known,
    a wage that's got an inbuilt hole
    through which our lifeblood flows
    and leaves us wishing we were dead
    because the penny in this hand
    is nobbut worth a pinch of sand.
    Amen. Amen. Amen.

DR LOCO: Well, James – what d'you think of that?

LILE JIMMY: That's the first work of art anyone's ever
    dedicated to me. Though I've given thousands of pounds
    worth of art to the people of this town, your piece just now
    is all I've ever received in return. Thank you, but all it's
    done is make me sad.

DR LOCO: Thank you, choir. His lordship was moved.
    (*He descends the ladder and puts it back in the pagoda, then sits
    down in a deck-chair.*
    *Two EDITORS enter as playful dogs with pencils between their
    teeth as the PRESS OPERATOR enters and sings:*)

PRESS OPERATOR: Lile Jimmy Williamson
    Tom Storey's at your throat,
    trying to poison your good name
    and catch the floating vote,
    we don't want him for our MP,

the man is such a pain,
we'll stick to thee, the Workers' Friend,
and vote for thee again.
(*TOM STOREY enters and gives a piercing whistle.*
The EDITORS sit down on their back legs, jostling each other
in front of him, panting, pencils at the ready.)
STOREY: Behave, Observer, you bad dog! Quiet Gazette,
you cur! Do as you're told!
(*The EDITORS whimper, cowed and obedient.*
STOREY feeds them titbits from his pocket.)
Get this down. Mr Williamson's latest damp thunderbolt...
(*The EDITORS scribble.*)
– the Elector's Guide, is stale rechauffé Irish garbage and
English gutter politics. Lancaster voters are tired of being
dictated to by this man. He has no right to think he owns
the seat in the Commons as a natural perquisite of his
business.
(*Barking off.*
LILE JIMMY enters with two EDITORS on leashes.
They lunge at STOREY's dogs, snapping and snarling.)
Keep those animals under control!
LILE JIMMY: They never hurt anyone, Tom. Just keep your
distance.
STOREY: They're mad.
LILE JIMMY: A word from me and they're nice as pie. I've
taught them a few tricks. Up, Guardian!
GUARDIAN EDITOR: Thomas Storey has all the rancour of
the pervert. (*Rolls over.*) Once an honoured Liberal leader
he is now a mere flunkey of the Tories.
LILE JIMMY: Come on, Times. Don't be outdone!
TIMES EDITOR: Thomas Storey has the bitter spleen of
disappointed ambition. (*Rolls over.*) Who can trust the
judgement of an envious man?
STOREY: Very impressive, Jimmy. You know how to train
animals, I'll give you that much – especially human
animals.
LILE JIMMY: (*Patting his dogs.*) It is not my way to indulge in
personal attacks and invective. All I put before the people
is my record and my principles...and my friends. (*Whistles.*)

(*Enter HODKINSON looking shamefaced, cap in hand, and
WALL, who is angry and sullen.*)
Mr Hodkinson, I believe you've got something to say on
behalf of the Trades Council.

HODKINSON: Well, yes…we've had a meeting and…er…
the upshot is, we see it is indeed in everyone's interest
to support your candidature. You are truly the Workers'
Friend.

(*A rolling dog-fight starts among the EDITORS. They run off,
barking.*)

STOREY: You've been conned, lads. The Workers' Friend?
Ask him who voted against an eight-hour day for miners!

LILE JIMMY: How can you expect a working man to vote
Tory, Tom? It's a contradiction in terms.

STOREY: (*Desperately.*) Listen lads, for years Williamson has
had Lancaster tied up with secret agreements between
himself and the other employers and the town council.
He's a sinister and dangerous manipulator. It's his intention
to own this town lock, stock and barrel! His influence is
evil! I beg you, don't elect him again. He's a man after
power for its own sake, not yours. He's bamboozled you
and you should hate him for it. You have before you
a ruthless dictator in the making. I plead with you to
recognise this fact.

(*Pause.*

HODKINSON and WALL look at the ground.)

He's done his job very well. What does your silence mean?
You don't believe me, or you daren't believe me? (*In a
sudden fury.*) He has only to put up his little finger and you
cringe and fawn before him! He overawes you! By God, we
have an idiot asylum here in Lancaster and I think it has a
great influence on the population! You act like imbeciles!

(*Silence.*

STOREY closes his eyes, aware he's gone much too far.)

LILE JIMMY: Thank you, Tom.

(*STOREY exits R, HODKINSON and WALL, L.*

DR LOCO steps out of the garden.)

DR LOCO: You won the seat again. Congratulations.

LILE JIMMY: Doctor, I've never felt so ill, so betrayed, so wretched.

DR LOCO: Oh, come on, James! You should be happy.

LILE JIMMY: There are four thousand and seventy-five men in this town who hate me. Some of them are undoubtedly in my employ.

DR LOCO: You've just been through a democratic process, James. Some people will always vote against you. We can't be liked by everyone.

LILE JIMMY: I can't go on. I must have peace. I can feel them working against me. I daren't go to London and leave them a free hand here. They'll destroy everything.

DR LOCO: Then don't go. Stay here. They won't miss you in the House of Commons. Tighten your grip. We can get the names of those four thousand and odd men who voted against you. We'll set up a concentration camp.

LILE JIMMY: You're mad.

DR LOCO: The mad doctor, or the doctor of the mad?

LILE JIMMY: I'm a sick man. Fifty, and look at me – haven't had a day's good health since I was a boy. Can't you do something for me, Doctor?

DR LOCO: Try taking snuff.

LILE JIMMY: Snuff?

DR LOCO: You need to vary your vices, James. They can't all be on such a grand scale. Yes, take snuff. Blast out all the cobwebs!

LILE JIMMY: Alright, we'll give it a try.

DR LOCO: It stands as good a chance of curing your ailment as anything else, James.

LILE JIMMY: Ah, you admit I've got something! Now you're talking!

DR LOCO: Oh, yes.

LILE JIMMY: My condition is one on its own.

DR LOCO: I'm not sure about that. But it could be contagious – especially in the House of Commons.

LILE JIMMY: You've given me fresh hope, Doctor. I feel better already. Perhaps you'll come down to London for a visit.

DR LOCO: Yes, I'd like that. There's some research I want
    to do in the largest asylum for the insane we have in these
    islands. It's situated in London.

LILE JIMMY: Oh? Where is that

DR LOCO: The House of Lords.

    (*LILE JIMMY laughs, shaking his head.*)

LILE JIMMY: Be away with you, Doctor. You're having me
    on.

    (*GLADSTONE and CABINET MINISTER enter as DR
    LOCO exits through the pagoda.*)

GLADSTONE: Mr Williamson, we have been defeated. The
    Home Rule Bill has been rejected by the Upper House.
    The main platform of our policy has been taken from
    under us. We must go to the country again.

LILE JIMMY: Oh, no, no! Not another election so soon!

CABINET MINISTER: We have no alternative, I'm afraid.

LILE JIMMY: The last one nearly killed me. (*Takes snuff.*)
    I was just starting to get over it.

CABINET MINISTER: You fought a brilliant campaign and
    won a decisive victory, James. We were all most impressed.

GLADSTONE: Quite outstanding. (*Pause.*) Er...my colleague
    will explain the position, Mr Williamson.

CABINET MINISTER: We have two problems, James. First,
    funds – much of our financial backing went with the split
    in the Liberal Party over Home Rule – second, the House
    of Lords. The Home Rule Bill is now stuck there. We need
    people on our side in that chamber. (*Pause as he scans LILE
    JIMMY'S face for understanding.*) James, we must change the
    Lords.

LILE JIMMY: You mean alter their privileges?

CABINET MINISTER: More their persons.

LILE JIMMY: Chuck some out? That would be revolutionary!

GLADSTONE: Heaven forfend.

CABINET MINISTER: James, we will be candid. You are a
    rich man – in fact, a very rich man. The Party is short of
    funds. Also, we must have some new peers in the Lords to
    counterbalance the anti-Home Rulers.

    (*Pause. LILE JIMMY takes another pinch of snuff.*)

LILE JIMMY: I paid all the election expenses of every
  Liberal candidate in Lancashire for the last election.
CABINET MINISTER: We know, James, we know.
  Remarkably generous.
GLADSTONE: Don't know what we'd have done without
  you.
CABINET MINISTER: Two problems, James. One – no
  money. Two – new peers. Look at them together.
LILE JIMMY: Wouldn't it make a mockery of the House of
  Lords if you stuff any Tom, Dick and Harry in there to get
  bills through?
GLADSTONE: Mr Williamson, there are men in the
  commercial world, great captains of industry, such as
  yourself, who are eminent by process of natural selection.
  They have risen to the top by merit. Such men are already
  peers to me.
  (*Pause as LILE JIMMY starts to catch on. He rapidly takes
  more snuff.*)
LILE JIMMY: Prime Minister, am I to understand…
GLADSTONE: Yes, Mr Williamson, you are.
LILE JIMMY: Me, a lord?
CABINET MINISTER: Look at your export record! You're
  covering the floors of the entire globe.
LILE JIMMY: I'm amazed!
CABINET MINISTER: Is it settled, then?
LILE JIMMY: I can't believe it!
GLADSTONE: There is one question remaining. Let us
  complete the business.
CABINET MINISTER: What d'you say? Is it to be Lord
  James?
LILE JIMMY: Prime Minister, I don't know how to thank
  you.
GLADSTONE: I do.
CABINET MINISTER: Couldn't happen to a nicer fellow.
  What can I put you down for?
LILE JIMMY: Eh?
CABINET MINISTER: How much?
LILE JIMMY: How much what?

CABINET MINISTER: (*Wearily.*) Two connected problems… peerages and money.

LILE JIMMY: But you said I deserved it – I'm a natural peer, a born aristocrat…I should get a free one, surely.

GLADSTONE: (*Now steely.*) We can offer elsewhere to people of lesser worth – (*Softens.*) – but we would rather a man like you enjoyed this eminence rather than some mercenary wretch with no principles. You will make a great Liberal peer. A great Liberal radical peer!

LILE JIMMY: But I have to pay for the privilege.

CABINET MINISTER: A baronage is ten thousand. You can choose your own title. Not Lancaster – that's already spoken for.

LILE JIMMY: To pay for even what we deserve.

GLADSTONE: Most of all for what we deserve. We'll expect your cheque. Goodnight.

> (*GLADSTONE and CABINET MINISTER exit R.*
> *LILE JIMMY ponders, taking snuff.*
> *The PRESS OPERATOR enters and starts to sing.*
> *LILE JIMMY exits during the song.*)

PRESS OPERATOR: Lile Jimmy Williamson,
> they're putting it around
> that you've forgotten all your friends
> and London's made thee proud,
> they say you crave to be a lord,
> a baron or a duke,
> that you can choose the one you like
> when in your purse you look. (*Exits.*)

> (*DR LOCO enters with binoculars round his neck, pushing LILE JIMMY in the wheelchair.*)

DR LOCO: While we're waiting for Lloyd George to contact you, let's do a bit of bird-spotting, eh? (*Uses binoculars.*) There's one in your weeping willow.

LILE JIMMY: Why isn't he singing?

DR LOCO: Perhaps he's sad about something. Here, have a look. (*Gives him the binoculars.*)

LILE JIMMY: Ah, yes. I see it – a little wren.

DR LOCO: A very shy bird with a perky tail. James, would you like me to transfer your condition to that tiny creature?

LILE JIMMY: Eh?

DR LOCO: Troglodytes troglodytes is its zoological name – so that's a good start. We'll give the trog your sickness and send it flying into space. How about that?

LILE JIMMY: What would happen to it?

DR LOCO: It would explode.

LILE JIMMY: Do it then.

DR LOCO: Christ transferred a man's madness into the Gadarene swine and sent them crashing over a cliff.

LILE JIMMY: DO IT! DO IT!

DR LOCO: First, the admission. Say after me, I am insane.

LILE JIMMY: No, I won't! I'm not. I'm a success!

(*DR LOCO puts his hands on LILE JIMMY's head and intones:*)

DR LOCO: I call upon the powers of the old earth to cause all the physical manifestations of madness to afflict this man. Let him be seen to be mad. Let him recognise himself for what he is.

LILE JIMMY: Take your hands off me! Maud, help, help!

DR LOCO: Maud is tinkering with the lock on her door with a hairpin. There's only me, James…and the jenny wren.

LILE JIMMY: You've upset me today. You always make it your business to upset me. Go away…go on. I'm annoyed.

DR LOCO: (*Moves to leave.*) Very well.

LILE JIMMY: But don't go too far.

DR LOCO: There are men suffering from your condition stalking through Europe, loaded with honours, free as air to do as they will.

LILE JIMMY: I think we should part company. I've got a good mind to sue you for professional malpractice.

DR LOCO: James, I appeal to your hypochondria. Do you really want to be left in your mental state without anyone to help you?

LILE JIMMY: You're fired.

DR LOCO: Go ahead. Be alone.

LILE JIMMY: I don't want to consult you again. You've allowed envy of my achievements to colour your attitude towards me. I will go elsewhere.

DR LOCO: Your complaint will get worse, James.

LILE JIMMY: The complaint doesn't exist. Who else ever had it?

DR LOCO: King Louis the Second of Bavaria.

LILE JIMMY: (*Quite pleased.*) Really? Anyone else?

DR LOCO: Napoleon.

LILE JIMMY: I'm in good company then. Oh, Doctor, I know you and your mischief. What would I do without you, eh?

DR LOCO: They might put you inside. But then you'd pay them not to, wouldn't you? Or perhaps you'd buy the asylum.

LILE JIMMY: Sometimes I think I do you some good, keeping you on your toes, eh? Come on, let's go and have a glass of champagne with Maud.

(*The wren starts to sing.*)

DR LOCO: There she goes. Whoosh! Watch out for the explosion!

(*LILE JIMMY laughs and shakes his head as DR LOCO pushes him off in the wheelchair.*
Lights fade to blackout.)

End of Act One.

ACT TWO

1928. Lights up on LILE JIMMY in the wheelchair and DR LOCO playing cards in the walled garden.

LILE JIMMY: Snap!

DR LOCO: You're too quick for me, James.

LILE JIMMY: You don't pay enough attention. I knew there were two Mr Breads the Baker coming up.

(*A TELEGRAM DELIVERY BOY enters nervously.*)

TELEGRAM BOY: Art thou Lord Ashton?

LILE JIMMY: Tell him to turn his face away when he's talking to me. I won't be stared at!

DR LOCO: Talk to me, boy.

TELEGRAM BOY: Art thou Lord Ashton, then?

DR LOCO: No, thank God.

LILE JIMMY: Take the thing off him. Get away, boy. Go on. And don't you dare look over your shoulder at me or I'll have you fired.

(*DR LOCO gives the TELEGRAM BOY a tip and takes the telegram off him. He runs off L.*)

LILE JIMMY: He did take a peep. Cunning little eyes he had.

DR LOCO: D'you want me to open this for you?

LILE JIMMY: It'll be an apology from Lloyd George.

(*DR LOCO opens the telegram and reads it.*)

A grovelling apology.

DR LOCO: Well, who'd have thought you had that kind of influence, James?

LILE JIMMY: What does he say, the slimy, two-faced equivocator?

DR LOCO: He's coming up to Lancaster today.

LILE JIMMY: (*Delighted.*) In person?

DR LOCO: How else?

LILE JIMMY: (*Very excited.*) I knew it! Oh, this is just the tonic I needed! I made him jump, didn't I? And won't it be wonderful having him here, Doctor? Some life at last! We can talk about the old times in the Commons. Oh, the fun we had! He must come to dinner. Tell Maud he's coming

to dinner. Tell her I want the best wines, only the best. I tell
you, Lloyd George and me have drunk a few together!
(*DR LOCO smiles and exits R.*
LILE JIMMY plays cards, slapping them down.)
Snap! Mr Black the Coalman! Knew he was coming!
(*RAMSBOTTOM, the Tory candidate, enters sporting a blue
rosette.*
*He stands a little way off as LILE JIMMY keeps playing. After
a while he clears his throat.*)
Snap! Mr Blood the Butcher! Are you any good at this
game, Ramsbottom?

RAMSBOTTOM: You asked to see me, Lord Ashton.

LILE JIMMY: Know how to play? Easy enough. It's like for
like. What did I want to see you for? What's your name?

RAMSBOTTOM: Ramsbottom, your lordship.

LILE JIMMY: Ah, yes. My doctor calls you Ewesanus. We
have a good laugh about that.

RAMSBOTTOM: Very droll, your lordship, but rather
childish.

LILE JIMMY: Lloyd George is coming to dinner tonight.
His favourite is meringues. D'you like meringues, Mr
Ewesanus?

RAMSBOTTOM: Ramsbottom, actually.

LILE JIMMY: I sent you a letter.

RAMSBOTTOM: Yes, you did. That's why I came.

LILE JIMMY: I want that letter printed on a poster and stuck
up all over the town.

RAMSBOTTOM: What a good idea.

LILE JIMMY: I want it everywhere – in Tory blue. I want
Lloyd George to see it when he arrives at the station…

RAMSBOTTOM: That doesn't give us any time to have it
printed.

LILE JIMMY: If you have any trouble with Mr Print the
Printer bring him up here and I'll sort him out. Take heart,
man. I'll pay your damn campaign expenses! Cheer up!

RAMSBOTTOM: If you say so, your lordship… Lloyd
George coming up here is a trifle worrying, I would have
thought…

LILE JIMMY: He'll be destroyed. One look at my town with my letter plastered all over it and, phut! he'll be ruined as a political force. Then we can relax and enjoy our dinner together.

RAMSBOTTOM: I'd better go and talk to the printer. Will you excuse me, your lordship?

LILE JIMMY: I want those posters BIG, d'you understand? As big as he can make them.

(*RAMSBOTTOM hurriedly exits R.*

DR LOCO enters L with SHED, the works manager.

LILE JIMMY gets out of the wheelchair and pushes it into the pagoda.)

SHED: I'm a little anxious about this medical exam, Doctor. It's years since anyone looked me over. What did you find?

DR LOCO: (*To LILE JIMMY.*) Here's Mr Shed to say hello, James. He's going to manage your factory for you. I'm glad you take my advice sometimes.

SHED: Am I a fit man?

LILE JIMMY: Mr Shed, I want that new system of quality control installed tomorrow, understand?

SHED: I haven't started work yet, your Lordship. I'll need a little time.

LILE JIMMY: You're fired.

DR LOCO: Take no notice. Are you sure you want this job?

SHED: It's the best I've ever been offered. It's a company with global ambitions.

DR LOCO: The salary is pitiably small.

SHED: That's my look-out. After I've proved myself I'll ask for a raise.

DR LOCO: (*Laughs.*) He'll work you into the ground. He'll tyrannise you. At the moment, you're healthy. Within six months you'll be a nervous wreck, hounded from pillar to post by this appalling megalomaniac. I feel guilty about your future because I suggested he should delegate...but he's left it much too late.

SHED: It will be an honour to serve his lordship.

LILE JIMMY: Good man.

(*DR LOCO sighs and shrugs, then exits.*

SHED goes into the pagoda and returns with a large ledger, the Red Book.

He works on it as the PRESS OPERATOR enters L and sings:)

PRESS OPERATOR: Lile Jimmy Williamson
Though t' old queen's dead and gone,
the empire and the glory,
go marching on and on!
We're living in a brand-new age,
the twentieth-century,
which promises a better life
for working folk like me.
(WALL and HODKINSON enter L.
They address their remarks obliquely to SHED.)

WALL: Brothers, first of all let's get one thing straight: we would never criticise Lord Ashton. *(Under his breath.)* Get that down, you spying bastard.
(SHED writes in the Red Book.)

HODKINSON: Never would we say a word against him.

WALL: Every man in the Independent Labour Party thinks the world of his lordship.

HODKINSON: We do that.

WALL: What we want to attack is capitalism.

HODKINSON: Capitalism's the thing.

WALL: We hear a lot of patriotic talk about the British Empire on which the sun never sets. That's all very well, but you should spare a thought for your wages. There's not much sunshine there, brothers. The average pay in some of our philanthropic industries round here is one pound and threepence a week. Who can bring a hungry family up on that?
(WALL and HODKINSON exit L.
SHED finishes writing his report of the meeting in the Red Book, then hands it over to LILE JIMMY.)

SHED: Apart from my daily report, your lordship, I have some general news. The South African War is over.

LILE JIMMY: Good. Those Boers will need lino for their huts before long. Tell the design department to come up with some ideas. You know, monkeys playing in the trees, crocodiles sleeping on a sandbank – that kind of thing. Nothing too complicated, mind.

SHED: I'll see to it, your lordship. (*Exits.*)

LILE JIMMY reads the Red Book.

(*JESSE enters, dressed up for an occasion.*)

JESSE: (*Agitated.*) James, I don't like to see you with that awful book! I don't like it at all!

LILE JIMMY: See what those Socialists call me now.

JESSE: Oh, not the Socialists again. If the world ended you'd say it was part of the Labour Party programme.

LILE JIMMY: A grocer drinking in the Wellington public house called me the uncrowned king of Lancaster. What d'you think of that?

JESSE: Why bother to have such nonsense brought to you?

LILE JIMMY: I have to know what they're saying about me behind my back.

JESSE: Having it recorded by sneaky informers diminishes you.

LILE JIMMY: I have a perfect right to know what's going on in my own town.

JESSE: Stop saying things like that! It's not your town!

LILE JIMMY: Where are you going?

JESSE: I have to attend a meeting at the Mission and give some prizes. I do wish you'd do more of this kind of thing. I seem to spend my entire life in public mouthing platitudes.

LILE JIMMY: I believe your little speeches are always well received.

JESSE: No doubt you have those recorded by your wretched minions as well!

LILE JIMMY: Jesse, there are thirty – THIRTY – Socialists sitting in the House of Commons these days. They are committed to the destruction of our society. Why do people elect them? If being an uncrowned king means I have a natural authority, I must use it to make the voters see sense. Socialism is an evil force. If it gets any more powerful, it will inflict enormous injury on trade and ruin the lives of the working class.

JESSE: Oh, be quiet, James. You're giving me a headache.

LILE JIMMY: Under Socialism, England as we know her, and love her, will cease to exist. But this town will survive. I'll see to that!

JESSE: Why d'you exaggerate all the time?

LILE JIMMY: The Socialists are determined to destroy my business by making huge wage demands.

JESSE: James, once you believed in these people. Now all you care about is the few who criticise you. What about the rest who still respect and admire you.

LILE JIMMY: Then why don't they drive those devils out? Jesse, you're a very trusting, simple-minded woman. You can't see how devious, underhand and unreliable people are. They blow with the wind. Look at the last election…

JESSE: You won!

LILE JIMMY: Aye, but with a reduced majority. After all I've done for this town, all the money I've spent, all the jobs I provide, they go against me in increasing numbers. How can they treat me in this way?

JESSE: When all's said and done, James, people have a right to make up their own minds.

LILE JIMMY: Go to your meeting.

JESSE: I do believe you seek the same monopoly over people's minds as you have obtained over making linoleum.

LILE JIMMY: That will do, Jesse. Go to your meeting.

JESSE: Why don't you make a take-over bid for all the awkward ideas we might ever have!

LILE JIMMY: You're out of your depth. They're waiting for you at the Mission, dear. Off you go. But watch them carefully.

JESSE: Why can't you respond to affection when it's honestly given? You used to…

LILE JIMMY: Jesse…enough.

(Exits L.

JESSE crosses to downstage R.

REVEREND MELVILLE enters and greets her.

The WORKERS enter, tidied up. One of them gives JESSE a bouquet.

She smiles and smells the flowers.)

REV MELVILLE: Firstly, let us offer our thanks to Lady
　　Ashton for finding time in her busy schedule to attend our
　　meeting. Now we will sing hymn two hundred and forty-
　　three: 'I vow to thee my country, all earthly things above.'

JESSE: Reverend, I feel a little faint. Has someone put
　　something in the flowers?

REV MELVILLE: They were picked out of my garden only a
　　while ago, your ladyship. Get a chair!
　　(*A WORKER brings a chair on and JESSE sits down.*)

JESSE: Thank you. My husband says I must be careful. Do
　　carry on.

REV MELVILLE: We'll skip the hymn. I have prepared a
　　short address. We can skip that as well, if you like.

JESSE: No, no. I'm sure it's most interesting. Please begin.

REV MELVILLE: Well, if you're quite sure…

JESSE: Yes, yes. I'm alright now.

REV MELVILLE: Sit down, please.
　　(*The WORKERS sit at his feet.*)
　　I have chosen as my subject, Christianity in our Daily
　　Life. Rachel, will you stop fidgeting! Let's ask ourselves
　　this question: if Our Lord was a Lancaster man, which
　　way would He vote in the forthcoming election? Tommy,
　　I'll send you out in a minute if you don't stop doing that!
　　What candidate would he choose to support? Can we, for
　　instance, imagine Jesus as a Tory?
　　(*The WORKERS burst out laughing.*
　　JESSE, already troubled, winces.)
　　No, no, I'm perfectly serious. They call themselves
　　Christians. But did our saviour go to Eton and Oxford?
　　Did He ride to hounds? Did anyone ever see Jesus drunk?
　　How did He talk? Did He seound like this thoysand of yars
　　ageouw?
　　(*The WORKERS go berserk with laughter.*)
　　Please, please, this is a serious matter. I ask you as thinking
　　individuals – could Christ ever be a Conservative?

WORKERS: NO!

REV MELVILLE: Well then, let's look at the major
　　alternative. Would He be a Liberal? The word itself means
　　two things: generous and loving freedom. I think Jesus

would accept both as fine qualities and well worthwhile.
But would He BE a Liberal as we know them? Is the
Liberal Party generous and freedom-loving? Look at them.
Would Our Lord be the rapacious owner of a limited
liability company? Would He be a pillar of the iniquitous
capitalist system under which we live? Is He in sympathy
with usurers and exploiters of working people? Does He
support the amoral plutocracy which racks and crushes this
country of ours for gain?

WORKERS: NO!

(*JESSE is shaken, looking about her as if trying to work out
how to escape.*)

REV MELVILLE: No! Christ would be a Socialist, as were
the disciples and apostles champions of the poor and
downtrodden! He drove the moneylenders from the
Temple, likewise He would kick the greedy, power-mad
manufacturers out of the seat of government. Jesus would
be the real Friend of the People... (*Glares at JESSE.*) The
real Workers' Choice!

JESSE: Ah...no...no...no...

(*JESSE collapses and dies.*
*The WORKERS and REVEREND MELVILLE carry JESSE
off L as LILE JIMMY and DR LOCO enter from the pagoda
wearing black arm bands.*)

LILE JIMMY: What a way for her to die – in public with
everyone gawping at her.

DR LOCO: An apoplectic seizure. It could have happened
any time.

LILE JIMMY: That minister's been fired. I've seen to that.

DR LOCO: I'll give you a sedative.

LILE JIMMY: She might just as well have been in the Roman
arena, thrown to the lions. But, by God, I'll see they
remember her. I'll build her a memorial that will outlive
them all!

DR LOCO: Go and play golf on your private estate, James.
Bash a little ball around and make yourself feel better.

LILE JIMMY: The biggest memorial ever raised in England!
Jesse's spirit will stand over this town. I'll build it at the

top of the park father gave to Lancaster. I'll show them whether I've got a heart or not!

DR LOCO: Golf, not grief, James. Come on. I'll give you a few tips.

(*DR LOCO gets a bag of clubs out of the pagoda and gives LILE JIMMY a lesson, adjusting his swing.*
WALL and HODKINSON enter L and watch.)

WALL: I hope he breaks his neck.

HODKINSON: You ought to take it up, Wall. It might teach you patience.

WALL: See where patience has got us. In Lancashire, we're a laughing-stock. All the other towns are going full steam ahead with union organisation – but not here. Oh, no – we might upset his lordship. Look at him. One little man, that's all he is.

HODKINSON: You don't understand power, Wall, and you don't understand money. If he closed his plant this town would die.

WALL: If he closed down because he had to have union representation in his workforce, what would that say about him?

HODKINSON: He is what he is and we have to live with it.

WALL: You see how assassins get made, don't you? Bang.

HODKINSON: You're heading for trouble, Wall. He knows what you say about him. Remember the Reverend.

WALL: I'm not bothered.

(*WALL and HODKINSON smoke cigarettes and continue watching the golf lesson.*
COLONEL WHALLEY and his wife, MAUD, enter R.)

MAUD: Good day, Lord Ashton. We are just taking our afternoon stroll. I hope you don't mind us crossing your land.

LILE JIMMY: By all means, Mrs Whalley.

WHALLEY: Well, we'll be off now, Williamson.

MAUD: Have a tot out of your flask, dear. The Colonel needs a pick-me-up now and then, don't you, dear?

WHALLEY: (*Taking a nip.*) Bloody terrible stuff, this. Got it in Malta, homemade in some whorehouse. I'll be glad when it's all gone. Not like the old French *eau de vie*. More like *eau de mort*. Want some, Maud? Keeps your pecker up if nothing else.

MAUD: No thank you, dear. You have it all.

WHALLEY: I'd offer you some, Williamson, but you know I don't drink with upstarts in trade.

LILE JIMMY: Feel free, Colonel.

WHALLEY: It's you damn cheapjacks selling your inferior goods to the bloody niggers all over the place who've done it. Free trade is a disaster.

MAUD: Don't you find living alone in that enormous house lonely, Lord Ashton?

LILE JIMMY: I'll get used to it in time.

MAUD: Have you ever thought of marrying again?

WHALLEY: Can't you see what you're doing to the country? We must have tariffs to protect us from wogs and dagoes and sweat-shop men abroad.

MAUD: Yes, dear. Have little more.

WHALLEY: Every bloody bedouin in the desert can send his filthy tat over here and undercut our fellers.

MAUD: Not his lordship, dear. No one ever undercuts him. Isn't that so?

(*LILE JIMMY smiles at her and shrugs.*)

WHALLEY: And the farmers, the farmers! How can we compete with slave labour? The foreigners have their mothers and fathers and grandmothers and bastards working their stinking land, paying them nothing! (*Takes a nip.*) God, this brandy is vile. It'll be the death of me. (*Spits.*) As for these Labour men you shelter in your bloody whorehouse of a factory, Williamson, they're even worse than Free Traders! I'd have them shot out of hand. (*Totters.*) Oooooh! Steady the Buffs! What's the bloody empire for, I say, if every slant-eyed bandit and atrocious bloody nigger can unload his trash on us when he feels like it! Maud, I'm talking!

MAUD: Of course you are, dear, and we're all listening to every word. Lord Ashton, it's been very pleasant passing the time of day, but we really must be getting home. Finish your flask, darling. Lighten your load.

LILE JIMMY: I'll bear your advice in mind, Mrs Whalley.

WHALLEY: Lord Ashton, my arsehole! Manners maketh man, Williamson. You're not one of us and you never will be. (*Totters.*) Damn these Chinese boots, they're making me walk sideways! (*Falls over.*)

MAUD: Oh, dear. Here we go again.

LILE JIMMY: Would you like some help with him, Mrs Whalley?

MAUD: I'm used to it. We'll get there in the end. Leave us to it, please.

LILE JIMMY: Good bye, Mrs Whalley.

(*LILE JIMMY and DR LOCO exit to the pagoda with the bag of clubs.*)

MAUD: (*To WALL and HODKINSON.*) I say, you fellows over there. Give me a hand, will you?

WALL: What's the matter with the old gentleman?

MAUD: Sunstroke.

(*WALL and HODKINSON help COLONEL WHALLEY to his feet.*)

WHALLEY: Who's this?

(*DR LOCO enters and retrieves a club left behind.*)

MAUD: A couple of kind fellows who are helping us, dear.

WHALLEY: Pair of gypos, I expect. See they don't pinch my wallet. God, I don't feel so good, Maud.

MAUD: Worse than usual, darling?

WHALLEY: A damn sight worse... (*Slumps between WALL and HODKINSON who struggle to hold him up.*)

WALL: He's dead drunk, doc.

(*DR LOCO examines COLONEL WHALLEY.*)

DR LOCO: No, just dead.

(*WALL and HODKINSON carry COLONEL WHALLEY off to the Dead March L and return with MAUD on their shoulders to the Wedding March.*
LILE JIMMY enters with a carnation in his button-hole.
WALL and HODKINSON put MAUD down in front of LILE JIMMY and exit L.)

MAUD: James, darling.

LILE JIMMY: Yes, darling?

MAUD: Would you do me a little favour?

LILE JIMMY: Anything.

MAUD: I want you to have that memorial to your first wife taken down.

LILE JIMMY: But it took years to build. It cost an enormous amount of money – the Taj Mahal of Lancaster.

MAUD: Nevertheless, I can't be expected to live with her breathing down my neck. We'll never have a life of our own. Why did you build such a huge monument to a woman who was so boring?

LILE JIMMY: Was she?

MAUD: By all accounts. Well? Are you going to have it demolished or not?

LILE JIMMY: It would be very embarrassing to knock it down. I gave it to the town.

MAUD: I think I'll go to London for a week. When I return I expect to see it gone.

LILE JIMMY: But Maud, it will make me look very foolish. A lot of fuss has been made of it. Architects compare it to many great buildings of the world…

MAUD: It's ugly, arrogant and I hate the thing. Either it goes or I go.

LILE JIMMY: We've only just got married, for God's sake!

MAUD: Plenty of people at our level of society get married and see very little of each other. It would arouse no comment at all. And you are an awful lot older than I am? I need friends of my own age.

LILE JIMMY: I'll tell you what I'll do – call it something else. I'll say it's been changed to a memorial to myself.

MAUD: But you're not dead yet, are you? Or do you mean, a memorial to the man you were?

LILE JIMMY: (*Stung.*) I've got an election letter to write. Why don't you go up to bed?

MAUD: Because it's half past eleven in the morning.

(*MAUD exits R.*

LILE JIMMY goes into the pagoda and brings out the wheelchair. He lowers himself into it as DR LOCO enters the walled garden from L.)

DR LOCO: We're not afraid, are we, James?

LILE JIMMY: I'm not afraid of any damn thing, Doctor.

DR LOCO: But you've never taken on Lloyd George before. He can be very destructive when he likes.

LILE JIMMY: He's a coward – a charming coward. Face up to him and he collapses. I'll sit him directly opposite me at table. You watch him fall apart.

DR LOCO: His courage will drain out of him?

LILE JIMMY: Exactly. First, I'll remind him of his broken promises.

DR LOCO: That should take a couple of hours.

LILE JIMMY: He'll have to beg my forgiveness. I'll be very stern.

DR LOCO: Keep him waiting.

LILE JIMMY: Deep down he's quite excitable. Guilt could produce a few tears.

DR LOCO: Lloyd George might weep? That would be astonishing!

LILE JIMMY: He's got it in him.

DR LOCO: Real tears from Lloyd George? Well!

LILE JIMMY: Take me inside, Doctor. I must get ready to receive the old devil. Oh, I'm really looking forward to this.

(*DR LOCO pushes LILE JIMMY off L in the wheelchair. The PRESS OPERATOR enters and sings:*)

PRESS OPERATOR: Lile Jimmy Williamson
who thought we'd see the day
when you were cursed in Lancaster
for giving such low pay,
when we were so afraid of thee
folk couldn't help but cower,
pride stifled in their hopeful hearts
by thy corrupting power.

(*LILE JIMMY enters on a penny-farthing bicycle with DR LOCO running alongside. LILE JIMMY does a few circuits.*)

DR LOCO: You've got the hang of it, James! Well done!

LILE JIMMY: I feel most unsafe up here, Doctor.

DR LOCO: It'll work wonders for your circulation.

LILE JIMMY: May I get off now?

DR LOCO: Go round a few more times.

LILE JIMMY: Won't cure anything though, will it? Ingratitude, for instance!

(*DR LOCO catches the penny-farthing and helps LILE JIMMY down.*)

DR LOCO: There we are. Something else you've mastered, James.

LILE JIMMY: I gave them a town hall with a clock that does the Westminster chimes. What do I get in return?

DR LOCO: (*Sings.*) I own this town as you can see, I pay my men one pound and three.

LILE JIMMY: I handed out thousands of tins of chocolates to the children at the opening of the new town hall – a majestic structure, it has to be said. Once they'd scoffed all the chocolates, the little blighters threw the empty tins over my wall full of dog excrement. My wife's picture is on those tins, Doctor!

DR LOCO: And then there's *Mr* Wall, as well. Oh, dear, James. That man has it in for you.

LILE JIMMY: He's a criminal. Held meetings right outside my house, calling me a thief and a robber! He must be dealt with.

DR LOCO: There's worse. He's standing for the town council in this ward, where you live. He's squaring up to you, James, challenging you to a fight.

LILE JIMMY: The gall of the man. I'll fix him.

DR LOCO: How will you do it? Bribe him?

LILE JIMMY: No, I wouldn't waste money on a man like Wall.

DR LOCO: Drive him out?

LILE JIMMY: I'll crush him.

DR LOCO: Is it right to do that, James?

LILE JIMMY: He's challenging me to a fight! You said so yourself just now. What am I expected to do? Let him walk all over me?

DR LOCO: Isn't it time you asked yourself if any of these charges laid against you are true?

LILE JIMMY: You just watch it, Doctor!

DR LOCO: None of us are perfect, James.

LILE JIMMY: I could stop your research work at the asylum tomorrow.

DR LOCO: But you'd still be my laboratory, James – my place of experiment and study. I'd have to write my paper on you.

LILE JIMMY: (*Interested.*) Really?

(*SHED enters with the RED BOOK.*)

Anything fresh about Wall's activities, Shed? What's he saying about me now?

SHED: He's canvassing hard, your lordship, but Hodkinson has told him to stop slandering your name.

LILE JIMMY: Isn't he mentioning me at all now?

SHED: No, your lordship. The Labour men say they don't want a dirty campaign. If you'll believe that you'll believe anything.

LILE JIMMY: Well, what's brought this about? (*Pause.*)

Tell Wall I'd like him to come and see me for a personal meeting – just us two, together.

SHED: Here? To the house?

LILE JIMMY: Yes. He must be by himself. Nine o'clock tonight.

DR LOCO: What are you up to, James?

SHED: He'll have been drinking by then, your lordship. Wall likes his pint. On an average day, by nine o'clock he'll have supped several.

LILE JIMMY: That's all to the good.

(*SHED gives LILE JIMMY the Red Book and exits R.*)

Standing as a Socialist right under my nose! On my own doorstep!

DR LOCO: What have you got planned for him, James?

LILE JIMMY: Doctor, you accuse me of all sorts and I think I take it in good part. I'm no fool. I know my power. I know my business. From your position, even as an independent man of science, you can't judge how I should react to something like this. (*Takes loose letters out of the Red Book.*).

It's something I've kept to myself.

DR LOCO: What is it, James?

LILE JIMMY: Poison pen letters. Some of them are delivered by hand, at night. They won't give me the benefit of a damn stamp, Doctor. After all I've done for them, do I not deserve a stamp?

DR LOCO: What do they say?

LILE JIMMY: (*Handing them over.*) Read them yourself, then see who's mad.

DR LOCO: (*Reading.*) Hmmm. Nasty. Passionate. Cruel.

LILE JIMMY: They would blow me up, kill me, see me suffer…why? Why? I can't bear any more of this…I can't…

DR LOCO: They certainly hate you, James.

LILE JIMMY: At this moment there's someone out there with a heart full of hate composing another one. But it's warped, the way they see me, Doctor. How can we stop it?

(*SHED enters R.*)

SHED: Wall says he'll come, your lordship.

LILE JIMMY: Well done, Shed. Did he make any comment about the invitation?

SHED: He mentioned walking into a spider's web. He reminded me how he'd stood for election twice before in other wards and you'd told everyone not to vote for him both times.

LILE JIMMY: But he's definitely coming?

SHED: That's what he says. I'll keep an eye on him from opening time onwards.

LILE JIMMY: I've been showing the Doctor our literature, Shed.

SHED: We've had a few more today down the office.

LILE JIMMY: Burn them. I don't want to see any more.

SHED: Best thing for them, your lordship.

LILE JIMMY: Shed, what do these people want from me?

SHED: You shouldn't take too much notice, your lordship. I wouldn't be surprised if someone like Wall was putting them up to it. And there's always a few loonies in any population.

DR LOCO: There we are, James. An explanation. Loonies crop up in all sorts of places, eh, Shed?

SHED: That's right, Doctor.

LILE JIMMY: I can see you sneering at me, Doctor! I know what you're thinking! This singling me out, attacking me, has to stop… (*Holds his head in his hands.*) I can't stand much more of it!

(*SHED backs out, embarrassed.*)

DR LOCO: Breaking down in front of an underling was very ill-advised, James. The poor fellow didn't know what to do with himself.

LILE JIMMY: (*Shouting.*) I can't help it if I get upset, can I?

(*MAUD enters from L.*)

MAUD: Don't bellow at the Doctor, James. What a way to treat a friend.

LILE JIMMY: I've got no bloody friends, you gormless bitch! Least of all you! Get inside!

MAUD: I will not. And I won't have you abusing me. Apologise immediately.

LILE JIMMY: Sorry.

MAUD: That's better, darling. (*To DR LOCO.*) I do pick them, don't I?

LILE JIMMY: Maud, they're watching every move you make.

MAUD: Oh, do be quiet. How do you put up with having to listen to all this, Doctor? It's so infantile!

LILE JIMMY: Every time you cast an approving eye on a man, Maud, they register the fact. Then they start talking.

MAUD: Don't be absurd.

LILE JIMMY: You have to think of your position, Maud. You must flirt less.

MAUD: Flirt? Me? James, I have to look at men if they're in front of me.

LILE JIMMY: They use your flirting to torment me. You're playing me into their hands.

MAUD: Doctor, shall we go and have a mild flirtation somewhere? Deep down, I think that's what my husband wants.

(*DR LOCO laughs and offers her his arm. He exits L with MAUD.*

LILE JIMMY puts the Red Book in the pagoda as WALL enters R.)

LILE JIMMY: Thank you for coming, Wall.

WALL: What d'you want to see me for? I'm a busy man.

LILE JIMMY: No nonsense. I like that.

WALL: Then let's get on with it. (*Peers into the pagoda.*) No witnesses. Just checking. I know you.

LILE JIMMY: Then you'll know I'm not an underhand man, Wall.

WALL: I know no such thing. You have spies everywhere. Come on – what is it?

LILE JIMMY: The local election and your candidature.

WALL: If you're going to tell me to pull out, the answer's no.

LILE JIMMY: On the contrary, Wall – I'm going to support you.

WALL: Support me? Why?

LILE JIMMY: I think you're the right man for the job.

WALL: I'm a member of the Labour Party! You know perfectly well what I stand for, and it's not what you stand for!

LILE JIMMY: I have principles, Wall. You don't have a monopoly on good intentions.

WALL: There's a catch in this, somewhere.

LILE JIMMY: No catch at all. In the long term, the only way we'll finally beat the Tories is through a Labour/Liberal alliance.

WALL: (*Laughing.*) You can't be serious!

LILE JIMMY: Never more so, Wall.

WALL: But what does this piddling little ward in a local election matter when you look on the grand scale? Labour and Liberal don't mix.

LILE JIMMY: We have to start somewhere. If we make the alliance work here, the national committees will have to take notice. What d'you say? Why shouldn't we shift things?

WALL: I won't be your creature. I'll be my own man.

LILE JIMMY: You'd immediately lose my respect if you were not.

WALL: I don't like some of your tactics and the way you work…

LILE JIMMY: I'll be guided by you, Wall. I think you could
go far in politics. There might be a few things I could teach
you, though.

WALL: That may be. (*Pause.*) And you'll publicly declare your
support?

LILE JIMMY: Not at this stage.

WALL: Ah! I knew there was a catch.

LILE JIMMY: Hold on, hold on. This is a working-class ward.
My employees live here. All you need to tell them is that
you've made representations to me on their behalf and,
single-handed, obtained my agreement to an increase in
the daily rate.

WALL: (*Astonished.*) You'll purrup t'wages?

LILE JIMMY: I have intended to do so for some time, but
I don't like being forced, Ward. But if we're working
together, that's a different matter.

WALL: But why are you doing this for *me*? We don't like each
other at all.

LILE JIMMY: I'm not saying you're my perfect choice.
You've said and done many things I don't approve of – but
I take you for an honest man. That goes a long way with
me.

WALL: Will you give me this promise in writing?

LILE JIMMY: Wall, if we're to work together, you'll have to
trust me sometime, but I'll prepare a statement. There's my
hand on it as a fellow-worker.
(*LILE JIMMY offers his hand.*
WALL hesitates, then takes it.)
Thank you for calling round. I'll be in touch. Goodbye.
(*WALL exits in a daze.*
LILE JIMMY watches him go, smiling.
Blackout and thunderclap.
Spot on the pagoda.
The KAISER steps out and clicks his heels.)

KAISER: With your permission, Herr Williamson. Like
myself, you are not fundamentally an aggressive person.
You are gravely misunderstood by virtually everyone who
knows you. You endure the trials of leadership unwillingly,
as I do. Duty and destiny are the key words, here. For the

sake of your kingdom and your people, sometimes you are forced, with many regrets, to destroy an individual.

(*The four EDITORS slink on as dogs through the darkness and sit around LILE JIMMY, begging, pencils in their mouths.*)

Journalists ask you to verify the claim Mr Wall made in the Wagon and Horses public house last evening shortly after meeting you, to the effect that he, by his own efforts, has got you to agree to an increase in wages for all those you employ. Journalists were waiting for him in the bar, tipped off by Mr Shed.

LILE JIMMY: (*To the EDITORS.*) Ask yourselves, would I announce such an important measure through a mouthpiece like Wall? He's talking utter rubbish.

(*The EDITORS run off yapping.*)

KAISER: A stroke of genius. You knew your man. Oh, I wish you were my Foreign Minister, Herr Williamson. But although Mr Wall loses the election, it is by one vote only. It appears there are many people who do not believe you. In fact they insist you are a liar. That is the fate of a great man.

LILE JIMMY: (*Shouting.*) SHED!

SHED: (*Running on.*) Yes, your lordship?

KAISER: In a masterly mood, you fire all Mr Wall's supporters from your works.

SHED: May I make a suggestion, your lordship?

KAISER: I like this Shed. In his simple, loyal way, he loves you.

LILE JIMMY: People love you for what they can get out of you.

SHED: Your lordship?

LILE JIMMY: A man likes to be loved for what he is.

SHED: Yes, your lordship. I was about to say that Wall works for the London Midland Scottish Railway and you're a director.

KAISER: Ah, I leave you in good hands, Herr Williamson. Auf wiedersehen.

(*The KAISER clicks his heels and enters the pagoda as DR LOCO come out reading. He closes the door behind him as he joins LILE JIMMY and SHED.*)

SHED: The town's solidly behind your lordship. People are sick of the way you've been treated.

LILE JIMMY: I should think so too.

SHED: Acting on my own initiative I've arranged one or two demonstrations of affection. Not in working hours, I hasten to add – during the lunch-break.

LILE JIMMY: Do we have a lunch-break?

DR LOCO: It says here, in one of our respected national dailies, that you've become a despot, James. A tin-pot despot. It makes the point that we're fighting a world war for the sake of freedom, yet we nurture dictators within our industries. This, it says, is a conundrum worth sorting out. Would you like to read all about it?

(*LILE JIMMY grabs the newspaper and crumples it up into a ball as the TRIBUNAL OFFICER enters with table and chair. He sits down facing LILE JIMMY.*)

TRIBUNAL OFFICER: Will your lordship make your case for exemption from conscription for military service?

LILE JIMMY: It's not me I want exempted, you idiot! It's my labour force.

SHED: Sir, Lord Ashton's firm has lost seventy per cent of its workers already...

LILE JIMMY: (*Raging.*) Lloyd George has deliberately started up a vast munitions factory in Lancaster to steal my men from me!

TRIBUNAL OFFICER: How does it do that?

SHED: Higher rates of pay, sir.

LILE JIMMY: Broken every agreement we employers ever had in this town! They're paying way over the top! It's a disgrace!

TRIBUNAL OFFICER: Lord Ashton, you're aware that the linoleum manufacturing business is classed as non-essential in terms of the war effort. A reduction in your output has to be accepted as a necessary corollary...

LILE JIMMY: Corollary? Don't you talk to me about corollaries! I'm being put out of business! I'll do anything for my country but I'm not being treated fair and square. I'm being singled out! Made a special target!

SHED: Our production levels are down to a quarter of pre-war levels.

LILE JIMMY: The Kaiser has liquidated my factory in Antwerp. Who cares? Who's going to compensate me for that?

TRIBUNAL OFFICER: That's outside my remit, Lord Ashton.

LILE JIMMY: To hell with your remit! You're in Lloyd George's pay.

TRIBUNAL OFFICER: Please calm down, your lordship. I'm empowered to come to arrangements.

LILE JIMMY: Bugger your arrangements, you stooge! You tell Lloyd George that he's ruined my town and it will never, never, be the same again!

(The TRIBUNAL OFFICER exits L with the table and chair as the PRESS OPERATOR enters and sings:)

PRESS OPERATOR: Lile Jimmy Williamson,
my man has gone to France,
he's off to throw his life away
in the Kaiser's bloody dance,
I've got his job, his army pay,
so much, it takes your breath,
but you can keep it at the price
of going dutch with death. *(Exits.)*

(MAUD enters.)

MAUD: Here on Christmas Day, Shed? Haven't you got a home to go to?

SHED: I have to keep his lordship up to date, Lady Ashton. The Americans have imposed punitive tariffs on linoleum imports. It'll reduce our transatlantic trade by half.

MAUD: Don't bore me with it. Go on, leave us. Pull a cracker somewhere.

(SHED exits L.)

LILE JIMMY: Maud, I hear you've been riding through town in the Rolls without the blinds drawn.

MAUD: Happy Christmas, Doctor. Isn't it a nice day? That sun's quite hot. We won the war. Isn't that splendid? I hope you haven't bought me too big a present, James. I'm afraid I forgot to buy you anything.

LILE JIMMY: That war cost me ten million pounds and my monopoly. Call that winning?

DR LOCO: Well, you'll have to build up the business again, make some changes. Modernise, James! Modernise!

(*DR LOCO goes into the pagoda and brings out a wheelchair.*)

LILE JIMMY: Things have never been worse. On top of that, we've got a 'flu epidemic that your lot has let get right out of hand. Our absentee rate has gone through the roof. They're dying on me in droves, deliberately.

(*DR LOCO sits LILE JIMMY in the wheelchair.*)

DR LOCO: Ever contemplated suicide, James?

MAUD: He hasn't got the imagination.

DR LOCO: This is the Rolls-Royce of wheelchairs, James.

LILE JIMMY: I don't need it! (*Struggles to his feet.*)

MAUD: You're rocky on your pins, darling. Do make use of the chair.

DR LOCO: Come on, sit down, James.

LILE JIMMY: Don't fuss! I can manage!

MAUD: Is the sun too much for you? Here, try these. (*She puts a pair of small round-lensed sunglasses on him.*)

LILE JIMMY: Now you've made everything go dark! (*He gropes around.*) I'll be alright if I'm left alone.

DR LOCO: Your eyes will adjust, James. Give yourself time.

LILE JIMMY: I don't want a damn wheelchair! (*Throws the sunglasses off.*) And I don't need these!

MAUD: How can we look after you if you're so difficult?

LILE JIMMY: I'm not a cripple. I'll stand on my own two feet, thank you! (*He falls over.*)

MAUD: Oopsadaisy, darling.

LILE JIMMY: I'll be back, you'll see. As they said at the Resurrection, you can't keep a good man down.

(*DR LOCO and MAUD pick him up and sit him in the wheelchair.*

MAUD put the sunglasses back on him.

SHED enters in haste.)

SHED: Lloyd George is at the station, your lordship.

LILE JIMMY: I knew he'd come running at my beck and call!

SHED: He's going to have a meeting at the Drill Hall.

LILE JIMMY: Is my advice to the electors posted up everywhere?

SHED: It is, your lordship – in Tory blue, like you said.

LILE JIMMY: Is it up at the station? Will he see it as soon as gets off the train?

SHED: It'll be the first thing he sees.

LILE JIMMY: He should have asked my permission if he's going to make a speech. Has my personal letter to each and every member of the work-force gone out?

SHED: It has, your lordship.

LILE JIMMY: Has Lloyd George mentioned coming here to dinner?

SHED: No doubt he'll send word.

LILE JIMMY: Maud mustn't dine with us. He'd be all over her like a rash.

SHED: D'you want me at the meeting, your lordship?

LILE JIMMY: What can he say that can hurt me? The man is totally discredited. Everyone knows what a charlatan he is. But you'd better go along and see what happens. Take a note of who's there.

SHED: Yes, your lordship. (*Exits L.*)

DR LOCO: He's a persuasive speaker, James. He can sway a crowd.

LILE JIMMY: This crowd still belongs to me, Doctor. It's been that way in Lancaster for nearly half a century. People can't remember when it wasn't the case.

DR LOCO: Thanks for that illumination, James. Now I can make a final diagnosis. You're not an amalgam of megalomania, hypochondria and paranoia at all. You simply suffer from being a moment of sanctified living history.

(*Blackout.*

A burst of cheering as a following spot falls on the pagoda and the door bursts open and LLOYD GEORGE, a Liberace figure, silver hair superbly coiffured, steps out in a sequined suit. He smiles and holds up a hand for silence as he walks to the front of the stage.

Pause. He addresses the audience.)

LLOYD GEORGE: Let me say at once that I have no quarrel
with Lord Ashton. He was an old colleague of mine in the
House of Commons when we were both Liberals. Times
have changed. I respect his age. I respect his achievements.
I would never be disrespectful to him. But this… (*He
shows the audience a letter, holding it between finger thumb as
if it were infected.*) I shall have to argue with this. I shall
have to protest against any man, whatever his power, his
authority, his influence, his wealth, who thinks he has the
right to dictate to free and independent electors how they
are going to vote. I read in the Tory press that I have come
here because Lord Ashton's letter has nettled me. I will
tell you before I have done who has been stung. I am not
a very thin-skinned person. If I were, I would have been
dead long ago. I suppose I must be about the best abused
man in the country and have been for such a long time that
I have got accustomed to it. Now, when I was in Brazil,
my daughter and I visited a snake-farm. They explained to
me how they inoculated horses against poison. They give
them a little dose of snake poison and then keep giving
them more until, at last, the horse can stand the venom
of a thousand snakes and be none the worse. As I said, I
would never say a word against Lord Ashton. None of us
would. None of us have. He has received more respect and
affection than any living man. But here, in this…thing, he
says that I have wrecked the Liberal Party, that my own
political associates do not trust me, that I am a dangerous
man who seeks power for its own sake, and that he now
supports the Conservative candidate. And this…thing,
has been sent to every worker, every foreman, and every
manager in his factories so that they will do the same.
(*Pause. He crumples the letter into a ball and tosses it over his
shoulder, then takes another out of his inside pocket and carefully
unfolds it.*) Now I will read you another letter. It was not
written by an old man living remote from the world, bitter
and resentful against all his fellow men. No, it was written
by a fine fellow in the best years of his life. This letter was
also sent out and circulated just as this…thing has. I think

it is a wonderful letter and I agree with every word it says, even though it was written nearly fifty years ago. I think so much of this letter that I always have it with me. I carry it here. (*Puts a hand over his heart.*) Let me read it to you. 'Dear Sirs, Allow me to remind you that every voter in my employ is a free agent. You must give your vote as you please and discharge your duty as a citizen conscientiously, without fear and free from any kind of undue influence. The suffrage is your birthright as Englishmen. Yours sincerely… (*Pause.*) James Williamson.' I think you knew him better as Jimmy.

(*LLOYD GEORGE carefully folds up the letter and puts it back in his breast pocket, giving it a pat, then turns and exits through the pagoda followed by the spot.*

As DR LOCO closes the door of the pagoda, the lights come up on the walled garden discovering SHED with LILE JIMMY and DR LOCO.)

SHED: And that was it, your lordship.

LILE JIMMY: (*Puzzled.*) Where did he dig that letter up from? That's a lot of nonsense about keeping it next to his heart. Lloyd George hasn't got a heart.

DR LOCO: It's all over. He's broken you.

LILE JIMMY: I don't remember writing that letter. He must have forged it. I'll tackle him about it over dinner.

SHED: He sent a message from the station, your lordship. He had to go back to London immediately and must decline your invitation. He sends you his apologies, regrets and best wishes.

LILE JIMMY: Scared to face me, eh?

DR LOCO: Obviously.

LILE JIMMY: Pity. I was looking forward to that.

DR LOCO: I do have another guest for your dinner table, James. He took the liberty of inviting himself.

LILE JIMMY: (*Agitated.*) No, no, I don't want strangers.

DR LOCO: He's no stranger, James.

(*DR LOCO goes into pagoda and pushes out a wheelchair with a skeleton dressed identically to LILE JIMMY sat in it. He positions the skeleton face to face with LILE JIMMY.*)

Here we are, gentlemen. I don't think introductions are needed. Come on Shed, we can leave these old friends together.
(*DR LOCO ushers SHED into the pagoda and exits with him, closing the door behind them.*
Pause.
Blackout.)

The End.

BUCK RUXTON

Characters

BUCK RUXTON, an Indian doctor

BELLE, his common-law Scottish wife

DR LOCO, a psychiatrist at the Moor Hospital

CORPORAL, an ex-Army man

MRS NELSON, Belle's sister

MARY, a maid

GARDENER, a solicitor

DANNY, an inmate of the Moor

VANN, Chief Constable

BOBBY EDMONDSON, a junior solicitor at the Town Hall

MAXWELL FYFE, prosecution counself for the Crown

HUTCHINSON, an expert witness

NORMAN BIRKETT, Buck Ruxton's defence counsel

WILLMAN, a painter

FREEMAN, VICKY, FOGG, patients

LAWLEY,

MIDDLETON, the Town Clerk

JUSTICE SINGLETON

GOVERNOR OF STRANGEWAYS

CHAPLAIN, of Strangeways Prison

PHOTOGRAPHER

THE TOWN HALL SET

Set in Lancaster and Manchester, 1930 to 1936

Buck Ruxton was first performed on 23 October 1975 at the Duke's Playhouse, Lancaster, with the following cast:

BUCK RUXTON, Stephen Boxer

BELLE, Fiona Victory

DOCTOR LOCO, Will Tacey

CORPORAL, David Boyce

MRS NELSON, Lyndsey Franklin

FOGG & DANNY, Alexander Wilson

VANN & MAXWELL FYFE, Paul Humpoletz

NORMAN BIRKETT, David Calder

TOWN CLERK, John Hartoch

EDMONDSON & PHOTOGRAPHER, Terry Iland

MARY & VICKY, Maureen O'Donnell

FREEMAN, GARDNER & LAWLEY, Charles Haggith

CAPTAIN, JUSTICE SINGLETON, WILLMAN & GOVERNOR, Leader Hawkins

The Town Hall Set played by members of the company

Director, John Blackmore

ACT ONE

Slowly dawning light behind silhouetted BUCK and BELLE at a café table. BUCK is sleeping with his head on the table, holding BELLE's hand. Pause. A little more light on the scene. BELLE wears a black waitress uniform with a small white apron and headpiece. BUCK is in an elegant light suit. BELLE gently disengages her hand and looks out the café window. She sighs. Pause. She walks back to the table and lightly strokes BUCK's head.

BELLE: Come on, Captain, wake up.

BUCK: (*Waking with a start.*) What? Oh, there you are.
I was dreaming about you and there you are.

BELLE: We talked nearly all night – then you got bored with me and went to sleep.

BUCK: Bored with you? Impossible!

BELLE: Oh, yes?

BUCK: How long have you been sitting with me?

BELLE: A couple of hours.

BUCK: Did I snore?

BELLE: No.

BUCK: I'd better take you home.

BELLE: There's no need.

BUCK: I should take you to your door. It would be most ungentlemanly if I didn't.

BELLE: (*Getting her coat.*) I'll take you home instead.

BUCK: You will?

BELLE: I will.

BUCK: So, which home will we end up at, if you're taking me home? Your home or my home?

BELLE: Yours. My landlady is very strict.

BUCK: I'm prepared to accept this compromise. My landlady couldn't care less.

BELLE: I have to lock up. See you in the street.

BUCK: Don't be too long. If I have to hang around too long, the police will arrest me thinking I'm up to no good.

BELLE: (*Kisses him.*) I won't be long. (*Exits L.*)
(*BUCK walks forward.*

The light spreads downstage.
BELLE re-enters from R in coat and hat and links his arm.
They walk slowly.)

BUCK: The best part of the day. It's so quiet and peaceful.
Edinburgh is a beautiful city.

BELLE: More beautiful than Bombay?

BUCK: God, yes. What a thought. Bombay, beautiful? You
don't know what you're saying.

BELLE: What time d'you have to be at the eye clinic?

BUCK: Ten o'clock – but they wouldn't miss me if I turned up
at eleven.

BELLE: No, you musn't be late for work.

BUCK: There are more important things than work. You, for
instance, are far more important.

BELLE: D'you really mean that?

BUCK: I declare it from the heart.

(*Lights up on a single bed, wash-stand, and a suitcase.*
BUCK ushers BELLE into his room.)

Here we are. Home sweet home. No palace by any means.
May I take your coat? Would you like some tea?

BELLE: (*Taking off her coat and hat.*) No, thanks.

(*She lights a cigarette and sits on the bed.*
Pause.)

I'm very nervous, Captain.

BUCK: I'll open a window for the smoke.

BELLE: No, don't. I'll put it out. Where shall I...?

(*BUCK takes the cigarette off her and holds it up, laughing.*
He shrugs then puts it out in the washstand.
BELLE takes her high-heeled shoes off.)

Ah, that's better. I wear such stupid shoes.

BUCK: My Belle. My belle Belle.

BELLE: It's a wee room for such a well-travelled man.

(*BUCK kisses her and pushes her back on the bed. She struggles*
free.)

(*Standing up.*) No.

BUCK: No? You are saying no?

BELLE: I musn't crease my skirt and blouse. I have to be back
at work at half-past eleven.

BUCK: One way out of the problem would be to take them off.

BELLE: I suppose it is. Turn out the light, please.

BUCK: Are you wanting to hide from me? I'm your doctor, remember?

BELLE: You're not my doctor. Turn it off, please.
(*BUCK switches off the light and keeps his back to her.*
BELLE gets undressed and slips under the covers.)
This bed is hard.

BUCK: I don't think they want me to stay too long.
(*BELLE laughs.*
BUCK undresses until he is only wearing a sada ceremonial shirt tied with a kusti cord. He starts to get into bed.)

BELLE: What are you doing?

BUCK: Getting into bed with you, my beautiful Belle.

BELLE: Not in that thing, you're not. What is it?

BUCK: A sacred garment.

BELLE: Sacred or not, you're not wearing it in bed with me.

BUCK: My religion forbids me to take it off. I must die in it.

BELLE: Well, that seems a very unhygienic arrangement. But if it's that important, you can sit there in your holy shirt while I go to sleep. I've got a full day ahead of me.
(*BELLE turns her back on him and pulls the covers round her.*
Pause.
BUCK stands up, undoes the cord and pulls the shirt over his head, then gets into bed with BELLE as lights fade to blackout.
Lights up on DR LOCO in military dress uniform, on a bench.
Brass band music can be heard faintly in the background.
CORPORAL enters in full dress of NCO in the Lancaster King's Own Regiment. He comes to attention in front of DR LOCO and gives him a salute.)

CORPORAL: Come to say tara, sir.

DR LOCO: (*Saluting in return.*) Out of the Army today, Corporal, thank God. No wonder the sun is shining. Sit down a minute.
(*He offers the CORPORAL a cigarette.*
They light up and smoke as they talk.)

What are you going to do with yourself? There's not much work in Lancaster.

CORPORAL: Got a job at the station, portering, sir.

DR LOCO: Once they discover your faults of character, what then? You, waiting for trains, Corporal? Are you suited to Civvy Street?

CORPORAL: I'll never find another doctor who understands me like you do, sir.

DR LOCO: Well, you'll have to find another confessor soon. I'm going to work at the mental hospital.

CORPORAL: That's bad news, sir. My case needs your special inside knowledge. Recurring malaria can make a man seem drunk when he's not.

DR LOCO: Who else will believe you?

CORPORAL: Being out in India did that, sir. Not my fault I ended up in the marshes. I didn't ask to go.

DR LOCO: None of us asked to go anywhere. We submitted to the general will that supports whatever the Army does. We obeyed, Corporal. You'll do well to remember the London Midland Scottish Railway will expect you to continue obeying. Well, come to think of it, I might have the right man for you. A friend of mine, ex-British Indian Army Medical Service, Iraq – we were in Baghdad and Basra together, '22, '23 – might be coming to Lancaster to set up in general practice. He understands the ways of the white man.

CORPORAL: (*Pause.*) Are we talking about a wog doctor?

DR LOCO: From Bombay.

CORPORAL: And he's setting up in Lancaster? Has no one told him?

DR LOCO: Yes, I've told him – but he's coming anyway.

CORPORAL: He must be out of his mind. They won't stand for it. It takes them all their time to talk to someone from Bradford, never mind Bombay.

DR LOCO: He possesses a certain kind of charm. Ever heard of charm?

CORPORAL: I've had contact with charm once or twice in my life, sir. As I remember, it doesn't always last long.

DR LOCO: Buck is an approachable human being. Sign on to his panel when he gets here and you'll be alright. But don't try his patience.

CORPORAL: A wog doctor with a temper. That promises fun and games.

DR LOCO: Old Army lead-swingers are his speciality. (*Stands up and offers his hand.*) Well, good luck, Corporal. Keep off the spirits and find yourself a good woman. No doubt we'll be bumping into each other.

CORPORAL: (*Shaking hands.*) Thank you, sir. See you around.

(*They exit R and L as band music fades with light to blackout. Lights up front stage on BELLE pushing a pram with BUCK beside her.*)

BUCK: When you look at a baby, there must be hope. (*Pause.*) I'm very fed up.

BELLE: Sorry you failed your surgeon's exams.

BUCK: Silly business. (*Looks at his hands.*) Look at these. I am a surgeon – made for it. But I can't keep taking exams time after time.

BELLE: Can't we stay here in London? We'll do alright, eventually.

BUCK: I must have my own practice. The Lancaster one is going cheap. And I have a good friend there who can help me.

BELLE: But Bommie, you're broke! How can you buy it?

BUCK: Finance companies give loans to doctors with qualifications. That won't be a problem.

BELLE: I'm not sure I like the sound of Lancaster. I don't like small towns.

BUCK: Belle, I'll need your help. In five years we can be doing very nicely – a big house, car, everything. Once I get going I'll build the practice up very quickly, you'll see. And you will be the perfect doctor's wife.

BELLE: We're not even married.

BUCK: Who will know? Forget your husband, forget everything. Just concentrate on the future.

BELLE: You don't consult me much. I've got a mind of my own, you know. I really don't fancy living up there.

BUCK: You'll be someone. You'll have status. Our house will be full of artistic objects. We'll have a lot of grand friends.

BELLE: I'm not saying yes. I'll think about it.

BUCK: (*With a touch of testiness.*) Well, don't take too long about it. If I lose the practice by shilly-shallying, you know who'll be to blame!
(*They exit L.*
Sounds of steam train pulling into platform.
CORPORAL enters in porter's uniform.
Slamming of carriage doors. Sounds of the train pulling out.
BUCK enters from R carrying suitcases.)

CORPORAL: Carry your bags, sir?

BUCK: How much?

CORPORAL: Shilling. (*Pause.*) You must have a shilling, sir.

BUCK: Don't be impudent, man. (*Puts the cases down and gives him a coin.*) Where's Dalton Square from here?

CORPORAL: I'll get you a taxi.

BUCK: I didn't say I wanted a taxi.

CORPORAL: If you're going to Dalton Square you'll be expected in a taxi. They're all nobs there.

BUCK: Is there a phone-box?

CORPORAL: Tuppence to phone. You could pawn your hat.

BUCK: (*Laughing.*) My God, what a cheek. I have a friend who could pick me up.

CORPORAL: I think I know him. (*Picking up the cases.*) It's against regulations, but I'll carry these all the way to Dalton Square for you for your shilling. Think yourself lucky. It's a good half-mile. (*Sets off L.*)

BUCK: Are you sure you can manage?

CORPORAL: Hard as nails, me, sir. Got all your instruments in here? They weigh a ton.

BUCK: Wherever you go, there's an old soldier. (*Walks ahead and exits.*)

CORPORAL: Hey, less of the old. (*Exits.*)
(*Lights up on frontstage where BELLE is ironing baby clothes. Her sister, MRS NELSON, sits in a chair reading a newspaper.*)

MRS NELSON: (*Putting the newspaper down.*) I can't help it. I don't like him. I don't like him at all. Mum and Dad would have hated him.

BELLE: See if I care. You're jealous because he's good-looking.

MRS NELSON: That's typical, Belle. You've got a one-track mind. Sex, sex, sex.

BELLE: You just can't stand the idea that something good could be happening to me.

MRS NELSON: He reminds me of a snake. And he fancies himself. I can't stand that in a man.

BELLE: You don't know him at all so why don't you just shut up.

MRS NELSON: Fancy living with a heathen. Father would have taken you to pieces.

BELLE: Fuck father!

MRS NELSON: God forgive you. You've got a mania for foreign men. Marrying a Dutchman, now this.

BELLE: Bommie believes everyone's the same underneath.

MRS NELSON: Does he? Well, he's got that wrong. (*Pause.*) There has to be a man. That's your weakness. You can't do without it.

BELLE: Oh, shut up!

MRS NELSON: He only wants you for a servant.

BELLE: Maybe.

MRS NELSON: That's what they do. They come over here, have their fun then go home. He'll desert you soon enough, abandon his kid. Those people have no feelings. (*Pause.*) He seduced you, didn't he?

BELLE: No one seduces me.

MRS NELSON: Oh, you think you're so tough. You're not. You let men wipe the floor with you. You've already had one husband walk out on you after only six weeks.

BELLE: There we are, then. I'm nothing special, obviously.

MRS NELSON: That doesn't mean you grab the next man to make a pass at you.

BELLE: (*Slamming the iron down.*) For God's sake, does it matter?

MRS NELSON: You'll burn those good clothes.

BELLE: I'm just a bloody left-over! Bommie can have me. And he'd marry me if he could. So lay off! (*Pause.*) He says he loves me. When did that thickhead husband of yours say that to you?

(*MRS NELSON gets up and takes the iron off BELLE.*)

MRS NELSON: Sit down. Go on, sit down. What a mess you're making, burning a good bib.

(*BELLE slowly sits in the chair and stares into space.*
MRS NELSON starts ironing the clothes.)

Well, I've had my say. I don't think you should stay here in London with us any longer if you've made up your mind. Go and live with him up there and take your chances.

BELLE: (*Absently.*) Yes…that's what I want.

(*Lights fade to blackout.*
Lights up on BUCK's surgery in Dalton Square.
He is sitting at an old desk with a phone and a few journals and papers.)

BUCK: Not one patient all day. Not one.

(*DR LOCO enters.*)

DR LOCO: How's tricks?

BUCK: Tricks are not good.

DR LOCO: It's only a matter of time. You've got very good premises here in Dalton Square – bang in the middle of everything. Town Hall and unhealthy aldermen opposite. Borough Club and apoplectic drinkers nice and close. Police Station up the road with supply of casualties. Potential customers constantly wandering in and out of these places. Perfect.

BUCK: Well, they haven't been in and out of here yet.

DR LOCO: You'll do them a world of good – give the town a dash of buccaneering exoticism.

BUCK: Don't tease me too much. I'm very nervous. The interest on the money I've borrowed is punishing our finances. We've no money coming in. But I don't want Belle to work. It wouldn't be the right note to strike.

DR LOCO: I'm sure you'll succeed. Having a wife and child helps give you a respectable image.

BUCK: Yes, my Belle is a great asset.

DR LOCO: So I don't put my foot in it, Buck, put my mind at rest. If I remember correctly, when we were in Iraq together, didn't you mention a wife?

BUCK: She is dead to me.

DR LOCO: But not actually dead?

BUCK: I was young when I married her.

DR LOCO: I see.

BUCK: She is barren, unfortunately.

DR LOCO: Are you divorced?

BUCK: Parsi law does not permit divorce.

DR LOCO: I'm sorry I had to bring it up.

BUCK: That's all behind me. From now on, my life is here with Belle and the children.

DR LOCO: Plural? Is Belle pregnant again?

BUCK: Yes, thank God. You can be a godfather if you like.

DR LOCO: The more I get involved with my patients up at the hospital the more I wonder about gods and fathers.

BUCK: You're doing great work, Jimmy. As an old friend I know what brilliant results you'll come up with. You're not as crazy as you pretend. You will find some answers in mental health.

DR LOCO: Come up and spend an afternoon with me sometime. I'll show you round my new kingdom. It's the biggest establishment of its kind in the north, packed out with the Empire's walking, talking wounded. You'll feel perfectly at home.

(*A knock at a door off.*)

Ah, a customer! I'll be off. Don't leave it too long.

BUCK: Enter!

DR LOCO: (*Loudly, so the arrival can hear.*) Thank you, Doctor. I'm completely cured. What a genius you are!

(*DR LOCO exits R as FOGG enters, a young working man with one hand held behind his back.*)

BUCK: (*Getting to his feet.*) Please come in and be comfortable, old chap.

(*BUCK brings a chair over so FOGG can sit down.*)

May I have your name?

FOGG: Fogg, Doctor.

BUCK: And your Christian name?

FOGG: Nathan.

BUCK: (*Writing it down.*) Nathan Fogg, esquire. What an interesting name. Are you wanting to sign on my panel?

FOGG: If tha'll have me.

BUCK: I will be delighted. Now, what's the problem you have, Nathan, my friend?

FOGG: (*Taking his clumsily bandaged hand from behind his back.*) It's this, Doctor.

BUCK: What have you done to it?

FOGG: Promise not to tell anyone.

BUCK: Who would I tell? (*Starts to carefully undo the bloody bandage.*) Let's have a look.

FOGG: Before you start, I can't be laid off work.

BUCK: (*Uncovering the hand.*) God, man, you've lost two fingers!

FOGG: It were always a bad machine, always slipping. Can you stitch them back on? Here, (*Takes a bloody bundle out of his pocket.*) I've brought them.

BUCK: (*Taking the fingers off him.*) When did this happen?

FOGG: An hour ago, at the end of my shift. I came as fast as I could.

BUCK: (*Getting a chair for him.*) Sit down, please.

FOGG: I won't, if you don't mind. Can you help me?

BUCK: Do as you're told, please.

(*FOGG obeys.*)

The best surgeon in the world could not give you your fingers back, and the worst doctor in the world wouldn't allow you back to work in this condition. I'm going to clean up the wounds then take you round to the Infirmary.

FOGG: Oh, no you're not! Give me my fingers back!

BUCK: Your employers will understand.

FOGG: You haven't been here long, have you? This hand must be perfect. I'm a millwright at Williamson's. They'll find a way to get rid of me. Come on, give it a try. Sew them on for me.

BUCK: I'll talk to the management. I'm sure you misjudge them. (*Pause.*) Alright then, if you insist. You're mad...but I'll have a go.

FOGG: Oh, thanks! Thanks!

BUCK: (*Taking equipment and a bottle from the desk.*) Lie down on the desk. I'm going to have to chloroform you.

FOGG: Fine! (*Lies on the desk.*) My mate said you might take a chance.

BUCK: (*Pouring chloroform on a pad then putting it over FOGG's mouth and nose.*) Did he, indeed? Count to ten and inhale deeply.

(*FOGG counts and passes out.*)

Only God will give you your fingers back. (*Starts to clean the hand.*) We're both being forced to take chances, my friend.

(*Fade to blackout as BUCK works on the hand.*

Dance band music – a quickstep.

Lights up frontstage where the TOWN HALL SET are at a formal dance.

To one side stand VANN, the Chief Constable, and MIDDLETON, The Town Clerk.

BUCK and BELLE enter in evening dress, self-conscious and nervous.

BELLE is wearing a kind of tiara. The music stops. The dancers clap politely, looking at BUCK and BELLE as they wander off the floor.

A tango starts. The dancers take the floor again. BELLE looks at BUCK. She wants to dance. He shakes his head. A young man, BOBBY EDMONDSON, asks BELLE to dance. She looks at BUCK. He's doubtful and doesn't like the idea, but nods curtly. BOBBY expertly leads BELLE into the tango.

BUCK wanders round to where VANN and MIDDLETON are standing and hovers, waiting to be spoken to. They ignore him.

BUCK smiles and speaks. They look right through him.

BOBBY and BELLE dance past, chatting and laughing.

BUCK storms off.

BELLE breaks away from BOBBY and follows BUCK off as VANN and MIDDLETON and the TOWN HALL SET laugh.)

MIDDLETON: You've upset the maharajah, Bobby.

BOBBY: She's alright.

VANN: Our new doctor holds himself well – served in Mesopotamia, I'm told.

BOBBY: Next time I'll teach her the Boston Two-Step.

VANN: Ruxton looks useful – the kind of man who doesn't stand much nonsense. You gets those in Army, Bobby – not that you'd know.

(*Blackout.*

Lights up on BUCK's bedroom as they enter.

He tears off his jacket and throws it on the bed.)

BUCK: You were all over that fellow like a rash! You behaved like a prostitute!

BELLE: (*Coldly.*) I'm making some tea. D'you want some?

BUCK: No, I don't want your bloody tea! I want an apology.

BELLE: For what? Knowing how to do the tango?

BUCK: What do I care about a stupid dance? You deliberately humiliated me in front of all those people!

BELLE: Stop working yourself into a lather about nothing.

BUCK: What were you talking about?

BELLE: What d'you think? Who am I…who is he…what do we do…that's all. You should learn to dance.

BUCK: I don't like it, you know that. I never have.

BELLE: Then why did we go?

BUCK: To meet people. We have to get started, socially.

BELLE: Which is what I was doing. The boy comes from a good family. He's a solicitor, like his dad.

(*Pause.*)

BUCK: You were right about this town. We should never have come.

BELLE: Your panel is building up. What else d'you want?

BUCK: Happiness with dignity.

BELLE: You're a card, Bommie. Come to bed and relax.

BUCK: There's no relaxing in bed with you. But you must take me seriously. (*Holds her.*) Say you do.

BELLE: I don't know what you're on about.

BUCK: Love must be serious.

BELLE: (*Kisses him.*) It's the funniest thing of all.

BUCK: All the best things are serious – a man's work, children, relationship with God. I must get your horoscope done – perhaps that will help. My Belle, you must respect life.

BELLE: When it starts to respect me.

BUCK: I love you. Isn't that respect? The other kind, you must earn. You don't get it for just being able to do the bloody tango!

(*A telephone rings off.*)

BELLE: That will be a call-out. No one ever rings us but patients.

BUCK: (*As he exits to answer the phone.*) They will. I'll make them.

(*BELLE lies on the bed and lights a cigarette.*

The telephone stops ringing.

As BELLE smokes the cigarette she hums the tango tune.

Blackout.

Lights up on DANNY wearing a strait-jacket in a padded cell.

He is crouched on the floor.

DR LOCO enters.)

DR LOCO: Danny, I've got a visitor for you.

(*BUCK enters.*

DANNY growls and stiffens, struggling to his feet.)

BUCK: Don't get upset, old chap.

DR LOCO: He's ex-Iraq, Buck. He was with the Army during the 1920 rebellion, then he was years on Ross Island in India on prison duty, guarding the Moplah rebels – a very wild bunch of Muslim extremists. Say hello to Dr Ruxton, Danny.

DANNY: Bollocks.

BUCK: Bollocks to you as well, dear fellow.

DR LOCO: He went into a Kurdish village just after we'd gassed them for harbouring insurgents. He found all the village children dead, with the teacher.

DANNY: It was their own fault.

DR LOCO: Didn't affect him at all – so he says.

DANNY: What could I do about it?

BUCK: So how did you end up here, Danny?

DANNY: Insanity in the family – on my mother's side.

DR LOCO: Well, as all your relatives are dead and gone, I can't prove that one way or the other.

DANNY: I inherited my problem.

DR LOCO: Doctor Ruxton and I were out in Iraq together when it first came into existence. That was an odd experience, being present when the idea of a new country is literally spirited out of the air, and the civilisation itself is so ancient.

DANNY: Those kids had toys with them – painted bits of wood. You can't get proper toys out there, not like you can here.

(*The CORPORAL enters in the white suit of an orderly. He carries a tea table which he sets down.*)

CORPORAL: Afternoon, Doctor Ruxton.

BUCK: I thought you were working at the railway station.

CORPORAL: They had to let me go.

DANNY: He was fired.

CORPORAL: I was being employed well below my abilities.

(*Exits and returns with chairs and tablecloth.*)

DR LOCO: In the regiment Danny was known as Mad Dog.

DANNY: Lots of us got called that.

CORPORAL: (*Pulling on a tea-trolley including a vase of flowers.*) There you are, then.

DANNY: What did they know about me? Nothing.

(*The CORPORAL sets the table for tea downstage of the padded cell.*)

DR LOCO: Dr Ruxton's wife is coming to have tea with us.

DANNY: (*Struggling to get to his feet.*) A woman, here?

DR LOCO: I'd like to believe you can conduct yourself in a proper manner while Mrs Ruxton is with us.

DANNY: I'll behave.

DR LOCO: What does that word *behave* mean to you?

(*Pause.*)

Take the strait-jacket off him, please.

(*The CORPORAL unties the strait-jacket and takes it off DANNY. Pause. The CORPORAL watches him warily.*)

Will you go and bring Mrs Ruxton up, Corporal?

CORPORAL: (*Whispers.*) Any trouble from you, Danny, and you'll answer to me. (*Exits.*)

BUCK: Belle will find this fascinating.

DR LOCO: Should I tell my colleague here, how bad you can be, Danny?

DANNY: If you like.

(*DANNY sits at the table. He smells the flowers.*)

BUCK: How long has he been here?

DR LOCO: Five years. It's obvious to me what caused his mental distortion, but he refuses to accept the analysis. He argues it's normal for a soldier to encounter bloodshed and death – part of the job. If he admits he cracked under the strain, it means he's not a man. Although he's been with us all this time under restraint, he finds imprisonment acceptable – something a man should be able to take. When you think of it, that makes sense for someone who worked in a prison. That's what he saw – men enduring pain, punishment and death.

BUCK: What can you do for him?

DR LOCO: His mind has adjusted around the trauma. It's healed the wound but the scar is everything. He thinks he absorbed the shock. This is a delusion. It twisted his psyche.

(*Enter BELLE ushered in by the CORPORAL.*

DANNY gets to his feet.)

Belle, how good of you to come. This is Danny.

BELLE: Hello, Danny.

DANNY: Hello. They got you some flowers.

BELLE: Good. I love flowers.

DANNY: How long are you going to stay?

CORPORAL: I'd better hang around – you know, with the lady present.

DR LOCO: I think we can manage, thank you.

CORPORAL: I'll be outside in the corridor if you need me.

(*Exits.*)

DANNY: My name isn't Danny, it's Daniel, and my surname name is Burton. Also, I have a middle name, a family name – Wells. So I'm Daniel Wells Burton.

BELLE: (*Gives him her hand.*) Pleased to meet you, Daniel Wells Burton.

(*DANNY shakes her hand but doesn't let go.*)

BUCK: That's enough, now.

BELLE: He's not hurting me.

DR LOCO: Let go.

(*DANNY releases BELLE's hand.*)

BUCK: Everyone loves my Belle.

DANNY: Memsahib, everything will be alright.

BUCK: She's made you feel better, hasn't she, old chap?
That's the effect she has on people.

BELLE: I'll be Mother, shall I? (*Pours tea.*)

DANNY: First, I'm going fishing. At high tide, I'll try off those
rocks with a sandworm. Then I'm on for punishment shift
at ten sharp. The Moplahs pray five times a day. They eat
no pig and never take a drink. They're strict, but love a
fight. Three Moplahs up for buggery today. A long flogging
job. They've been chanting and singing all night, keeping
us awake. God knows what it'll be like next week. We've
got several hangings. Then you'll hear a din you won't
forget in a hurry.

BELLE: It sounds as though you've been around.

BUCK: Strange that homosexuality isn't mentioned in the
Koran. There's no guidance.

DR LOCO: Prison changes the sexuality of men. They make
do.

BUCK: This isn't worrying you is it, Belle?

BELLE: Not at all.

BUCK: Unnatural vice is the only crime Zarathustra, our
Parsi prophet of God, said must be punished instantly. The
discoverer of the act, whether between men or women,
has to decapitate, skin, disembowel and dismember the
offenders and scatter the pieces over the land.

BELLE: Puts a lot on the shoulders of a nosey parker.

BUCK: It is open and shut – an unatonable crime. No
forgiveness.

DR LOCO: That makes it very hard for the weak-minded.
Aren't they the ones who most need forgiveness?

BUCK: The god who made them so vulnerable is the one who
needs the forgiveness.

DR LOCO: Is that what Zarathustra says?

BUCK: No, that's what I'm saying. Sexual insult and pain is a terrific force, an invasion of the mind by the body. D'you remember in Baghdad? A hundred murders a week, nearly all of them women only suspected of adultery. Never mind your wars and insurrections! Usually it was the husband, father or brother who killed the women, carving out their parts with knives. Night after night, the same old thing at the hospital, butchered females. When the guilty party got caught the sentence was laughable – six months at the most. As a crime it was condoned.

DANNY: Me and Bonzo are going to shoot seagulls this evening. You've got to have something to do once those fucking Moplahs start chanting and singing and getting on your nerves.

BUCK: Hey, less of that bad language in front of my wife!

DANNY: Eh?

BUCK: You should have your mouth washed out with soap, man!

BELLE: Come on, Buck. He can't help it.

BUCK: He can watch his Ps and Qs with me! I won't have it!
(*DANNY lowers his head onto the table and weeps.*
Pause.)
Old chap, I'm sorry I shouted at you. (*Pause.*) I shouldn't have come. Too many memories. And it's not my field. But they have to be told!

BELLE: What can you do for Daniel? (*Pats him.*) Come on. Don't cry.

DR LOCO: Don't touch him, Belle. (*Pause.*) Sedatives. And experiment. How d'you heal his kind of wounds? He thinks he's hard. He thinks he knows the world. In his way, he's arrogant. But how do we disprove his case? He's partly right. Violence solves as many problems as it creates. Ask the military. But a void is left through which we stumble towards our animal past. Now I'll be quiet.

BELLE: Well, after that, I think we'd better get back to the children, Buck, and stop them tearing each other apart.

DR LOCO: You took your time accepting my invitation, but I'm glad you did come, finally. You can see what we're up against here in our quiet little backwater. Now you can drive back down the hill in your limousine and rejoin civilisation.

BUCK: I'd like to stay on a bit, if that's alright, Jimmy?

DR LOCO: By all means.

BUCK: You take the car, Belle. I'll walk back.

BELLE: I'll see you later then, Bommie. Bye Daniel Wells Burton.

(*DANNY groans but doesn't look up.*)

Good luck. (*Exits.*)

(*DANNY weeps again.*

BUCK and DR LOCO sit looking at him.)

BUCK: Bloody India. Bloody Iraq. Bloody everything.

(*Blackout.*

Lights on magic mirror ball.

Dance band plays 'Red Sails In The Sunset'.

BELLE enters dancing the slow fox-trot cheek to cheek with BOBBY.

Cross fade to BUCK's surgery.

He sits at an ornate brass-bound Buhle desk in an imposing gilded chair.

FREEMAN, a middle-aged, rough-dressed man, sits in a chair with VICKY standing by his side.)

It would be more suitable if the girl's mother was with us.

FREEMAN: She's dead.

BUCK: I'm sorry to hear that. This is a delicate matter.

FREEMAN: It's straightforward enough. Girl's having a baby.

BUCK: I could ask my wife to come along. Would you prefer that, Vicky?

FREEMAN: No, she wouldn't. Look, Doctor, she's not wed and we don't want it. (*Pause.*) We don't want it because we couldn't manage. Do I have to spell it out for you?

BUCK: Please.

FREEMAN: We have to get rid of it.

BUCK: I'll pretend that wasn't said here, in my own house. What do you say, Vicky?

VICKY: I dunno. My dad says…

BUCK: I've heard very clearly what your father says. He's insulted me very considerably. I'm not an abortionist.

VICKY: If he won't have it in the house, what can I do?

FREEMAN: We don't want it. There should be some help we can get from someone, surely!

BUCK: (*Standing up.*) You will leave now, please.

FREEMAN: Don't get shirty with me! Where you come from you must have to deal with this kind of thing all the time.

BUCK: Your daughter is three months gone, Mr Freeman.

FREEMAN: She didn't tell me until today.

BUCK: That child in her womb has a soul. It has a place with God.

FREEMAN: Then let God look after it.

BUCK: (*Losing his control.*) You will get out now, if you please.

FREEMAN: Come on, Vicky. We'll have to go elsewhere. This high and mighty feller's no use to us.

BUCK: I will have you watched. The police will be informed if you interfere with the natural process of this baby's birth.

FREEMAN: What chance does an unwanted child have? What kind of a life? Never mind the police. Help us.

BUCK: You stay behind, Victoria. I have things to talk about with you.

FREEMAN: I'll pay what I can.

BUCK: (*In an outburst.*) *Allez-vous en!* Get out you insulting bastard!

(*FREEMAN backs off, frightened.*)

VICKY: Do as he says, Dad.

FREEMAN: Alright, alright…I'll wait outside. (*Exits.*)

(*Pause. BUCK is still trembling. He sits down again.*)

BUCK: I'm sorry. I get so appalled, you know, so upset. People are so brutal when they like. I've never really got used to it.

VICKY: Doctor, don't blame him too much. He's fed up to the back teeth with me.

BUCK: You must have your baby, and be healthy, live a long life, be well. If it's out of the question for you to keep the child, it can be adopted.

VICKY: Oh, I don't know about that.

BUCK: How do you know this child won't grow up to be
a very famous man or woman? A composer, a general,
a great beauty, a hero of some kind. We must give it its
chance.

VICKY: It's his, Doctor.

BUCK: (*Groaning.*) Oh, God, no!

VICKY: It will be deformed, I know it will.

BUCK: I must tell the police.

VICKY: What's the point of getting him put in prison? I'd
have nobody. He was drunk.

BUCK: Is everybody in this town drunk all the time?
Everywhere I look, drunk, drunk! No self-control.

VICKY: Please, Doctor, don't report him.

BUCK: Although I refuse an illegal abortion, under these
circumstance I might be able to get official permission for
you to have one.

VICKY: Then we'll forget about it.

BUCK: Forget about it? This is a terrible situation. That foetus
is alive. It is already someone. What does it know of your
father's crime? God, how tragic… People! What can you
do with them?

VICKY: If it's a monster I'll kill myself.

BUCK: Vicky, I am about to become a father for the third
time. My wife is carrying a child, like you. How do I know
it will be perfect? How do I know it won't be a monster? It
will be what it will be. If there is a design, it is God's. I will
take care of you.

VICKY: How will I be able to be a proper mother to it?.

BUCK: If I read you right, you'd be a damn good mother.
Although we say of babies, he's the father and she's the
mother, are they, really? We come ready-made out of
nowhere, my dear girl. When your baby is in your arms it
will have its own existence, never mind parentage. Come
on, let's go next door and I can have a good look at you.

VICKY: You'll stay with me right through?

BUCK: To the end. Be strong, lass. I have never lost a baby
yet, or a mother. That is my record. I have the highest
first class honours in gynaecology, that's childbirth and

midwifery. The main thing to remember is that even this one is completely natural.

(*As BUCK ushers VICKY off R, BELLE enters dressed to go out.*)

BELLE: I'm just off, Bommie, darling. Let me make a call... (*Dials on the desk telephone.*) ...I'll be back about six or thereabouts... Mary will give the children their tea.

(*BUCK gives her a disapproving look as he exits.*)

(*On the 'phone.*) I'm on my way. I'll be there in about ten minutes... Well, yes, I am quite hungry, actually.

(*Lights fade as she puts the telephone down.*
Night.
DR LOCO cycles across front stage with lights on. His bicycle has a basket.
BUCK enters from the opposite direction.)

DR LOCO: What's this? A prowler? (*Stops.*) What are you looking for?

BUCK: I am taking a contemplative stroll after a hard day in my surgery.

DR LOCO: Glad things are going well for you. I hear great things. You seem to be very popular with your patients. Do they pay up?

BUCK: When they can. My panel is the poor majority, Jimmy – a lot of consumption, cancer, bronchial, heart disease. This isn't a rich town. The middle-class is quite small and they don't seem to like me for some reason. I find it strange that the most educated people in this country are the most prejudiced. What do they get taught in school?

(*DR LOCO gets off his bicycle and props it up on the back of a bench. He sits down with BUCK, chatting quietly as lights come up on WILLMAN's studio.*
There is an easel, a canvas, a Chinese screen and a dais.
WILLMAN, a painter, is preparing his brushes as BELLE enters, drunk.)

BELLE: Hello, Captain Willman. Sorry I'm late. I was detained by some friends.

WILLMAN: Hello, Mrs Ruxton. (*Clocks her condition.*) If you'll get ready we'll make a start. I'll try not to keep you too long today.

(*BELLE goes behind the Chinese screen and undresses.
WILLMAN prepares his canvas.*)

DR LOCO: Belle is becoming quite a socialite.

BUCK: She is a wonderful woman. Let us not argue about
that.

DR LOCO: Do you like the company she keeps?

BUCK: Not entirely. But who else is there for her?

DR LOCO: I wouldn't choose to spend time with the Town
Hall Set – not that I'd be invited to. But then…they're
useful contacts, I suppose.

BUCK: I don't like them either. They drink far too much.
But there you are. A man can't choose his wife's friends.
(*Pause.*) Jimmy, the woman has changed. She doesn't want
this baby she's having. Six months before it's born and she
hates it.

DR LOCO: That will pass. Women get depressed because
they think childbirth ages them. It does.

BUCK: There's something dark at the centre of my Belle.
She doesn't care what happens. It's a very painful business
loving such a lady, I can tell you. Now and then it makes
me feel very bitter. Why was she put in my path?

DR LOCO: Is this really a good place for you to be, Buck?
You work with the poor. She mingles with the well-off.
Where do you touch?

BUCK: In bed. Where else?

(*BELLE comes out from behind the screen in a diaphanous
garment, carrying a book. She gets onto the dais.*)

BELLE: What d'you want me to do now?

WILLMAN: Dr Ruxton has a very definite idea how you
should look, based on an Italian Rennaissance painting he
knows.

BELLE: Have you seen this painting yourself?

WILLMAN: No. It's of some goddess or other, he tells me.

BELLE: Reading a book? Do goddesses read books? Oh, he's
so cultural, my husband.

WILLMAN: If you would recline for me…

BELLE: For the artist, anything. (*Lies down.*) Now what?

WILLMAN: The left hand propping your chin...the right turning over the pages of the book...the left knee little closer to the right...

BELLE: (*Adjusting.*) I won't be able to stay like this for long if you want me to say awake.

WILLMAN: Would you be so good as to open your dress a little more at the neck? The Doctor specified as much in his instructions.

BELLE: Bommie told you to do that? Wow!

WILLMAN: Your husband is very serious about this piece of work, Mrs Ruxton, especially the classical allusions.

BELLE: Well, let's not dodge the issue, then. (*Takes a breast out.*) He should realise that goddesses have no shame. They do as they like.

WILLMAN: That's not quite what he had in mind, Mrs Ruxton. He says this is to hang in your drawing-room over the fireplace.

BELLE: What will the neigbours think? Go on! Paint! What does it matter? How much is this nonsense costing him?

WILLMAN: (*Annoyed, as he starts.*) I'm really not at liberty to say.

BELLE: But you know a pretentious mug when you see one.
(*WILLMAN ignores her, frowning as he sketches in.*
BELLE laughs.)
Men and their fantasies. What a sad lot you are. I'm no goddess, I can tell you.
(*She shakes her head, flipping over the pages of book.*)

DR LOCO: Must be off home now, Buck. (*Gets on the bicycle.*) Stick with it.

BUCK: Jimmy, that woman is gambling on horses. She has over thirty pairs of shoes. It's cheques here, cheques there. Can you lend me a hundred pounds?

DR LOCO: (*Laughing.*) You must be joking! Where would I get a hundred pounds?
(*He rides off, lights wavering.*
BUCK crosses to the studio scene and peers in. He reacts violently.)

BUCK: What the devil is going on here? I said it was to be based on Corregio's *Reading Madonna* in the Bologna Nunciata. You've got her looking more like the Whore of Babylon!

WILLMAN: Doctor Ruxton! I'd be obliged if you wouldn't come barging in here while I'm working!

BUCK: You're making love to my wife!

(*BELLE laughs.*)

WILLMAN: I most certainly am not. The extra nudity was your wife's idea, not mine.

BUCK: This is supposed to be the Mother of God, the Madonna. Cover yourself up!

(*BELLE gets off the dais, covering up.*)

BELLE: Mother of God, my arse! So, you're following me now, Pa – checking on me!

WILLMAN: Would you both care to leave? I can't possibly work in this kind of atmosphere.

BUCK: (*Looking at what he's sketched out.*) Ah, you've not managed to corrupt this man, Belle. Here, he's got you decently dressed. Thank you, you honourable man. You see the kind of bitch I'm in love with. What a fine woman. Look at her, a super woman, eh?

WILLMAN: I have some urgent business to attend to. Please show yourselves out. I will be returning your deposit, Doctor Ruxton.

BUCK: Please don't be too hasty. As you can see, someone has been plying my wife with drink. This will not happen again.

(*BELLE laughs as WILLMAN leaves in high dudgeon.*)

BELLE: What an old yellowbelly! He didn't even make a pass at me! I'm very insulted.

BUCK: Next time, Belle, please behave. This picture is important to me. Your beauty should be remembered in the art world.

BELLE: Bommie, I use the mirror. I'm no oil-painting. Stop dreaming.

BUCK: Now, with child, you are the Earth.

BELLE: I'll get dressed.

BUCK: Let me come to you.

BELLE: Here? (*Laughs.*) What if he comes back?

BUCK: He needs inspiration. We'll charge up the atmosphere for him. Get the electrons whizzing! Back on the dais. Look like you did when I came in. Why should artists have all the fun?

BELLE: Bommie, you'll never make an English gentleman.

(She lies on the dais and holds out her arms.

BUCK goes to her.

Blackout.

Lights up on VICKY lying on a mattress. She cries out.

BUCK enters hurriedly with his bag.)

BUCK: How often? How often?

VICKY: It's one after the other!

BUCK: (*Examining her.*) Not long now. Here, feel that? The head in the birth canal. Don't relax.

VICKY: Relax?

BUCK: You must work. Push.

VICKY: How long will this go on for? Aaaah! It's no joke!

BUCK: Whoever suggested it was a joke? Keep wound up!

VICKY: It's too big. It'll never get out of me!

BUCK: I bet you it does, and very soon. Don't forget, you're only doing half the work. Behind you is Mother Nature pushing hard.

(VICKY cries out.)

The pains will get heavier in a moment as the head of what I'm sure is a perfectly normal child is followed into the birth canal by the shoulders, and torso. Then you must bear down as hard as you can and push the baby along.

(VICKY screams in labour.)

Bear down! These are good pains.

VICKY: It can't get out!

BUCK: Oh, yes it can. I will save you. Come on, come on. It's nearly here.

VICKY: Oh, God!

BUCK: Oh, dear it's gone back. What a character – in and out. I think you may be a little tight. I'm going to open the door a little… (*Takes out a slip-knife.*) Don't worry, it won't hurt.

VICKY: Yes, please make it easier. Oh, why is it taking so long?

BUCK: Pant. Pant like a dog.

(*She pants. BUCK makes an incision.*)

Good girl. Now we can make headway. Relax, relax. Don't go rigid on me. Here we go again. Yes, I can see ears! Come on, BEAR DOWN, BEAR DOWN...wonderful! You're doing it! Congratulations!

VICKY: I want to see...I want to see...

BUCK: Lie back. Pant.

VICKY: (*Panting.*) Does it look alright? Is it normal?

BUCK: The worst is over. I have the head. I am turning the head round, Vicky, so I can see the eyes... Oh, yes, wide open, very bright. Where am I? How did I get here? What's going on? (*Laughs.*) Gotcha! It's a boy. (*Baby cries.*) A fine boy! Who knows, Vicky – perhaps he'll be a great man. He doesn't need a slap. He's breathing on his own. Let me get his mouth clean.

VICKY: Please God, don't let him look like my dad.

BUCK: As of this moment, he is purely himself. Now we will just wait for your blood to stop flowing to him, cut this useful pipe here which has kept him going for so long, make a nice neat bow, then out will come the afterbirth. There we are. God heard us. Look.

(*He wraps the child and holds it up to her.*

She stares, then turns her head away.)

(*Commanding.*) Woman! Look at what you have done! He's yours. Magnificent!

VICKY: What will he be like inside his head?

BUCK: (*Giving her the baby.*) Take him. He need never know how he came into being. He can assume he's like everyone else. (*Cleans up.*) Ask yourself about Adam and Eve. How did they have grandchildren? Work it out. Myself, I don't know what's inside people's heads. Trust in God is my motto.

VICKY: Look at his hands. What sweet little hands.

BUCK: (*Looking at his own which are bloody.*) Hands. Strange how women focus on the hands.

VICKY: He's lovely, Doctor, but I musn't get too fond of him if he's going to be adopted. When will you want paying?

BUCK: I never want to hear that mentioned again.

VICKY: I'm going to keep him!

BUCK: (*Gently.*) Vicky…rest now.

VICKY: He's going to stay with me, no matter. I'm not by myself now.

BUCK: No, lass, you're not.

(*Blackout.*

Lights up on BELLE frontstage, dressed up, being photographed for a newspaper with VANN, in uniform.)

PHOTOGRAPHER: I need a few notes to go with the picture. Here we go…Mrs Belle Ruxton, wife of the popular Dalton Square doctor, assisted by Chief Constable Vann attended the children's Christmas treat…

VANN: Alright, alright, you know the form. You don't need to spell it out.

PHOTOGRAPHER: I've got everything I need. Many thanks. Should make Friday's. (*Exits.*)

VANN: Went very well, I thought. Good to see the little ones having such fun. We all need a bit of fun sometimes, eh, Mrs Ruxton?

BELLE: How right you are. And how seldom we get it.

VANN: It's been a pleasure. Good evening to you.

BELLE: Good evening.

(*VANN exits.*

BELLE lights a cigarette.)

(*Muttering to herself.*) Two-faced bastard.

(*DR LOCO enters.*)

DR LOCO: Hello, Belle. You look very elegant. Been somewhere stimulating?

BELLE: Very. Charitable work. Exciting stuff.

DR LOCO: How's Buck?

BELLE: Working.

DR LOCO: Do you still give him a hand?

BELLE: Oh, no. He has a nurse.

DR LOCO: May I have one of your cigarettes? I only smoke other people's.

BELLE: You have a hard life, Jimmy.

DR LOCO: How are the kids?

BELLE: Very well. They're at home with Mary, our nursemaid.

DR LOCO: Lots of servants you have these days.

BELLE: We're doing very well, thank you. Plenty of money rolling in. He's got more than two thousand patients on his panel now.

DR LOCO: And your new friends – how are they?

BELLE: Yes, I've made a few friends. Anything the matter with that? He won't let me work.

DR LOCO: The mentally deranged gossip a lot. They pick up all the dirt. The people at the town hall would be astonished what accurate information circulates through the hospital system. There's no censorship, you see. We're very close to the sources of human interaction.

BELLE: Did Bommie ask you to do this?

DR LOCO: I can't think of anyone else in a position to talk to you this way. Belle, you're publicly humiliating your husband

BELLE: You're taking a lot on yourself.

DR LOCO: Everyone knows about your affair. It seems as though you want everyone to know. Why is that?

BELLE: Have you finished?

DR LOCO: I lived close to Buck for two years in Iraq. I've seen him pushed beyond the limit.

BELLE: I've got a temper of my own. I can let off steam too, Jimmy. I'm not afraid of Buck.
(*Pause.*)

DR LOCO: I'd like to leave it at that, Belle, but I can't. He's a notable man. You may not understand how his concept of honour works. This is a small town and you live in the public eye. If you keep shaming him, he'll blow, I warn you.

BELLE: Why don't you fuck off and mind your own business!

DR LOCO: It would be a mistake to take him for granted, Belle.
(*DR LOCO exits pushing his bike.*

Lights up on the dining-room where BUCK is walking up and down reading a textbook.
BELLE enters the area.)

BUCK: Surgery is over. I needed you. Where have you been?

BELLE: With Chief Constable Vann at the children's treat. Safe enough for you? And I bumped into your friend, Jimmy Loco, who was good enough to abuse me.

BUCK: I don't believe that. But I'm sorry I forgot you had to go to the children's treat.

BELLE: To represent you.

BUCK: As I said, I'm sorry...but I had thirty people in the waiting-room.

BELLE: I'd be obliged if you'd stop telling everyone I'm having an affair with Bobby Edmondson, by the way.

BUCK: I will when I know you're not. (*Pause.*) Tomorrow morning I'll be needing your help at surgery.

BELLE: I won't be there. I'm going out.

BUCK: You are not going out.

BELLE: Hire a nurse. You can afford someone. Just because that girl had to leave it doesn't mean I have to go back to working at surgery. Get another female who won't fall in love with you.

BUCK: What am I going to do with you, Belle?

BELLE: Stop telling lies about me for a start. Bobby Edmondson is no use to me. He's a mere child. What would I want with him?

BUCK: You're becoming a sarcastic bitch, my Belle. I know you are transferring your affection to that one young man. You have his photograph.

BELLE: So what? I have my grandfather's photograph. And one of the pope.

BUCK: You know what I mean. You keep it in your handbag.

BELLE: Now you're going through my handbag? This gets better and better.

BUCK: It is breaking my heart, this business. (*Pause.*) You say you've been out doing good works with the children but I can smell drink on your breath. You've been out drinking with someone, as if I didn't know who. (*Pause.*) Give him up, Belle. Don't destroy our family.

BELLE: If I was looking for a lover, it would be an experienced man with hair on his chest, not a boy.

BUCK: You say that kind of thing to hurt me.

BELLE: Och, wee Bobby is no use to me, Pa. Forget him. My dreamboat would never live in this godawful town! Jesus, how I hate this place!

BUCK: You shouldn't drink. You can't handle it. It makes you very foolish and unpleasant to live with.

BELLE: Don't you want to see the real me, Pa?

BUCK: The real you is someone I adore. This other woman, I detest.

BELLE: There's nothing to be done about it! I am what I am. If I didn't drink, I'd die of boredom. Bommie, it would help if you found yourself a bit on the side – someone else to put on a pedastal so I can be myself.

BUCK: Oh, do shut up. Lie down for a while.

BELLE: I can't. I have to get ready for tonight.

BUCK: Tonight? Where are you going tonight?

BELLE: Nowhere. My friends are coming here.

BUCK: Oh, no. I'm not having those horrible people here. Belle, why are you tormenting me? What have I done to deserve it?

BELLE: I've invited them for dinner so they can see our fancy house. I've told the cook...given her a menu, even! It's very French, very sophisticated. You'd better supervise the wines. I can't be trusted in that department.

BUCK: I hope you told them to dress for dinner. If you didn't, I refuse to have them here.

BELLE: They'll be correctly dressed, Bommie.

BUCK: And no Bobby Edmondson. I won't have him in the house.

BELLE: As it happens, he can't come. I did invite him, though.
    (*BUCK exits L, BELLE R as lights fade to blackout.*
    Lights up on the TOWN HALL SET in white tie dress,
    frontstage, glasses in hand. They talk amongst themselves.
    A gramophone off plays 'Red Sails in the Sunset'.
    Enter DR LOCO to a spot downstage extreme L.
    He addresses the audience as if at a convention of psychiatrists.)

DR LOCO: Colleages, my paper has the title: Imperial
   Homecomings. Lancaster, where I work, has a formalized
   social structure built around repression in various guises.
   Forget the cachet attached to that name, Lancaster. It is
   not a royal burg is any way whatsoever. The king would
   never be seen dead in it. It's essentially a mill town,
   gritty, working class, slow-moving, rough, plus lots of old
   soldiers and half-cured patients from the many hospitals
   serving the county. The bourgeoisie is represented by
   a mere handful of solicitors, doctors, factory owners
   and the like, very much a self-protecting, self-regarding
   clique. There is the prison, which is a medieval castle.
   There are two very large mental hospitals. Not long ago
   they would have been called asylums. There is still a
   garrison, reminding us people need to be overawed. It is
   a tough town with an image of itself. Though deferring
   to traditional authority, Lancaster's cap in hand always
   has a brick in it – but socialism has not been taken too
   much to heart. Punishment, incarceration and arduous
   employment churning out linoleum for low pay have been
   the mainstays of its economy. If I were to describe the most
   unpromising place on earth for a foreigner of different
   ethnic type to try to set up as a professional man, it would
   be Lancaster. But the story I have to tell is heart-warming
   – one of extraordinary success, against the odds. At a time
   when we must brace our spirits for the humiliations of the
   post-Imperial epoch, when Ghandi is the devil incarnate,
   the conquest of prejudice achieved by a young Indian
   doctor in ingratiating himself with the common people of
   this grim northern fastness is remarkable, and worthy of
   close study. What type of personality could break down all
   those barriers, those deeply ingrained attitudes? If there is
   ever going to be a multi-racial society, the subject of my
   research, who we will call Mr Zed, is the kind of man who
   will lead the way.
   (*Lights up on the dining-room laid for the meal.*
   BELLE enters.)
BELLE: Will you come through?

(The TOWN HALL SET go to the table and check name cards.
They make a game of it.
BUCK enters, superbly turned out.
Pause.
The TOWN HALL SET eye him.)

BUCK: Good evening, everyone. Welcome to my home. I trust you've been well looked after by my wife. I had a late surgery and needed a little time to get ready.

(A murmur of subdued greeting from the TOWN HALL SET.)

I see you have a drink. Is it sherry, Belle?

BELLE: I don't know what the poison is. It's alcoholic, that's all I know.

BUCK: It should be sherry. I have quality amanzanilla, fino, amontillado, oloroso…all types. I drink very little myself but when I do, I like it to be right.

(The TOWN HALL SET murmur, not sure what to say in reponse.)

Perhaps we should change to the correct glasses? They are Waterford crystal.

BELLE: For God's sake, leave them to drink what they've got.

BUCK: Or we could have Barsac as an aperitif. Would you prefer that? I've been fasting myself so Barsac wouldn't be a good idea. Too rich for an empty stomach, you know.

BELLE: *(Hissing.)* Stop showing off!

BUCK: I study everything, you see. Wine, and medicine. You can appreciate how a doctor who is serious about his profession must spend many hours keeping up. For the sake of his patients, he must keep abreast of new developments.

BELLE: Oh, all this lot keep abreast as much as they can.

BUCK: D'you like my room? I love this Buhle furniture, all the brass. It is French, of course. My own mother is French. On my father's side, my ancestors are Persian, from the line of the great kings.

BELLE: What does it matter where you came from? Me? I came from nowhere – and I'm going nowhere.

BUCK: Would you like to hear some Persian poetry?

(The TOWN HALL SET are both bemused and amused at BUCK.
They smile and murmur encouragement.)
'Makun bidar ai saqi ze khab I naz nargis ra,
ke badmastand o barham mizanand filhal majlis ra.'
This poem was put in the mouth of Jahan, queen of Persia.
Like my Belle, she was celebrated for her beauty and
intelligence.
(A ripple of laughter from the TOWN HALL SET.)
Oh, don't laugh, please. My Belle is queen of this house.
Would you like to know what the poem is saying? 'O, cup-
bearer, refrain from awakening my narcissus-like eyes from
their amorous dream for they are intoxicated and with
their bewitchment will instantly plunge the assembly into
tumultuous disorder.'
(The TOWN HALL SET laugh and give him a little round of
applause.)
(Pressing on, not letting anyone else get a word in.)
I was schooled in Paris. French is my first language.
I think all my thoughts primarily in French, then translate
into English. Each day I do an hour to keep up my
grammar. French is a very strong and virile language, so
expressive of emotion, as well as being the language of
culture and good society. English is much more workaday,
I find it difficult to feel sophisticated in English, if you
know what I mean...

BELLE: *(Cutting in.)* Give us an earful of the language of love,
Bommie. We'd all like that, wouldn't we?
(A murmur of assent from the TOWN HALL SET.)

BUCK: Certainly. Let me think of something appropriate. Ah,
yes. *'Boire sans soif et faire l'amour en tout temps madame; il n'y*
a que ça qui nous distingue des autre bêtes.'

BELLE: We picked up the mention of *l'amour.* Our ears
pricked up immediately, didn't they, gang?

BUCK: It was written by Pierre Augustin de Beaumarchais – it
comes from *The Marriage of Figaro.*

BELLE: Feeegaro! Feeegaro! Oh, yes! We all know that one,
don't we? Feeegaro! Feeegaro!
(The TOWN HALL SET join in with more feeegaros.)

175

BUCK: (*Icy cool.*) If you will pardon me for correcting you, Belle, your favourite aria is from *The Barber of Seville*, not *The Marriage of Figaro*. There is a character called Figaro in that masterpiece by Rossini, but my quotation is from Beaumarchais' satirical play, set to music by the immortal Wolfgang Amadeus Mozart.

BELLE: Get away. See how ignorant I am, folks? Christ almighty! (*Shouting.*) Bring in the bloody soup before I go mad!

BUCK: There is no soup, Belle, no dinner. Your friends are welcome to my wine, my Persian, my French, but not to break bread with me. They are misleading you so badly – bringing out the worst in you, turning you against me. Before I dismiss you all from my house, which I regret, but my cruel woman here has driven me to it, let me translate what Beaumarchais was saying: 'Drinking when we are not thirsty and making love at all seasons, madam; that is all there is to distinguish us from other animals.' Goodnight. (*Exits.*)

(*Pause.*

BELLE wildly rubs the make-up from her face, tears the combs out of her hair.)

BELLE: Call yourself friends? You let him do that to me! Get out, you useless, stupid bastards!

(*The TOWN HALL SET put their glasses down and exit hurriedly, murmuring, laughing.*

Pause.

BUCK enters with a Service revolver.)

BUCK: I told you Bobby Edmondson was not to come into my house.

BELLE: Didn't I mention it, Pa? He found he was able to come after all.

BUCK: That was a dirty trick done to upset me.

BELLE: Oh, put that rusty old thing away, or get some bullets for it. I get tired of seeing you wave it around.

BUCK: It is loaded. You have shamed me for the last time.

BELLE: Then let's get it over with, Bommie.

BUCK: I mean it! We can't carry on like this, Belle!

BELLE: I'm tired of life, Bommie. Oh, so fucking fed up with it all! Can't stand the pretence. Having my brains blown out would be a relief.

BUCK: Stop swearing! It ill becomes a woman. (*Pause, he lowers the revolver.*) If you will promise not to see that young man again...

BELLE: If I'm dead I won't be able to, will I? (*Peers at the revolver.*) Hey, things are looking up. Bullets at last! This is much more exciting. But you still have to pull the trigger, Bommie. Can you do that?

BUCK: If I can cut off a man's leg while he's looking at me, I can pull a trigger.

BELLE: The woman you love so much? The Madonna? (*Laughs.*)

BUCK: The whore who tortures me. The bitch who wants to destroy me. I do love you, but it has become suffering and misfortune. (*Raises the revolver again.*) I think I have to do it, Belle.

BELLE: (*Pause.*) Why take up with the most worthless woman you could find – a discard, another man's leavings? You've no taste in women, Bommie, that's for sure. Or did you just want a white wife, regardless?

BUCK: Your mind is rotten, Belle. I cannot stand the shame of being married to an alcoholic any longer.

BELLE: (*Calling.*) Mary!

BUCK: This has nothing to do with Mary!

BELLE: Mary! He's going to kill me!

BUCK: (*Putting the revolver down.*) Oh, be quiet, woman. Stop this noise. It's me. How could I ever kill you? You're everything to me. Come to bed.

BELLE: I'd rather sleep in the gutter than with you, you dirty half-caste bastard!
(*BUCK slaps her.*
She falls.)

BUCK: Shut your foul mouth!

BELLE: I hate you, you and your coloured children!

BUCK: How could abuse our wonderful children? You must hate yourself.

BELLE: Not as much as I hate you!

(*BUCK grabs her by the hair, shakes her and drags her round the room screaming incoherently with rage.*
MARY runs in.)

MARY: (*Struggling with BUCK.*) Let go, Doctor! You're hurting her!

BELLE: (*Screeching.*) I'll go where I fucking like! I'll do what I fucking like and you won't stop me!

MARY: Doctor, please stop it! The children can hear.
(*BUCK suddenly drops BELLE, turns on his heel, and walks out. MARY helps BELLE to her feet.*)
There, there, it's all over. He's gone.

BELLE: That's it. I'm leaving him. Tomorrow, I'm off.
I can't stand being in the same house.

MARY: (*Seeing the revolver.*) Is this his?

BELLE: Haven't you see that before? He's always waving it around to frighten me. He had it in the Army. Don't touch it. It's loaded. If you hadn't come, he'd have killed me.
(*Picks the revolver up and puts it to her head.*) This is what I feel like doing, Mary.

MARY: Don't play games, Belle.

BELLE: What's a woman like me doing with children, eh? They'd be better off as orphans. I'm quite close to pulling this trigger. It would solve everyone's problems, including mine.
(*Snap blackout and simultaneous gunshot.*
Lights up frontstage on VANN with a smoking shotgun at his shoulder, MIDDLETON at his side, also with a shotgun.)

MIDDLETON: Missed.

VANN: This jacket is too tight under the arms.

MIDDLETON: We haven't hit much between us.

VANN: More than can be said for Dr Ruxton. The belle of the ball's been down to the station complaining about domestic violence.

MIDDLETON: Well, I'd say that man has a short fuse.

VANN: Perhaps, but he gets plenty of provocation?

MIDDLETON: Even if he does, that doesn't justify violence. He should sort her out.

VANN: How d'you sort out a woman like that?

MIDDLETON: Lancaster isn't exactly Mayfair, Vann.

VANN: Indians have a lower boiling-point than us. Ask anyone who's been out there. To someone excitable, ours is an alien culture.

MIDDLETON: It's up to him to control his wife and control himself.

VANN: A young man in your town hall office is pushing his luck with Dr Ruxton. He should know better.

MIDDLETON: That's just rumour, Vann.

VANN: When he's at work, they wave to each other from windows across Dalton Square. They don't care who knows what they're up to.

MIDDLETON: Maybe they're in love. What can you do about that? They're adults, Vann. I'm not giving anyone a sermon. If Dr Ruxton can prove infidelity, let him divorce her

VANN: Having a doctor's wife on hand can be quite handy. She can get at the goodies in the dispensary cupboard.

MIDDLETON: Now your imagination is running away with you. That's a very serious allegation.

VANN: And I'm very serious about making it. Just tell that mob to watch out because I've got my eye on them. I don't like lotus-eaters. I don't like playboys. And I don't like decadence.

(*Clatter of grouse flying.*
VANN throws up his shotgun and fires.
Blackout.
Lights up on BUCK and BELLE sitting together on a sofa.
BUCK has his arm around her.)

BUCK: My best friend. I love making up with you, Belle.

BELLE: So you say.

BUCK: You're wondering why it happens? It's human nature.

BELLE: Bommie, we have a row every day.

BUCK: Married couples have disagreements. We always make up, don't we? Sometimes I think we have rows so we can make up.

BELLE: It's not normal, Bommie. We're not suited.

BUCK: You are my fate, darling. I knew that from the very beginning.

BELLE: I don't think you know me at all.

BUCK: Of course I know you.

BELLE: I think you just decided you were going to find a
woman you could make into a respectable doctor's wife.
How you ever thought that could be me, I've no idea.

BUCK: That's nonsense. These are only ups and downs, my
darling.

BELLE: Not only don't you understand me, Bommie – you
don't understand yourself. You're so arrogant.

BUCK: I have faults, but arrogance is not one of them.

BELLE: What have you got to be arrogant about? You're a
doctor – so what? You're nothing special. D'you know
the only special thing about you? You're Lancaster's only
Indian. That's a hell of an achievement, isn't it?

BUCK: Belle, there are two thousand plus English people on
my panel. That is not because I'm an Indian. It's because
I'm a good doctor.
(*Pause.*
*BELLE takes BUCK's arm from round her shoulders and stands
up, moving away.*)

BELLE: Alright, I admit I envy you, Bommie. I envy your
work, I envy the way you apply yourself. But what am I
good for? Keeping your fantasies going? I don't think that's
doing me much good.

BUCK: You are all I want. You are my woman. You share my
life.

BELLE: I want something of my own. Everything I do has to
be for you. It's not enough to be your woman. This isn't
India!

BUCK: Will you pray with me to ask God to help us find a
way out of this?

BELLE: Oh, don't be ridiculous.
(*BUCK gets down on his knees and clasps his hands together,
praying hard, eyes tight shut.*
BELLE ruffles his hair as she passes on her way out.)
Poor old Pa. (*Exits.*)
(*BUCK gets to his feet, rolls up his sleeve, fixes a hypodermic
and gives himself an injection in the arm.*
MARY enters as he is doing this.)

MARY: Good night, Doctor. I'm going to bed now.

BUCK: (*Mumbling.*) Good night, Mary.

MARY: Are you alright?

(*BUCK laughs as he rolls down his sleeve.*)

BUCK: I've taken morphine for the pain she is causing me, Mary. That's very unprofessional, I know. But I didn't start the corruption. I think Belle has been stealing morphine and cocaine for her friends.

MARY: I don't believe she'd do that.

BUCK: (*Sharply.*) You mean Mrs Ruxton wouldn't do that!

MARY: Yes…I'm sorry.

BUCK: She is the cat's mother. (*Pause.*) Two of morphine would kill me. It's a thought.

MARY: A wicked one, Doctor.

BUCK: I have six thousand pounds of life insurance. If I'm driven to suicide, Belle will get the money and go off with Bobby Edmondson. That's their plan.

MARY: You don't know what you're saying, Doctor.

BUCK: I've seen them together. Everyone has seen them together. They are going to live in Blackburn. Down the road is the school where my babies will go. They will have a new life, without me. My body will be thrown on the rubbish-heap.

MARY: Please sit down, Doctor. I don't like to see you in this mood.

BUCK: (*Sitting down.*) You shouldn't conspire with them, Mary. I've always treated you properly – never harmed a hair on your head.

MARY: It's nothing to do with me. You're not well, Doctor. I can see that in your eyes.

BUCK: That is the morphine. We only have to worry when it wears off and the pain starts again. You have no idea how bad it gets.

MARY: It's so sad to watch two people you like always hurting each other…

BUCK: Yes, everybody watches. They get a lot of amusement out of my pain, Mary. (*Pause.*) Here am I, despised, mocked, yet I am a more civilized person than all of them.

In spite of everything, I pray for everyone around me. I say hallowed be thy name for every patient who comes through my door, praying in their religion. Not only that, I pray for the other doctors in Lancaster who hate me because I'm so succesful.

MARY: Yes, Doctor. I'm going to bed now. Goodnight.

BUCK: You'll go when I say so.

MARY: (*Upset.*) I'm very tired.

BUCK: What do they think of me, Mary?

(*Pause.*)

MARY: They think you're a fine doctor, and they're right, you are.

BUCK: But as a man...as a husband and a father?

MARY: They mind their own business.

BUCK: My father was a doctor, and his father, right back – but they were also men of honour.

MARY: May I go to bed now, please?

BUCK: Mary, you are a good-hearted girl. Today the children let it slip that they're going to live in Blackburn with a new daddy.

MARY: (*Cries.*) Oh, I'm so sick of the whole mess. Those poor little children... What kind of a life are they going to have?

BUCK: It's tomorrow you all go, isn't it? That's why I'm taking the morphine – so I don't make a scene. So I don't care. They can do what they like with me, walk all over me. I've accepted my fate. It's finished. Off to bed, my child. You are close to my heart.

(*MARY crosses to her bedroom across stage.*

Lights up on the area. She undresses quickly and gets into bed, but sits up, listening apprehensively.

BUCK dozes on the sofa.

BELLE, in a nightdress, enters MARY's bedroom.)

BELLE: Where is he?

MARY: Downstairs. He's taken morphine.

BELLE: Good. That'll keep him quiet. God, it's freezing cold in here. Shove over. (*She gets into bed beside MARY.*) Oh, Mary, it's going to happen. I'm leaving him. I'm going to be free.

MARY: He knows everything. The children told him about tomorrow.

BELLE: Christ! I told them not to say anything!

MARY: He says he doesn't care any more. He's given up.

BELLE: I wish I could believe that but it's only the morphine talking. (*Pause.*) You will join us in Blackburn, won't you? I'll need you more than ever.

MARY: I'll bring them over but I can't stay. It's too far for me to be away from mum and dad. And I'm not sure what you're doing is right.

BELLE: (*Laughs loudly.*) Right? It's survival! If I stay here the bastard will kill me. He's mad enough to do it, believe me!

MARY: Ssssh!

(*BUCK stirs.*)

BELLE: We'll have a good life over there. We'll be able to pay you more than the pittance he gives you.

MARY: It's not all that bad, Belle. And, I have to say, Blackburn might be your idea of Paradise, but it's not mine.

(*BUCK starts to cross to MARY's bedroom area.*)

BELLE: Alright, but think about it. There's plenty of time. You've been such a good friend to me. God knows what I'd have done without you.

(*BUCK enters as BELLE puts an arm round MARY.*)

BUCK: Belle! What is this? With Mary as well?

MARY: Doctor! This is my room!

BELLE: (*Hugging MARY.*) Keep him away from me!

BUCK: Woman with woman! It is unnatural vice!

MARY: Doctor, we were just talking…

BUCK: Silence, you pervert! Belle, I have tolerated you doing it with men. But this cannot be forgiven!

MARY: (*Getting out of bed.*) I've had enough of this nonsense. I've got to be up at six…

(*BUCK pounces on her and hurls her to the floor. She lies still, knocked unconscious.*)

BUCK: Belle, you have been very corrupt with Mary. You must both be punished. As the one who discovered you I am bound by the law.

BELLE: Poor Mary. You've knocked her out cold. (*Gets out of bed.*) Do something for her.

BUCK: With my babies in the next room you couple like she-asses. It is unatonable, Belle.

BELLE: Oh, be quiet.

BUCK: You defile the earth.

BELLE: (*Sensing real danger.*) Come on, lie down for a minute. Mary will be alright, I'm sure You've got the wrong end of the stick.

BUCK: (*Sitting on the bed beside BELLE.*) Why did it have to be me who found you? What a burden to impose on a man who loves his wife! But it is the judgement of God. You've no idea of the hard work ahead…two of you! Complete dismemberment and cut into very small pieces…think of the work! And the mess! It will take hours. My darling, I don't want to cause you pain. Would you like chloroform?

BELLE: Look, forget all that business about Blackburn…

BUCK: And tomorrow I was going to drive up to the Border country to keep out of your way while you got all your stuff together and left. Oh, how I wish I hadn't come up those stairs and found you. Goodbye, my Belle.

(*BUCK strangles her.*

At first she doesn't resist as though a willing victim, but then fights. It is a long struggle.

When BELLE is dead BUCK sits holding her hand for a while, then gets to his feet, rolls up his sleeves, picks BELLE up and carries her to a bathtub.

Music, very faintly – dance band plays 'Red Sails in the Sunset'. He returns to the bed, strips off the linen and throws it in a bundle beside the bath. He then exits for a moment and returns with a pile of newspapers and old clothes and towels, plus a box of tools and a set of surgical instruments.

Bending over the bath he takes off BELLE's clothes. He takes a scalpel, stands upright by the bath, raises his arm.)

Let the law take its course.

(*Snap blackout.*

'Red Sails in the Sunset' plays on for a few bars, then fades.)

End of Act One.

ACT TWO

BUCK, unkempt and unshaven, in his surgery, writing at his desk. His left hand is bandaged. DR LOCO and the CORPORAL enter in white coats and stand behind him.

DR LOCO: In the aftermath, Buck sent off for a horoscope. Having done his duty to God, he felt the need to plan a future. He sat down and composed a letter to a complete stranger.

CORPORAL: 'To Altair, astrologer, 111 Finchley Road, London NW1, I am interested to know how long I will live and what are my money prospects. How do I stand professionally?'

DR LOCO: 'They say that the exalted moon in mid-heaven in the tenth house assures dignity. I list my primary directions and transits for my entire existence on a separate sheet.'

CORPORAL: 'I am very fond of the fineries of life. I am very faddy. I must have the best of everything. I might say I am ultra-artistic in my household. I am always financially embarrassed but somehow manage to keep afloat.'

BUCK: 'I have never been happy in my married life. I came across a worthless woman who has left me for another man.'

CORPORAL: 'Remember to let me have length of life and mode of death.'

DR LOCO: 'I should also like you to advise me as to the locality in England where I should reside. What sort of house should I live in? A corner one or one in the middle of a row?'

CORPORAL: 'Without any intention to blow my own trumpet, I might say, just to help you, Altair, that I have had a most brilliant career, first-class honours in everything. I speak five languages. I observe total abstinence from alcohol and am even very moderate in my sex-life.'

(DR LOCO and the CORPORAL take off their white coats and fold them over their arms.

BUCK looks up from the letter, then puts it away in a drawer.)

DR LOCO: What have you done to your hand?

BUCK: I was trying to open a damn tin of peaches for my children's tea.

CORPORAL: Cuts off tins can be very nasty. You want to take care of that.

BUCK: Belle has left me.

DR LOCO: I'm sorry.

BUCK: She's made no contact since she went.

DR LOCO: Hard to believe she won't worry about the children.

BUCK: Who knows with that woman? She's so strange.

DR LOCO: You look tired.

BUCK: *(Testy.)* Of course I'm tired! I work very hard. I have over two thousand patients on my panel. As the most popular and successful general practitioner in the town I have a right to be tired! And Belle messes me about as much as she can!

DR LOCO: Alright, alright.

BUCK: I'm sorry, Jimmy. *(Pause.)* I can't even offer you refreshment. When Belle left me she took the nursemaid for the children with her.

DR LOCO: Why take Mary Rogerson and leave the children behind?

BUCK: How the hell do I know? Perhaps they are conspiring to procure an illegal abortion somewhere! Any more questions? I've had the bloody nosey police here this morning driving me mad. It's damaging my practice. The lower classes don't like to see the police on their doctor's doorstep. What do I know about bodies in Scotland? Bodies in Lancaster, yes. I have to know plenty about those, but bodies in Scotland? The police are always so stupid. I have complained about this harassment, of course, but no one takes any notice.

DR LOCO: I'll come back some other time. Try and get some rest. You look all in. If you need me, you know where I am.

BUCK: (*Holding up a few letters.*) See these unpleasant things? Not all bills, Jimmy. Poison pen letters already. It's amazing how quick off the mark people are. They love the pain others feel, damn them!

DR LOCO: We're up the hill if you need us.

(*DR LOCO and CORPORAL walk frontstage.*)

CORPORAL: Terrible stink in there, sir.

DR LOCO: Yes.

CORPORAL: No doubt in your mind, sir?

DR LOCO: Everything is too late now.

CORPORAL: Did you hear the BBC news this morning, sir?

DR LOCO: I did.

CORPORAL: Bits of bodies in Scotland – they found them scattered all over a popular tourist spot called the Devil's Beeftub.

DR LOCO: D'you remember Bombay?

CORPORAL: We had a roaring time in old Bombay.

DR LOCO: The Towers of Silence?

CORPORAL: You wouldn't forget them, sir – not once you've been downwind of one or two.

DR LOCO: That's where the Parsis put their dead so the vultures will clean up. The prophet Zarathustra forbids the burial of the dead. They must be scattered by the action of birds. That religion has a definite distributive theme – Nature fertilizing new life with old, like farming, and gardening really…

(*MIDDLETON enters with a briefcase, on his way somewhere.*)

What news, Town Clerk?

MIDDLETON: There hasn't been any positive identification.

DR LOCO: Being a solicitor, you'll know the French legal system recognises *crime passionel.* We don't have that here. Instead we have *crime municipal.*

MIDDLETON: Oh, be your age, man! You find excuses for everything.

(*DR LOCO and CORPORAL exit.*

BUCK leaves his desk and comes forward, tossing his car keys in his good hand.)

Off for a drive, Doctor Ruxton?

BUCK: I have to go on my rounds.

MIDDLETON: Not going far, then. Not a long journey.

BUCK: Good Lord, no. Just round the town.

MIDDLETON: I think Chief Constable Vann is hoping for a word with you.

BUCK: I've already had his minions pestering me. He'll have to wait his turn. My patients come first.

(*VANN enters.*)

VANN: Any news of your wife, yet, Doctor?

BUCK: No. Complete silence.

VANN: We've had no news either.

BUCK: Belle has done this before. She will turn up somewhere.

VAN: Nothing you can think of that might help us find her?

BUCK: Well, where is her boy-friend today? Check on him. Ask him some questions. They spend a lot of time together. He might lead you to her.

(*Pause.*

VANN gives MIDDLETON a look.)

MIDDLETON: If you keep talking like that, Doctor, you could ruin a young man's life.

BUCK: His future is not in my hands, but mine has been in his for some time, unfortunately.

(*BUCK exits tossing the car-keys in his good hand.*)

VANN: He left a trail a mile wide. Once they've identified the bits and pieces up there – which won't be easy – I'll arrest him.

MIDDLETON: If you're that sure, arrest him now. He might run off.

VANN: If he was going to run off he'd already have gone, wouldn't he? The doctor thinks he's smarter than we are. He's going to bluff it out.

MIDDLETON: God, what a shambles.

VANN: How right you are, Town Clerk. (*Pause.*) He wrapped some of the bits up in a Lancaster newspaper, would you believe? Plus old clothes with labels we've been able to trace back. You'd think he wanted us to catch him. And I'm afraid it gets messier by the minute. I've received a copy of a statement by Mrs Ruxton's sister saying Bobby

Edmondson and Mrs Ruxton were in Edinburgh together
ten days ago.

MIDDLETON: I know all about this,Vann. It was a family
excursion. Bobby's mother and father also went along.

VANN: As chaperones? You know the score. Ruxton's never
liked all her pally stuff with that family. He followed them
all the way in his car. She lied to him, saying she'd stayed
with her sister when she hadn't. The four of them stayed
in a hotel. Does that sound odd to you? Ruxton spoke to
Bobby Edmondson about it.

MIDDLETON: I don't care what you say, nothing justifies
what he's done. It's a vile, horrendous crime. And why kill
the nursemaid?

VANN: Does he look like a sane man to you?

MIDDLETON: I never thought it would go this far. I thought
Ruxton would have the sense to leave Lancaster before
things got out of hand. He's never fitted in here.

VANN: Lots of people like and respect him. His guilt may
be an open and shut case, but the verdict needn't be so
straightforward. Ruxton's been wound up like a clock. A
good defence barrister could put certain elements in this
town to shame.

(*Blackout.*

*Lights up on BUCK in the surgery, treating his hand while
talking to a JOURNALIST.*)

BUCK: Do me a favour, old chap. Tie a knot in that for me.
(*The JOURNALIST obliges.*)
A double knot. I don't want it to keep coming undone.
Thank you. Now, what is it your readers want to know?
Something about my life? Usual stuff?

JOURNALIST: Some people are saying the disappearance
of your wife and nursemaid could be linked to the
dismembered corpses found in the Devil's Beeftub on the
Moffat-Edinburgh road. Have you any comment to make?

BUCK: The first thing to know is I was born under the royal
constellation of Leo. My Moon and Venus are exalted. My
second house of wealth is occupied by Jupiter. Are you
taking this down?

JOURNALIST: Could those bodies be your two?

BUCK: My Belle is off on her travels. She gambles on horses. Also she has been trying to set herself up as a bookmaker. (*Raises his voice.*) For God's sake, this house is mortgaged up to the entire hilt! Tell the public that, if you like!
(*The JOURNALIST realises he has entered the lion's den. He makes to leave.*)
You're not at all interested in my problems. What kind of a newspaperman are you?

JOURNALIST: Excuse me, I must get back to the office.
(*DR LOCO and CORPORAL enter.*)

CORPORAL: Out, you!

JOURNALIST: I was just going.
(*The JOURNALIST hurries off.*)

DR LOCO: What did you say to him, Buck?

BUCK: Nothing. He's just sniffing round.

DR LOCO: We don't have much time. I want you to trust me.

BUCK: If it's a loan you want, Jimmy, you'll have to look elsewhere.

DR LOCO: I want you to come to the hospital.

BUCK: Why?

DR LOCO: Don't stay here. We can give you a kind of sanctuary while everything is sorted out.
(*Pause.*)

CORPORAL: Better let us look after you.

BUCK: Be quiet, man! Do not presume to address me as an equal.

CORPORAL: Sorry, sir.
(*Pause.*)

BUCK: The laws of God cannot be disobeyed.

DR LOCO: Buck, I remember in Basra you told me how extreme it was that Zarathustra decreed anyone found maltreating a bitch in pup should receive fifteen hundred lashes – a virtual death sentence. At the time, you said – who can make sense out of that?

BUCK: Now I know – the bitch in pup.
(*LAWLEY enters, a geriatric patient.*)
Now you must excuse me. Come in, Mr Lawley. My colleague is just leaving.

LAWLEY: I can wait, Doctor.

BUCK: No, no, you come first. Bye, Jimmy.

> (*DR LOCO and CORPORAL exit.*
> *BUCK gives LAWLEY a chair.*)

LAWLEY: Sorry to hear about your trouble, Doctor.

BUCK: Never mind my trouble. What about yours?

LAWLEY: Well, not much change. That stuff stops the pain. I don't like the feeling it gives, I must say – cuts you off from everything.

BUCK: But it is merciful to cancer patients, Mr Lawley. God put these opiates in Nature to help us with our pain. A long, lingering death is not something we should have to endure.

LAWLEY: That other doctor codding me, saying it was indigestion. You don't throw up night and day with indigestion. (*Pause.*) It's my wife's sent me. She says she has to know how long I've got.

BUCK: At a guess, I'd say less than six months.

LAWLEY: Thank you. I'll tell her that.

BUCK: I'll put you in hospital for the last few weeks. You will need constant sedation. How is your wife?

LAWLEY: We get on better. I don't mind a bit of sympathy from her.

BUCK: Open your shirt and let me have a feel around.

> (*LAWLEY undoes his shirt and BUCK examines him.*)

The wasting is quite advanced now. Thank you.

LAWLEY: (*Doing up his shirt.*) You know we're with you, Doctor. We know what you've been through. You can count on us.

BUCK: I'm grateful for your support, Mr Lawley, but I don't particularly need it in this case. I am innocent.

LAWLEY: Yes, Doctor. They shouldn't have given you the run-around. You're worth ten of them.

BUCK: (*Pause.*) If you feel any powerful bouts of pain in these next few weeks, strong surges, you must get hold of me immediately. Don't punish yourself. I can help you through the worst.

LAWLEY: You've a lot on your plate, Doctor.

BUCK: You are my responsibility. I'm going to be with you through to the end. D'you need another prescription?

LAWLEY: No, Doctor. I've got plenty of stuff to take.

BUCK: I'll see you out.

(*VANN enters.*)

VANN: On your way. I want a word with the Doctor.

BUCK: (*Taking LAWLEY's arm and ushering him out.*) Give my regards to your wife. Tell her not to worry. She can come and talk to me any time.

(*LAWLEY exits.*

BUCK returns.)

Don't you dare come barging in here when I'm with a patient in future!

VANN: I'm sorry, Doctor. I was anxious to let you know we've got somewhere with our enquiries.

BUCK: I've been slandered, you know, and libelled – poison pen letters.

VANN: It could be said you've been doing a bit of slandering yourself.

BUCK: Me? How so?

VANN: The way you've been talking about Bobby Edmondson makes it sound as though you think he might have murdered her.

BUCK: What rubbish! Why should he? He can do what he likes, that boy. He has your protection. But he is a home-breaker and the curses of my three children are on his head!

VANN: Eighteen months you've been making accusations, with no proof. Bobby and his father faced you with it, and you backed down and apologised.

BUCK: I had to or be destroyed. They rule this town, with your help. It has been my bad luck to settle in a place that is corrupt. No one is free from it. (*Pause.*) Anyway, what have you discovered about this silly woman of mine? Where is she?

VANN: Oh, we reckon she's dead, sir.

BUCK: (*Laughing.*) Belle, dead? Out of the question. Look again and you'll find her having a jolly good time in a dress shop somewhere.

VANN: Yes, sir, and we think you killed her, and Mary Rogerson.

BUCK: I'm a busy man. There are calls I must make. Don't waste my time. You're paid to find my Belle, not talk stuff and nonsense.

VANN: Would you be so good as to step over to the station?

BUCK: What a farce!

(*As VANN conducts BUCK to downstage L and a spot, the TOWN HALL SET and DR LOCO, CORPORAL and DANNY in military dress enter and dance to 'Red Sails In The Sunset'.*)

Where do they find people to do these jobs? Mr Vann, you are making yourself appear very foolish.

VANN: You are charged that between l4th to 29th September l935 you did feloniously and with malice aforethought kill and murder Mary Jane Rogerson and Isabella Ruxton.

(*In red specks of light from the rotating mirror ball, BELLE and MARY enter and join the dance.*)

BUCK: Most emphatically not. Of course not. The furthest thing from my mind. What motive and why?

VANN: You have a lawyer, Dr Ruxton?

BUCK: Several.

VANN: I would advise you to contact one of them. Would Mr Gardner do? He's acted for you in the past, hasn't he?

BUCK: Hardly worth the trouble, old man. This is an aberration caused by your ambition to be number one policeman in the country.

VANN: You have your rights, Doctor. Shall I call Mr Gardner for you?

BUCK: I'm loath to bother him but I suppose you might as well.

(*VANN takes BUCK to a police cell.*
The dancers circle around him.
BUCK suddenly slumps, defeated.
DANNY breaks out into a wild dervish dance.)

The music fades and the dancers exit.
VANN leaves the cell.
Pause.
GARDNER enters.)

GARDNER: Doctor Ruxton… (*Offering his hand.*) I cannot tell you how distressed I am about this.

BUCK: (*Shaking hands, straightening.*) Mr Gardner, we must keep a clear head. The first thing to do is to sell the furniture.

GARDNER: (*Pause.*) Yes…of course. We must raise money for your defence. As you know, Doctor, your affairs are perilously close to bankruptcy, and now this.

BUCK: Sell everything – but not the Reading Madonna. We will hold that in reserve. Every day it appreciates in value. Connoisseurs are after my Belle's picture.

GARDNER: The police court hearing was a travesty. We will get you a good man, Doctor, don't worry.

BUCK: The prosecution case is comical. They have stuck together those bodies in Scotland and claim they are my Belle and Mary. That's very amusing. They are taking my house to pieces. It is all fragments now, my life, Mr Gardner. My God, what am I thinking? I forgot to greet you. How are you?

GARDNER: Deeply upset, Doctor. We all hoped this would never happen.

BUCK: Pardon me for being slow, but what d'you mean?

GARDNER: It could have been prevented. Everyone was aware of what was going on. It was infamous behaviour on their part.

BUCK: Innocent men are charged with fearful crimes every day. All we must do is prove my innocence. It should not be difficult.

GARDNER: Doctor, I must be frank. I have the greatest regard for you as a professional man, immense respect. I have witnessed the good you do. Other members of your profession are far less caring. You are a compassionate man, and deserve compassion. (*Pause.*) Like everyone else, Doctor, I know the background…

BUCK: Not Guilty is the plea, Mr Gardner. I must leave the court without a stain on my character.

GARDNER: Good people like yourself can be driven to commit the most terrible crimes without meaning to.

BUCK: Those two bodies have nothing to do with me. They are not Belle and Mary.

GARDNER: Then where are Belle and Mary? The case is news headlines. They would know what position you're in and come forward.

BUCK: That is easy. Belle wants me dead. She has already tried to poison me several times.

GARDNER: Oh, Doctor, I think I must get a colleague of mine to take the case as your solicitor. He's more used to criminal matters…I'm a family lawyer, really. I'm not sure I can cope.

BUCK: Norman Birkett is the man for me. I hear he's the very best. Not that we'll need him. The case will be laughed out of court.

GARDNER: Birkett would be very expensive.

BUCK: I have war service for this country. Does that not carry any weight? I'm the top general practicioner in this town. No jury in Lancaster would convict me.

GARDNER: The trial will be in Manchester. You must think clearly. This is the Law we're dealing with. If you plead Not Guilty your character has little use. What matters is the evidence against you. (*Pause.*) I have to ask you – are you sure of that plea?

BUCK: (*Angrily.*) God man, you as well? Can't you see it's one damn thing after another? Life is being made impossible for me. I cannot bear it much longer! Who is at the bottom of this damn thing? It is racial prejudice and I condemn it. Is there no justice in the world? Do I look like a murderer? My religion would not permit me. I don't smoke and I don't drink. I cannot help the way I am. What a code of morality you have in this country!

GARDNER: Very well, Doctor. Not Guilty it is. I'll try to get you Birkett.

BUCK: Believe in me like my patients do. Doctor Buck
Ruxton is innocent. Think that way, Mr Gardner.
(*GARDNER exits.*
Lights fade on the police station cell and fade up on DANNY in
the padded cell. He hums 'Red Sails in the Sunset'.
DR LOCO works on notes at a table nearby.)

DR LOCO: Okay, Danny. Can we have some quiet?

DANNY: You brought him here one day with his wife, didn't
you? The one he chopped up.

DR LOCO: One of the few advantages of a man in your
position, Danny, is no one would see the sense in bringing
an action against you for slander.

DANNY: That's right. Mad people can say what they like.

DR LOCO: But they can't do what they like.
(*CORPORAL enters.*)

CORPORAL: They've moved him down to Strangeways
in Manchester. But the good news is, he's got Birkett. Mr
Gardner and a few others somehow guaranteed the money.
I won't tell you what the furniture sold for. It would break
your heart.

DR LOCO: Norman Birkett may be the best, but he's going to
have his work cut out if Buck doesn't change his plea. You
never bothered to deny what you did, did you, Danny?

DANNY: They said I had the body of a man of twenty-five
and the mind of an eight-year old. Some eight-year old, eh,
Doctor? What age of mind has your friend got?

DR LOCO: At a pinch, I'd say about three thousand years.
(*Blackout.*
Lights fade up on BUCK in his cell with BIRKETT.)

BIRKETT: You must allow me to call this young man
Edmondson to the stand.

BUCK: Whatever for, Mr Birkett?

BIRKETT: The prosecution case is based on your jealousy,
unfounded, according to them. You did suspect him
of adultery with your wife. You said so on numerous
occasions.

BUCK: That may be so, but as I'm innocent I don't see how
putting Bobby Edmondson on the witness stand is going to
prove anything.

BIRKETT: He will deny it. I know I can break him down because there is enough evidence, circumstantial perhaps, to put his credibility in doubt. Every prosecution witness I can discredit is to our advantage.

BUCK: This is a very roundabout way of proving I'm not guilty of these murders.

BIRKETT: Are you not? Even under strong provocation.

BUCK: I thought I had made this absolutely clear.

BIRKETT: Then whom can you suggest might be?

BUCK: That is not my place. We are all instruments, Mr Birkett. Also, it would be most ungentlemanly of me to put poor Bobby's reputation under pressure. He is a young man at the beginning of what I hope will be a brilliant and prosperous career.

BIRKETT: That's very magnanimous of you – but it may cost us some advantage. English juries, in general, don't take a shine to small town playboys.

BUCK: If there was anyone at fault it was Belle. She has a taste for young men – not that I'm so ancient.

BIRKETT: Before you were arrested you told the police to ask Edmondson where Belle was. Why did you do that?

BUCK: A little justice of my own. But that case is closed.

BIRKETT: And that is your final decision? You will not let me put the man who caused you so much suffering on the stand? Shouldn't he be held to account? (*Pause.*) You're making this very hard for me.

BUCK: If you believe I'm innocent, it should be easy.

BIRKETT: The doctors here at Strangeways have been visiting you, I understand.

BUCK: Two and half hours every night. Their questions drive me crazy! What do they want?

BIRKETT: Did you kill your wife and Mary Rogerson?

BUCK: No.

(*Pause.*)

BIRKETT: Your wife's infidelity was public knowledge.

BUCK: Then ask the public! They know me. Belle is an attractive, headstrong woman. She likes male attention. She drinks too much alcohol. She should never touch it.

But you can't keep such a female locked away. The door
will be broken down.

BIRKETT: Doctor, I must be candid. The Home Office
medical authorities have been examining you here to
ascertain whether you're fit to plead. They say you are.

BUCK: They're right!

BIRKETT: Very well, but now we have to look closely at this
mountain of evidence which the prosecution has against
you.

BUCK: I have complete confidence in you.

BIRKETT: To enter a plea of Not Guilty when you have been
found fit to plead means that if the verdict goes against
you, they will hang you. (*Pause.*) If you plead Guilty, I
can show the court how you were driven to murder by
the most relentless cruelty, that the provocation was
unbearable, that there are thousands of your patients in
Lancaster who swear by you, who are ready to do anything
to help you, that your previous character is excellent...

BUCK: (*Holding up his hand.*) I am fit to plead and I am
innocent. Those are your instructions.

BIRKETT: We'll talk again tomorrow. If you change your
mind, don't feel ashamed. It often happens.

(*Lights fade on BUCK in his cell as BIRKETT crosses to a room
and card table set for three.*

*Lights up on the table as SINGLETON, the judge, and
MAXWELL FYFE, prosecution counsel, both in casual dress,
enter and join BIRKETT.*

They sit down.

MAXWELL FYFE deals four hands for bridge.)

MAXWELL FYFE: You take the dummy hand, Birkett. It
would fit your mood, I should think.

SINGLETON: No teasing in front of the judge. No shop.

MAXWELL FYFE: No chance of keeping Ruxton out of the
conversation. What a performance in the dock! Ranting,
crying.

SINGLETON: Why did he burst into tears when you
mentioned his Army service, Fyfe?

MAXWELL FYFE: God knows. Half a crown a point?

BIRKETT: One feels the entire set-up isn't able to deal with such a man.

SINGLETON: I can't follow what he says half the time. What awful cards you've given me.

MAXWELL FYFE: Birkett thinks he's mad, of course.

BIRKETT: He is, believe me.

MAXWELL FYFE: Always the easy way out.

BIRKETT: The Home Office psychiatrist says he's sane. Ruxton himself says he's sane. Our Sunday newspapers seem to understand him perfectly. Who am I to decide?

MAXWELL FYFE: No bid. If you were faced by a native of New Guinea straight out of the Stone Age, a headhunter, up to his ears in a cannibal feast, how would you determine his sanity?

BIRKETT: Two spades.

SINGELTON: Hold on, Birkett. I haven't bid yet. I must say it makes me very uncomfortable trying an Indian in an English court.

MAXWELL FYFE: It's a foul and terrible crime, a hideous business. I don't think the public would countenance him merely being put away. No bid.

SINGELTON: No bid. That argument is irresponsible, Fyfe. Madness either exists or it does not. There is a man in his right mind and a man in his wrong mind, or, at least, not in his right mind. And let us not forget a man in a killing war and a man in peace. We get knocked about in all kinds of ways. Take the dummy, Birkett. You're a clever fellow.

BIRKETT: A clash of cultures can produce a divided mind. The rate of lunacy in the British Army in India has always been very high. Lots of suicide amongst our men.

MAXWELL FYFE: He is a cruel, cunning, merciless killer, no matter where he comes from. He means to get away with it if he can. That proves he's sane. If you can cheat, you're sane.

BIRKETT: I don't accept that for a moment. Deviousness and lying belong to the human race as a whole, in all conditions. It's part of our animal cunning.

SINGLETON: As we listen to your towering case against him, Fyfe, it's difficult not to come to the conclusion that this man is so inept, so obviously guilty, that he must be mad to think he'll get away with it. Interfering with witness! Giving away bloodstained clothes! Cleaning the house up with help! I ask you.

MAXWELL FYFE: He's a chancer and a charlatan. He has no respect for our law.

BIRKETT: Fyfe, his qualifications prove his intelligence. So what has happened to it? Let me tell you – it has cracked clean in half.

MAXWELL FYFE: He acted very deliberately in his attempt to cover up the killings. Every identifying feature was taken off those bodies, down to peeling off the finger-tips so there would be no prints. Imagine doing that, the time, the care, the cold mind behind it.

SINGLETON: Not all identifying features, Fyfe, or you wouldn't be in such a strong position. His plan failed. He must have been in a frenzy.

MAXWELL FYFE: He didn't reckon on his own technology – medical science. He can't have been keeping up with his reading. The forensic work on this case is a real leap forward.

SINGLETON: I have to say, when you consider they only had seven stone of minced remains to work on, they've done a magnificent job.

BIRKETT: What you're avoiding, Fyfe, perhaps what we're all avoiding, is that Ruxton has a different concept of innocence to ours, to do with honour.

MAXWELL FYFE: Cutting two women into pieces can't be honour.

BIRKETT: You feel no qualm of conscience in claiming Ruxton had no cause for sexual jealousy while, at the same time, declaring it the prime motive for the murders?

MAXWELL FYFE: He was wrong about her. Edmondson says he was friendly with Mrs Ruxton in the ordinary social way.

(*BIRKETT laughs.*)

(*Annoyed.*) Well, you haven't proved otherwise!

BIRKETT: He won't let me! But I could, and you know it.

MAXWELL FYFE: And the killing of Mary Rogerson? What provocation was there for that? She caught him murdering his wife and he killed her to keep her quiet. That's the kind of man he is. Ruthless and cruel.

(*Pause.*)

SINGLETON: I need to share this with you. I have received a parcel during the trial, postmarked Lancaster – a translation from the Persian of ancient laws held sacred by Parsis. A place was marked for me to read – the punishment for unnatural vice, which exactly matches what was done to those two women. (*Pause.*) I only mention it to you as colleagues. To admit it to my consideration would mean I couldn't serve English law.

BIRKETT: If Ruxton changed his plea to Guilty and the whole sordid business of what he had to endure in Lancaster was brought out into the open, he could never be hanged.

SINGLETON: But perhaps he wants to be. Have you thought of that?

(*Lights soften to red.*
'Red Sails in the Sunset' can be faintly heard.
SINGLETON, BIRKETT and MAXWELL FYFE are dressed for court.
BUCK leaves the cell and stands before them.)

SINGLETON: The court will come to order.

MAXWELL FYFE: Call Doctor Arthur Cyril William Hutchinson.

(*HUTCHINSON enters.*)

HUTCHINSON: I am Dean of the Edinburgh Dental Hospital and hold dental qualifications. On the sixth of October, I examined Exhibit 139.

MAXWELL FYFE: The Prosecution claims that Exhibit 139 is the head of Mrs Isabella Ruxton.

(*The exhibit is projected onto a screen.*)

Doctor Hutchinson, did you find that certain teeth had been removed for a considerable time before death?

HUTCHINSON: Yes, I'll start with the upper jaw. On the right side: the first premolar and the first and third molars.

On the left side: the first premolar, the first molar, the lateral incisor and the canine. In the lower jaw, on the right side: the canine, the second premolar, the first and second molars. On the left side: the second premolar and the first, second and third molars. Fifteen teeth in all.

MAXWELL FYFE: And what teeth had recently been removed?

HUTCHINSON: In the upper jaw, on the right side: the central and lateral incisors, the canine, the second premolar and the second molar. On the left: the central incisor and the second molar. In the lower jaw, on the right side: the central and lateral incisors, the first premolar. On the left: the central and lateral incisors, the canine and first premolar. Altogether there had been fourteen recent extractions.

MAXWELL: With regard to those teeth recently extracted, what would you say was the time of removal.

HUTCHINSON: Death or just after death.

MAXWELL FYFE: The teeth were taken out when the woman was dead.

HUTCHINSON: Yes.
(*Pause.*
Lights fade until only Exhibit 139 is left, then snap blackout.
Lights up on the court.)

SINGLETON: Buck Ruxton, you have been convicted of murder upon the verdict of the jury. Have you anything to say why sentence of death should not be passed according to law?

BUCK: Subject to the point that I be allowed to appeal in the administration of justice – I submit that to your lordship and the jury. I want to thank everybody for the patience and fairness of my trial. I have never attempted to pass any special restrictions. I should like to hear whatever his lordship says about it.
(*SINGLETON puts on the black cap.*)

SINGLETON: Buck Ruxton, you have been convicted on evidence that can leave no doubt upon the mind of anyone. The law knows but one sentence for the terrible

crime that you have committed. The judgement of this
court is that you shall be taken from this place to a lawful
prison and thence to a place of execution and that you
be there hanged by the neck until you are dead and that
your body be afterwards buried within the precincts of the
prison, and may God have mercy upon your soul.

BUCK: (*Saluting, arm raised, palm out.*) Hail thou. May thou
prosper though I wither. The Fates have spoken. Be it so.
(*Snap blackout.*

Lights up on the cell and BUCK changing into prison garb.
GARDNER enters.)

GARDNER: My dear Doctor, what can I say.

BUCK: You could try good morning, Mr Gardner. I trust you
had a pleasant drive down from Lancaster. How is the old
place? (*Plucks at the prison garb.*) I have to wear this now I'm
condemned. Very ill-fitting. Rough material. No sense of
style.

GARDNER: I'm desperately sorry about losing the appeal.
They wouldn't even consider our new expert witnesses.

BUCK: Oh, I suppose they've had more than enough of
doctors and dentists.

GARDNER: A petition is being organised in Lancaster.

BUCK: Now that is a good idea.

GARDNER: It will give everyone an opportunity to show
what they think. It's disgraceful how far from the truth
everything has got. It seems very unreal to me.

BUCK: I want all my children to be doctors – professional
people.

GARDNER: We are doing everything we can to help them.

BUCK: Thank you.

GARDNER: Painful though it is for me to have to be so petty
at a time like this, we must discuss money, I'm afraid.

BUCK: Ah, money, money, money. If there is a universal law,
it is that. Sell the Reading Madonna and raise an education
fund for my children.

GARDNER: You are insolvent, I'm afraid. And Birkett's fee
alone is two thousand.

BUCK: Perhaps my children should be lawyers instead of
doctors.

GARDNER: I've guaranteed the sum. It has to be paid somehow.

BUCK: I wonder if there are any further humiliations in store for me? What have I done to deserve all this? Did I ask to be born? (*Pause.*) What about my beautiful Buhle furniture? Haven't you sold it?

GARDNER: I didn't have the heart to tell you during the trial. The auction of all your household effects fetched only five hundred pounds.

BUCK: No! Five hundred? For all my treasures? My magnificent home? It cost five times that! How horribly mean! Damn them all!

GARDNER: With the Depression, there's not much money in Lancaster these days. We must be practical. We have a week to May the twelfth.

BUCK: They are taking my name from my beautiful children. All I will leave them is debts. How much could you get from a newspaper for my confession?

GARDNER: I would not accept less than three thousand.

BUCK: Give me something to write on, please.

GARDNER: (*Giving him paper and pen.*) Will you back-date it, please, Doctor?

BUCK: Back-date it?

GARDNER: To cover me. I'm not supposed to take out anything I don't bring in. Prison regulations.

BUCK: Very well. What date should I put?

GARDNER: May I suggest October 14th, address, Lancaster? That's just after you were charged remember. I can say you lodged it with me with strict instructions it wasn't to be opened until after your demise.

(*BUCK writes swiftly and decisively, then gives the note to GARDNER who wafts the ink dry.*)

Thank you. I will be taking the petition down to the Home Secretary myself.

BUCK: Who is signing?

GARDNER: We already have six thousand signatures – most of them ordinary people.

BUCK: The salt of the earth. I wish I could thank them all personally.

GARDNER: That will be communicated.

BUCK: They're good folk, the lower orders. If only they weren't so powerless. I hope my back-dated cheque clears my account. However, it does not amount to my saying that I am guilty.

GARDNER: With all the sympathy in the world for your predicament, it's difficult to think otherwise.

BUCK: Guilty by your law, which is the law of Man, but not by my law, which is the law of God.

(*Lights fade on the cell.*

Lights up on Dalton Square – CORPORAL and VICKY carry a banner: SAVE DOCTOR RUXTON above a table where DR LOCO is collecting signatures from FOGG, LAWLEY, DANNY and others, watched by VANN, MIDDLETON and the TOWN HALL SET.

DR LOCO leaves the table and goes over to VANN and MIDDLETON.)

DR LOCO: What thoughts can be running through your minds, gentlemen? Regrets, I hope. Poor Buck. To have had one more person committed to our care at the hospital wouldn't have been an intolerable burden. We'd have managed.

MIDDLETON: The law has taken its course.

DR LOCO: Not irrevocably, as yet. I hear the police have in their possession a statement from a Blackpool landlady attesting to the fact that Bobby Edmondson and Belle spent a night together at her establishment. (*Pause.*) I'm told – though I can hardly credit it – that under our law, the prosecution don't have to make material not used in their case available to the defence. Is that so?

VANN: If such a statement did exist, what difference could it possibly make?

DR LOCO: Added to our petition, it would make a forceful argument for commuting the sentence.

VANN: They might have been playing cards.

DR LOCO: What would it cost Bobby Edmondson to own up? I mean, more than he's had to pay already?

MIDDLETON: Exactly! He has paid! Put yourself in his place.

DR LOCO: No, you put yourself in Buck Ruxton's place.

VANN: You're sticking your neck out, Doctor. You're interfering with justice. This is the worst killing I've ever had to deal with. Ask those Scottish policemen who spent days gathering up those bits what they think.

MIDDLETON: I'm on your board, remember. I count your attitude as very unprofessional behaviour.

DR LOCO: What will Buck's death achieve? You know he was driven over the edge by our ways. He fights our wars, loves our women, tends our sick, but he's a man born under a different sun. Having driven him mad, we could have looked after him, at least. Life is all we have.

VANN: Tell that to those two women.

(Lights fade on Dalton Square. Crowd and all characters remain on stage.

Lights up on BUCK with the GOVERNOR of Strangeways. BUCK is holding his sada shirt.)

GOVERNOR: You asked to see me, Ruxton.

BUCK: Yes, Governor. Thank you for sparing me a few minutes of your valuable time. It is about my execution tomorrow morning. I have a little request to make about dress.

GOVERNOR: Yes, what is it?

BUCK: I would like to die wearing this shirt and be hanged with the cord you confiscated.

GOVERNOR: I'm sorry but I can't help you there. Prison issue is standard.

BUCK: Sir, I am of a different faith and upbringing to your other prisoners. I have a right to die properly in the eyes of my own religion.

GOVERNOR: Very well, the shirt I'll allow, but not the cord. It won't do the job properly. It's quite a techincal business.

BUCK: Then I will accept that, if I may wear the cord as well.

(The GOVERNOR nods.)

Thank you so much. A man needs all the comfort he can get at a time like this.

GOVERNOR: As you're not a Christian, shall I tell the prison chaplain he need not attend?

BUCK: Oh, I wouldn't exclude him. Let him come along. The more the merrier. Now, this business of being buried inside the prison walls couldn't be altered in my case, I suppose?

GOVERNOR: I'm afraid not. That's part of the sentence. Anything else?

BUCK: Is it true you'll be putting quicklime in my grave?

GOVERNOR: That will be attended to in the regular manner.

BUCK: Put lots in mine – lots and lots so I melt away very quickly.

GOVERNOR: Will that be all?

BUCK: I think so, thank you. Did you know the good people of Lancaster got up a petition for me? Wasn't that kind of them? It failed, of course. Petitions to anyone but God cannot alter a man's fate.

(*Lights change.*

The gallows box is on stage.

BUCK puts on the sada shirt.

The crowd sing 'Abide With Me'.)

GOVERNOR: It's time, Ruxton. Here's your cord.

BUCK: (*Tying the kusti cord around his waist.*) I am completely prepared and anxious to get it over with.

GOVERNOR: Mr Pierrepoint will be here shortly. He will secure your hands and cover your head.

BUCK: Oh, dear, I seem to be always asking for favours. Would it be possible to leave off the cover for my head?

GOVERNOR: Ruxton, it's better with it on, believe me.

BUCK: For you or for me? (*Pause.*) If I may explain without appearing to waste your valuable time – I must sing.

GOVERNOR: This is a terrible piece of work we must do, Ruxton. Don't imagine we feel good about it.

BUCK: I know, I know, and you need my cooperation, but I still have to sing my prayer. I cannot possibly sing if my head is in some bag.

GOVERNOR: I can't help you there.

(*DR LOCO comes forward to the front of the stage and addresses the audience.*)

DR LOCO: Albert Pierrepoint's train has been cancelled. Anyone for the hangman's job? (*Turns to the crowd.*) How about it? Not much to it, really. Positioning the knot under the left ear is like tying a dicky-bow for a friend. Pulling the lever? A child could do it.

DANNY: Over here, Doctor. I'll help out. Had to do a few Moplahs without making a balls of it. I'll help the man on his way. If you'll kindly step over over here, sir.
(*DANNY ties BUCK's hands behind his back.*)

BUCK: I forgive you.

DANNY: I should think so too. I'll let you off the bag. None of the Moplahs had a bag to put their head in.

CORPORAL: Come on, Doctor. Old style. Cocky to the last. Show them what you're made of.
(*DANNY opens the gallows box and positions BUCK on the trap, then adjusts the noose round his neck.*
The crowd sing the 23rd Psalm.
BUCK sings the Gatha prayer before death.
DANNY slams the door, marches round to the lever, waits until BUCK stops singing, comes to attention, then pulls it. The sound of the trap and the thud of the body.
'Red Sails in the Sunset'.
Blackout.)

The End.

A TALE OF TWO TOWN HALLS

Characters

HARVEY, Mayor of Rougerossbergh

BRENDA, his wife

BIRCH, the Town Clerk

BUNNY LEGGE, the Member of Parliament

SIR ALPHONSE BOURGE, an industrial magnate

RODRIGUEZ, his manservant

McALLISTER, editor of a local newspaper

STURGEON, managing director of a vodka distillery

NELLIE, a designer and convenor

KILROY, a bookseller

GROOT, the Town Clerk of Kleine-und-Zeine

SLINGER, Mayor of Kleine-und-Zeine

PIERS & KLAUS, a nite-club comedy act

SHAND, a professor

PRIVATE EYE, a character in a film

CUSTOMS OFFICER

AIR HOSTESS

SINGER

CLOG-DANCER

*Set in Rougerossbergh, Lancashire and
Klein-und-Zeine, Germany, 1976*

A Tale of Two Town Halls was first performed on 18 November 1976, at the Duke's Playhouse, Lancaster, with the following cast:

HARVEY, Ted Richards

BIRCH, David Boyce

BUNNY LEGGE, Linda Janiec

SIR ALPHONSE BOURGE, David Calder

BRENDA, NELLIE, AIR HOSTESS & SINGER,
Lyndsey Franklin

RODRIGUEZ, PRIVATE EYE & KLAUS, Terry Iland

McALLISTER & PIERS, John Hartoch

STURGEON, Charles Haggith

KILROY, Gary Yershon

GROOT, Paul Humpoletz

SLINGER, David Ericson

SHAND, Alexander Wilson

CUSTOMS OFFICER, David Plimmer

Director, John Blackmore

ACT ONE

Several acting levels with architectural touches from Victorian to post-war brutalism. Fade up lights on HARVEY in his pyjamas staring into a glass of white liquid in his hand. BRENDA enters, dressed for bed.

HARVEY: I can't turn it down, love. But what else is there for me? A man of principle would refuse. That lets me out.

BRENDA: Sleep on it.

HARVEY: The choice will still be there in the morning.

BRENDA: Drink that stuff. Stun your ulcers and turn in. Go to sleep, dream about something to look forward to – triumph in the Quiz League tomorrow night.

HARVEY: If I accept, I'm selling out. They'll just use me.

BRENDA: Rest your brain. (*Going to him.*) Be honest, don't you feel honoured? Number one citizen! That's something.

HARVEY: I do feel honoured – but in what part of my make-up? Is it a worthwhile part?

BRENDA: God, no.

HARVEY: That's my woman. So like my mother.

BRENDA: Alright. Ask yourself the question: what's the point of anyone being mayor?

HARVEY: A figurehead – that's all I'll be, Brenda – a municipal totem pole, with everyone dancing round me while I do nothing but stand there. I'll have no real power.

BRENDA: But you will have position.

HARVEY: You were always good at distinctions.

BRENDA: It might compensate for us having no kids.

HARVEY: No power, no potency.

BRENDA: Be a status symbol, full of history, and proud of it.

HARVEY: (*Hugs her.*) Love you, Brenda. You understand me so well. (*Drinks the medicine.*) Thank God I had the sense to marry you. In the maze you are my ball of string.

BRENDA: Quiz League tomorrow. You'll have to be on your toes. The Unicorn team is mustard. Capital of Peru?

HARVEY: Caracas should be the capital of somewhere.

BRENDA: Can't change the world to suit yourself. Have a go at Abraham Lincoln's assassin.

HARVEY: The Merchant of Venice?

BRENDA: You'll be a good mayor as long as you don't believe you can win. It's a bribe to keep you quiet. That's their mistake. You can never be quiet.

HARVEY: The local mafia will carry on running the town and I'll be helping them do it.

BRENDA: Perhaps you should have joined the Masons when they asked you?

HARVEY: Yes, that was slow of me. Greater men than I have been embraced by the Brotherhood – Mozart, Jack the Ripper, for instance. But I'm a class snob. If I knew the Royal Family was Masonic, now, that would be different! I'd join like a shot.

BRENDA: Come to bed. (*Leading him off.*) What were the Cayman Islands called originally?

HARVEY: The Tortugas, after the green turtles that thrive there.

BRENDA: (*Kisses him.*) How many men would know that? Sheer genius.

HARVEY: As long as you're behind me, I'll be alright.

BRENDA: I won't let them laugh at you.

HARVEY: Ho-ho-ho! Look at him in his funny hat! Hasbeen!

BRENDA: Ho-ho-ho!

HARVEY: Ho-bloody-ho!

(*Fade to blackout as they exit R. Lights fade up on BIRCH at his desk sporting a Remembrance Day poppy in his lapel. An intercom buzzes.*)

BIRCH: (*Answering it.*) Yes?

INTERCOM: Mrs Bunny Beresford-Legge is here, Town Clerk.

BIRCH: Let her in.

(*BUNNY enters wearing a large poppy of the kind usually reserved for car bonnets.*)

BUNNY: Don't get up.

BIRCH: I wasn't going to. Westminster is putting years on you.

BUNNY: You're depressed. I can tell.

(*BIRCH opens his desk and takes out a bottle of whisky and two glasses.*)

BIRCH: God, when I think of it: thirty years! Thirty years! Never ending! (*Pours whisky.*) Well, nice to see you. Not getting anywhere.

BUNNY: Darling Frank, I don't like to see you cast down.

BIRCH: Losing is such a fag.

BUNNY: I won't have you talking like this. Come on, buck up!

BIRCH: I'm thinking of emigrating.

BUNNY: At your age? (*Pause.*) Where would you go?

BIRCH: East Pakistan.

BUNNY: Don't you listen to the news? East Pakistan no longer exists.

BIRCH: Exactly. Aren't they lucky, those East Pakistanis? Ever heard of the Thirty Years War?

BUNNY: Someone mentioned something…

BIRCH: It happened in Germany in the early seventeenth-century, long before it was unified. Town fought town, village village. It went on until they were reduced to eating children.

BUNNY: How disgusting!

BIRCH: Why? British children are now eating the grown-ups, metaphorically. What an infantile society we live in, Bunny.

BUNNY: Stop being so gloomy. (*Pours two more whiskies.*) We'll come through. We always have.

BIRCH: I thought the Fifties was bad enough, but then along the came the Sixties. This can't get any worse, I thought, but the Seventies proved me wrong. I simply cannot face the Eighties, Bunny. We're standing on the threshold of something terrible. Would you like a surprise?

BUNNY: That's better. I love surprises.

BIRCH: It's a beauty.

(*BIRCH opens a desk drawer, takes out an antique barometer and hands it to her.*)

What d'you think of that?

BUNNY: Oh, Frank, it's lovely! Where did you get it?

BIRCH: Blackpool junk shop. Under a pile of Edwardian
tennis racquets. Everything's here: Extreme Heat, Desert
Conditions, Tropical Sultry, Sunny Spells, Overcast, Blood
Warm, Bearable Cold, Bitter Cold, Arctic White Death…
pure poetry.

BUNNY: A Swiss Disselbaumer! 1766! Vintage. You lucky devil!
I must have it off you! How much d'you want for it?

BIRCH: I might swap for your Tramper and Taylor. But yours
doesn't work – and this does.

BUNNY: No self-respecting barometer works. Look at the
craft in this. The calligraphy of the facia! The winds puffing
out their cheeks! Lovely!

BIRCH: We will negotiate, over lunch some time.

BUNNY: (*Putting the barometer down on the desk.*) Now you're
more relaxed – tell me what's eating you.

BIRCH: I'll explain at the meeting.

BUNNY: Who else is coming?

BIRCH: The Mayor.

BUNNY: That awful man, Harvey?

BIRCH: Bunny, you know Harvey is now the Mayor, much
as you'd rather not believe it.

BUNNY: A few nights ago I had a wish-fulfilment dream. He
was beaten to death by power-station workers.

BIRCH: Behave yourself or you'll have Brenda to deal with.
(*Intercom buzzes. BIRCH listens.*)
The Mayor has no right to be early… No, I will not
discuss any other matter except the business of the special
meeting… Definitely not, tell him… Be firm. Don't let him
push you around!
(*HARVEY enters wearing a poppy. He heads straight for
BUNNY, holding out his hand.*)

HARVEY: My favourite politician. Like your outfit. As your
ideas get older, you seem to get younger.

BUNNY: (*Shaking his hand.*) Morning. We're in the middle of a
private conversation.

HARVEY: (*Picking up the barometer and giving it a tap.*)
Expecting a hurricane?

BIRCH: Please don't touch that! It's very valuable.

HARVEY: Pressure's going up, Town Clerk. (*Sits down.*) I was musing during the Remembrance Service – how long should we keep old wars in mind? How long after they were fought did people forget the patriotic wars we fought against the Romans, Angles, Saxons, Jutes, Vikings, Normans, French and Spanish? Did they have buttonholes for those? When will we mentally let go of the two World Wars? Can't go on with these for ever, can we? (*Puts his poppy in the waste-paper basket.*) I've never liked artificial flowers.

BUNNY: The ceremony means a lot to many people.

HARVEY: With things as they are, Mrs BL, couldn't we do with a remembrance service for the future?

BUNNY: Oh, do be quiet. Have a drink. Here, use my glass. (*She pours him a drink.*)

HARVEY: Quality bacteria in your saliva will do me a lot of good, Mrs BL.

BUNNY: Do me a favour – either give me my full title, or call me Bunny as if you were a friend. I don't like Mrs BL.

HARVEY: To a miner it means Blasting Licence. You've always had one of them. If there's a problem – blow it up. Oh, don't sulk. We know you'd go through hell for this town. Good to see you. Cheers! (*Knocks back the whisky.*) Is Sir Alphonse coming to the meeting? (*Holds the glass out for another.*) Nothing can be decided without him.

BIRCH: He will arrive at ten, Harvey – the time for which the meeting was called.

HARVEY: So you were having a little get-together with our parliamentary representative, purely social…climatic but not climactic.

BIRCH: That's correct.

HARVEY: Glad to hear you two are still so close. While we're on subtle power-plays – will you do something about my wife's chain now she's agreed to wear one?

BIRCH: Later, later.

BUNNY: Brenda is going to wear a bauble? She's becoming compliant?

HARVEY: Menopausal idleness of mind. Get a silver chain, Town Clerk. A simple, elegant design, not too heavy or ornate.

BIRCH: The one we've got has been acceptable to the wives of our mayors for over a hundred years.

HARVEY: Brenda has dress sense. She won't wear a necklace of little gilt rolls of lino. If you don't give her something stylish, at every function, on every photograph, she'll have that face. You know the one I mean.

BUNNY: We do, we do.

BIRCH: As a regalia alteration, it will have to go before the General Purposes Committee Protocol sub-committee… (*Looks at a diary.*) That meets only once a year.

HARVEY: Bring it forward.

BIRCH: It met last week. They broke the record for the shortest committee meeting of 1976. Three minutes dead.

HARVEY: Well, you call an emergency meeting and tell them my Brenda's frontage is the main agenda. I'm prepared to be a vacuous historical emblem. I'll stoop to being a gesture. But I won't compromise on what lies across my Brenda's bosom, where any god would rest, given half a chance.
(*INTERCOM buzzes.*)

BIRCH: Yes?

INTERCOM: Sir Alphonse is coming in. The whisky needs secreting.
(*BIRCH hurriedly puts the bottle and glasses away.*
BUNNY and HARVEY stand to attention as RODRIGUEZ
pushes SIR ALPHONSE in.)

SIR ALPHONSE: Morning all.

BUNNY: Good morning, Sir Alphonse.

BIRCH: Morning, sir.

HARVEY: Morning.

SIR ALPHONSE: Thank you, Rodriguez. Smell anything?

RODRIGUEZ: Malt whisky… Inner Hebrides…mmm… Mull…Tallisker, peat soaked in diesel…suggestion of gannet droppings.

BUNNY: Bang on. What an incredible nose.

SIR ALPHONSE: My intellectual and sensory mentor, this man. Put me over by the Mayor. The fumes are too strong this side.

(*RODRIGUEZ repositions the wheelchair.*)

Very moving ceremony, I thought. The Last Post always goes right through me (*He notices the poppy in the waste-paper basket and picks it out.*) Well, some unsentimental person doesn't waste much time.

BUNNY: Not me. I'm still wearing mine.

(*BIRCH fingers his poppy in his buttonhole, looking across at HARVEY.*)

SIR ALPHONSE: How impatient you are to move on, your worship. After the service I remained behind. When I was reading the lesson I noticed a strange verse in the first book of Esdras – chapter 13, verse 12. Perhaps you can help me understand? Give it to them, Rodriguez.

RODRIGUEZ: Women are strongest...

SIR ALPHONSE: Is that so, Bunny?

BUNNY: Well...in a manner of speaking...childbirth and all that.

RODRIGUEZ: Woman are strongest but Truth beareth away the victory.

SIR ALPHONSE: What can old Esdras have been thinking about? What had happened to the old prophet? Why write that down? Curious. By the way, why aren't you in the Freemasons, Mr Mayor?

HARVEY: Me? I'd never be seen de...

SIR ALPHONSE: Bunny, you should join the Lodge. England's future is in its women. Make use of the existing male infrastructures. You can do anything through the Masons.

BUNNY: Well, I can but offer myself...

SIR ALPHONSE: And you, Harvey – our fastidious symbol, our lost post-Stalin socialist saint caught in a web of capitalist sin. If not the Masons, what outfit should you join?

HARVEY: The Union of Abstractions.

SIR ALPHONSE: (*Laughs.*) Good, eh, Rodriguez?

BIRCH: Sir Alphonse, may we start the meeting?

(*Snap blackout and clash of cymbal.*
Spot on SIR ALPHONSE as he whirls his wheelchair round
to face KILROY, the bookseller, who is caught in a blue spot
of his own.)

SIR ALPHONSE: To bring pornography into a town of
decent, uncorrupted folk, is the murder of morality.

KILROY: Your honour, be fair, soft pornography...

SIR ALPHONSE: As magistrate, in passing sentence I shall
be most severe.

KILROY: Why be so serious about a joke? Bums and tits are
a scream.

SIR ALPHONSE: Of all commercial crimes, peddling filth is
the most disgusting and degrading.

KILROY: You can't blame people for their animal instincts.

SIR ALPHONSE: Be quiet!

KILROY: I have a right to speak.

SIR ALPHONSE: Go on, then – incriminate yourself further.

KILROY: People come into my bookshop to brighten up
their lives with books and mags. Innocent pleasures of the
imagination, popular since the Ancients. Without porn, the
existence of many solitary males would be lacklustre and
inert. Sexually lukewarm men find the inspiration to be
fathers through those pages. We're told there's a population
crisis, declining birth-rate, massive upsurge in oldies...

SIR ALPHONSE: Enough! You self-righteous wretch! Fined
three hundred pounds with fifty pounds costs. And think
yourself lucky.

(*SIR ALPHONSE swings the wheelchair away.*
Blackout.
Lights up on GROOT and SLINGER L looking at a document
together.)

SLINGER: Our twin town is in the north-west. It makes
heavy-duty textiles, floor-coverings, and a few other items.
Very old, very historical, linked to the Queen but she never
bothers to go there. There is a big castle, which is still used
as a prison. There are salmon in the river, and shrimps in
the sea.

GROOT: The pound sterling fell another two points against the deutschmark yesterday. Britain is in deep, deep trouble with the IMF.

SLINGER: So, to us, their floor coverings are cheaper by the day.

GROOT: Are the inhabitants of Rougerossbergh pleased to be linked to Kleine-und-Zeine in this way?

SLINGER: They say so.

GROOT: It took the government long enough to sort it out. Didn't we ask for somewhere in the south-east – a rich commuter town within striking distance of London?

SLINGER: Well, we've been told it must be Rougerossbergh.

GROOT: Get me all the facts you can about it. Everything you can find. Thirty years after the war ended, the British are beginning to realise that was the last time they won anything.

(*Blackout.*

Lights up on McALLISTER and STURGEON sampling.)

STURGEON: Our new vodka! What d'you reckon?

McALLISTER: It's red. Vodka isn't red.

STURGEON: It is when it's made from beetroot.

McALLISTER: I wondered what that aftertaste was.

STURGEON: We're calling it North Country Blunt.

McALLISTER: Bingo! Hey, that'll sell!

STURGEON: How about this: Get Down To Fundamentals With North Country Blunt. Good, eh?

McALLISTER: Like a sock on the jaw. Can I use that in the piece?

STURGEON: Just hold on for a few days. We've made an introductory discounted offer to distributors in our new twin town in Germany. If they take it up, I want to make as much initial news impact as possible.

McALLISTER: Is this the Kleine-Und-Zeine deal?

STURGEON: That's the one. It's near Hamburg. Big drinkers, the Hamburgers. But you can mention beforehand that we've already had success further east – sold a thousand bottles to the Moscow Armed Services Association.

McALLISTER: They'll drink anything, those Ruskies.
Hamburg, eh? Lot of vice in Hamburg.

STURGEON: So?

McALLISTER: Ceaseless working of the optic in the bars and
bordellos of the notorious Reeperbahn. Sex, debauchery,
bad behaviour, and North Country Blunt.

STURGEON: Mmmmm. Sounds tasty.

McALLISTER: It's what they're going for these days.
I think we'd better get started. (*Puts on an apron.*) This is a
wise move of yours.

STURGEON: Thanks for sponsoring me.

(*BIRCH enters, putting on apron.*)

BIRCH: Hello McAllister. Sorry I'm late. Everything well with
you, Sturgeon? Going great guns I hear. This won't take
long.

STURGEON: I hear you're off to Germany next week.

BIRCH: Indeed I am. A trip I'm looking forward to. I'll be
taking a trade delegation with me. The Germans have laid
on a private jet.

McALLISTER: Shows how seriously they're taking this twin-
town business, doesn't it?

BIRCH: There's quite a lot of room aboard – for the right
people.

STURGEON: It's a big market, Germany. Wonderful
opportunities. I went to Moscow, you know? Did well. Got
what I wanted – foot in the door. Cracked the Soviet trade
barrier.

BIRCH: I think we're ready to begin.

(*McALLISTER starts assembling pieces of a cardboard maze
on the floor.*)

Sturgeon, before we rehearse your initiation, d'you know
what you're doing?

STURGEON: I do.

BIRCH: Repeat after me: a man does not join the Masons in
order to get useful business contacts.

STURGEON: A man does not join the Freemasons in order
to get useful business contacts.

BIRCH: Tell me, what is Freemasonry?

STURGEON: Freemasonry is a science which comprehends the principles, practice and institutions of a secret brotherhood.

BIRCH: And again – what is Freemasonry?

STURGEON: Freemasonry is an art founded on the principle of geometry and directed to the service and convenience of mankind, also the cultivation and improvement of the human mind.

BIRCH: What is our common faith?

STURGEON: The Grand Lodge of England accepts the T.G.A.O.T.U.

BIRCH: Do you accept the T.G.A.O.T.U.?

STURGEON: I do.

McALLISTER: The right arm of the candidate is made bare. Roll up your sleeve to show you are ready to labour. In order the sex of the candidate may be distinguished beyond doubt, take down your trousers.
(*STURGEON takes down his trousers.*
BIRCH puts a hand on his genitals.)

BIRCH: The sex is male.

McALLISTER: Unbutton your shirt, exposing the left breast.
(*STURGEON complies.*)

BIRCH: At this point in the ceremony you will be pricked with the poignard.

McALLISTER: Roll your left trouser leg up above the knee, and put this slipper on your right foot.
(*STURGEON complies.*)

BIRCH: (*Leading him in a circle.*) In this manner, neither naked nor clothed, slipper-shod, the candidate will be led around the Lodge in this humble, halting posture to represent his seeming state of distress and poverty.

McALLISTER: (*Lighting a candle.*) Down on your hands and knees. You must go through the maze.
(*STURGEON complies as light fade down.*)

BIRCH: (*Taking the candle and handing it to STURGEON.*) Find your way through by this solitary light. It is a man in this world, guided by his principles.
(*STURGEON crawls on hands and knees through the maze with the candle.*)

> Don't get lost. Don't make any rash moves. Look out
> for blind alleys. Be cautious. Be prudent. Find the right
> turning. Avoid the wrong angle. While you struggle and
> blunder, the anthem will be sung:

BIRCH / McALLISTER: (*Sing.*)

> The world is in pain our secrets to gain
> And still let them wonder and gaze on,
> They ne-er can divine the word or the sign
> Of a free and accepted Mason.
> 'Tis this and 'tis that, they cannot tell what,
> Why so many great men of the nation,
> Should aprons put on and make themselves one
> With a free and accepted Mason.
> Great kings, dukes and lords have laid by their swords,
> Our mysteries to put a good grace on,
> And ne'er be ashamed to hear themselves named
> As a free and accepted Mason.

STURGEON: (*Still looking for the exit to the maze.*) Is this the
way to Germany?

> (*Blackout.*
> *Lights up on NELLIE in a white overall beside a tall, sheeted*
> *rectangle.*
> *SIR ALPHONSE, BIRCH, HARVEY, SHAND and BUNNY*
> *stand as a group.*)

NELLIE: May I begin, Sir Alphonse?

SIR ALPHONSE: Take it away, Nellie.

HARVEY: What have you got there? Let's have a peep.

NELLIE: Lady and gentlemen…

HARVEY: Not only the best designer Bourge Floor-Coverings
have ever had, but the best works convenor.

NELLIE: D'you mind, Mr Mayor? I'm trying to get the
unveiling under way.

HARVEY: Unveil! Unveil!

SIR ALPHONSE: Early carpet technology comes from the
East. Not only did they put them on the floor, the Persians
– they hung them on the walls as works of art.

NELLIE: Am I running this or are you, Sir Alphonse?

SIR ALPHONSE: I am silent, but bear in mind another point. The Bayeux Tapestry tells a story. Everyone loves a story.

NELLIE: Finished?

SIR ALPHONSE: As I said: I am silent.

NELLIE: We of the Research and Design Department have been working on this for seven years. We're very proud of it. A lot of thought has gone into it. Sir Alphonse's instructions were – make me a world-beater, and that's what we've done.

SIR ALPHONSE: You don't walk on a good story, you'll wear it out. You hang it up. Let's hear from our friend, Professor Shand of University Marketing Department. (*A projection onto the sheeted rectangle:* $MV + M' V' = PT$)

SHAND: Some things are more important than the universe. Einstein knew a lot about relativity but nothing about money. The purchasing power of the pound abroad has taken a nose-dive. We are trying to export goods to countries where they can make them cheaper. If they do buy them at our export prices, it can only be because they're British. There's an identifiable culture-cachet there, and it's worth something. By studying it, we can determine in absolute terms the value of our civilisation. If we have a similar article manufactured both here and in another country to the same quality, and ours is sold in that country at a premium over and above the locally manufactured article, that premium is the price put on our history. To put that concept in a broader context, we turn to my formula, the product of many years of cogitation. Let me explain: Where M is the currency in circulation, M' is the average volume demand for credit. V and V' are different aspects of the velocity of turnover and P is the index number of prices on a sliding scale. T is the total aggregate of goods and services exchanged. Even with its limitations, my formula goes a long way to identify factors in the economy that affect, directly or indirectly, all the factors balanced in the equation. This can lead to great success. A final caution: if the premium price of British goods in export markets is brought too close to parity with the product of foreign competitors, respect will be lost, followed by collapse of culture-cachet. This will lead to the accelerated decline of our civilisation, which is still, in spite of everything, the envy of the world.

(*Pause.*)

HARVEY: Well, who'd have thought it?

SIR ALPHONSE: I agree with the analysis. It backs up my own reading of the situation entirely.

HARVEY: The professor knows his onions.

SHAND: The solution to Britain's economic problems is to continue to insist on the superiority of British exports, and do what we know best!

(*Fanfare.*

NELLIE whips the sheets off the blank rectangle. A large box is rolled on. She lifts the lid.)

NELLIE: The Bourge Mural-Maker!

HARVEY: Well, isn't that ingenious!

NELLIE: In essence, a do-it-yourself wall-hanging carpet kit that brings owning a tapestry within range.

BUNNY: What a masterstroke!

NELLIE: I pick up a piece – a numbered detail of the picture I want to make. It is already impregnated with a special adhesive for this prepared surface. I hold the detail, so,

(*Demonstrating on the rectangle with a detail of a pair of feet.*)

I affix the numbered piece to the space numbered for it, then firmly, smoothing from the centre outwards to get rid of air bubbles, press it into place in the composition.

BUNNY: Ah, I see! It's a jigsaw!

SIR ALPHONSE: A combination of jigsaw and painting by numbers would be more accurate.

HARVEY: Are you aiming upmarket with this, Sir Alphonse?

SIR ALPHONSE: The opposite. This is a quality product for the masses. Go into the houses of the common man everywhere. Look at what's on the walls. Kitsch!

BUNNY: Ducks flying nowhere. Women with green faces.

NELLIE: Would you all like to help complete the picture now you've got the idea?

HARVEY: What fun! (*Takes a piece.*) I think I recognise these
hills. Isn't that Cawsey Pike?

SIR ALPHONSE: There speaks an observant man.

BUNNY: Imagine a whole family doing this together on
Christmas morning.

BIRCH: Can't fail, Sir Alphonse. They'll go mad for it.

SIR ALPHONSE: Thank you, Town Clerk. As I see it, a firm
could get its directors to make one for the board-room
while the workers make one for the canteen. Schools,
colleges and universities...churches...all kinds of groups
and societies...creatively it will bring people together.
They take pieces out of the box at random and stick them
number to number on the rectangle.

BUNNY: I've got some bare knees.

BIRCH: Are we in a garden?

SIR ALPHONSE: You are. Keep going.

BUNNY: An abdomen. In fact, two abdomens.

HARVEY: A snake's head. Beautiful handiwork. Or should
we call it a serpent, perhaps?

NELLIE: You're good at this.

BUNNY: Good Lord, more body parts. You've certainly
managed to capture the skin-tones very well.

HARVEY: Fruit, animals in the leaves, man and woman in a
state of innocence... Is that an angel's wing? I know where
we are!

RODRIGUEZ: The Garden of Eden.

SIR ALPHONSE: How quick you are, you two, at seeing
things whole when they are only half-completed. Yes, it's
going to be Paradise.

HARVEY: Come on. Let's have it finished.
(*They rapidly fill in the spaces. BUNNY and BIRCH are left
with the sexual parts of Adam and Eve in their hands.*)
No blushing. We're all grown up here, aren't we? Without
those pieces of the jigsaw, where would we be?

SIR ALPHONSE: Who are those two people, Nellie? They
have very individual faces. Were they modelled on real
persons?

HARVEY: Well, Adam reminds me of the Minister for
Overseas Trade after a body-building course...ah, I see

what you're up to…and the upper half of Eve could be based on Noreen from the Wagon and Horses. I've never seen the lower half because she's always behind the bar.

SIR ALPHONSE: And where are they? What's the actual place you used in the design?

RODRIGUEZ: Sir Alphonse, this is a fictional garden. They are fictional people in a fictional garden. Don't be over-specific.

SIR ALPHONSE: No, you skeptic – the garden exists. It is here. How could the concept exist if there was no reality to base it on?

RODRIGUEZ: A preposterous claim! We dream what we like!

SIR ALPHONSE: Our town is Paradise, or as close to it as any of you will ever get. And our ordinary people have it in them to be the parents of mankind.

RODRIGUEZ: Pooh, this is fantasy. Time for your pills.

SIR ALPHONSE: I love this land, dammit! When the world hangs this on its walls, we'll return to our innocence and start all over again…aah…

RODRIGUEZ: (*Giving him pills to take.*) These will ease your heart, but not your madness.

(*Strip music.*

NELLIE unbuttons her white overall. Underneath she wears three red Lancashire roses. SHAND sheds his cap and gown and is left with one bonnet-sized rose. He puts on a bowler, picks up an umbrella, and dances a routine with NELLIE.

SIR ALPHONSE and RODRIGUEZ exit.

GROOT and SLINGER sit at a nite-club table with BUNNY, HARVEY and BIRCH watching the act.)

GROOT: We are delighted to have you here as our guests in Kleine-Und-Zeine.

HARVEY: She's a fit piece.

SLINGER: Mr Harvey is obviously a connoisseur.

BIRCH: (*Producing a bottle of North Country Blunt from his briefcase.*) Might I make a contribution to these heart-warming celebrations of fraternal feeling? One of our local distillations, famed for its flavour and potency.

SLINGER: Ah, yes – the North Country Blunt. We have
　　heard of the reputation of this wonderful drink.

HARVEY: Above all things – to thyself beetroot.

SLINGER: *Kennst du das Land wo die Zitronen bluhn?*

BIRCH: Got you.

HARVEY: What's going on here?

SLINGER: You don't like Goethe?

　　(*BIRCH pours glasses of the red vodka.*)

BIRCH: Gentlemen, sophisticates might wonder why we
　　emulate the beverage of the Russian peasant.

GROOT: Not at all. Ten per cent unemployment. Chronically
　　bad industrial relations. The lowest productivity per head
　　of the Western world. In desperation you'll try anything.
　　I'm joking, of course.

BIRCH: There are wine lakes. There are butter mountains.
　　Our subsidized farmers have provided an *embarrass de
　　beetroot,* and we're doing something practical to shift it.
　　Cheers!

　　(*They knock back the vodka.*)

GROOT: *Mein Gott, das is absuleich!*

BIRCH: I thought you'd like it.

SLINGER: It is ironical, is it not, that the modern architecture
　　you have admired so much today on your visit was
　　made possible by the pin-point accuracy of RAF Bomber
　　Command. Without them we would be still living in our
　　medieval slums.

BIRCH: (*Pouring.*) Another?

HARVEY: My grandfather fought in the Great War. He
　　reckoned if the Germans and the British had got together
　　instead of fighting each other, they'd have conquered the
　　world.

GROOT: That's what our twinning will achieve, I believe.

SLINGER: You like my establishment?

BIRCH: It has style, Herr Slinger.

SLINGER: As does this nectar of the gods you have brought
　　us. (*Sips.*) We have read your proposals carefully.

BIRCH: Are you at all interested?

SLINGER: On a reciprocal basis.

BIRCH: Well, we're all ears.

GROOT: We are prepared to order two large scale Mural-
Makers – one for our Town Hall, and one for Herr
Slinger's emporium here. But we would like to order our
own subjects. Is that possible?

HARVEY: You don't fancy the Garden of Eden?

GROOT: We're more hard-headed over here. The war taught
us many things. One was to be suspicious of Paradise.

BIRCH: I'm sure something can be worked out.

GROOT: In return we would like assistance in marketing
the product of our prestige publishing company which
specialises in art books.

HARVEY: Tit for tat?

SLINGER: You have sea-traffic, a port on a tidal estuary
with a mixed bag of cargo – biddable customs officials,
local men you must know very well. Help us import a few
special books and magazines. The UK market would boom
for us if only we could get round your petty restrictions.
(*Knocks back the vodka.*) *Gesundheit!*

BIRCH: What d'you think, Mr Mayor?

HARVEY: (*Pours himself a glass and knocks it back.*) There,
moral sense anaesthetised, I can think. My nephew
Rodney is in the customs.

GROOT: There we are! Perfect! We will get North Country
Blunt into every bar, every liquor shop, every supermarket.
We will arrange a massive trade exhibition centred on the
Mural-Maker and encourage all our big institutions to have
one – the university, schools, banks…

BIRCH: You're asking us to corrupt public servants.

GROOT: Do you want to save the British economy or not?
Does your disorganised and dispirited council really care
about your little town? Perhaps you want a golden future
with no risks? Even as we speak, the pound is slipping
deeper into the *schmutz.*

HARVEY: We'll be making a come-back, sometime. The tide
will turn!

GROOT: But you will have to be afloat to benefit. How low
must you sink before you face reality? You've seen those
ancient ruins in the desert? Ghost towns! Is that what you
want to happen to your town?

BIRCH: We may be desperate, but we can't entertain such an idea.

(*Drum roll. Lights spin as another act begins at the nite-club.*
KLAUS and PIERS enter as English and German city gents.)

PIERS: I say, I say, I say – will you lend me five pounds?

KLAUS: Lend you five pounds? Lend you five pounds? Why should I lend you five pounds?

PIERS: I'll give you ten pounds back next week.

KLAUS: But you owe me two pounds from last week.

PIERS: If you lend me another five pounds I'll be able to give you your two pounds back and keep the other three pounds towards your ten pounds next week.

KLAUS: But you'll still owe me seven pounds.

PIERS: Alright, then lend me eight pounds on top of that.

KLAUS: Eight pounds? Why eight pounds?

PIERS: So I can pay you your two pounds and ten pounds and have a pound left over for myself.

KLAUS: So it's gone from five pounds to twelve pounds you want. I'm not sure I can afford it.

PIERS: Alright, let's not beat about the bush. Lend me an extra seven pounds more to sort things out.

KLAUS: Seven pounds more? If I lend you five pounds and eight pounds and seven pounds I won't have any money at all.

PIERS: Then I'll lend you five pounds.

KLAUS: Hold on. I'll end up owing you five pounds.

PIERS: Which is all I asked for in the first place.

KLAUS: Look, why don't I just give you the pound for yourself and we'll call it quits?

PIERS: A pleasure to do business with you, old chap.

(*PIERS and KLAUS exit.*)

GROOT: I'm sure you'll forgive our little joke. All in a spirit of fun. Upon reflection, are you prepared to give our proposal consideration?

BIRCH: Well, Mr Mayor? You're in this. What do you say?

HARVEY: (*Drunk.*) We have to believe in something, comrades, God knows. With me it comes down to RGE and GEGA.

SLINGER: RGE and GEGA? What is this?

BIRCH: What are you rambling about, man?

HARVEY: Rosy Glow Economics... Gives Everything Go-Ahead.

(*Falls face down on the table.*

Blackout.

Music over tannoy.

Sound of jet engines before take-off.

Lights up on HARVEY and BIRCH in two aircraft seats centre stage – both hung-over.

An air HOSTESS stands behind the seats.)

HARVEY: Could we have a drink?

HOSTESS: Service will start after take-off, sir. Please fasten your seat-belts and extinguish all cigarettes and smoking materials.

HARVEY: We're dying here.

HOSTESS: I will now demonstrate the use of the oxygen equipment which may be called into operation at high altitudes. Through an automatic system triggered by decreasing air pressure the oxygen hose and face mask will appear.

(*Two masks on snake hoses tumble down in front of BIRCH and HARVEY, they put them on and inhale.*)

Oxygen helps hangovers. The serpent has its uses.

(*The jet takes off. The oxygen masks are withdrawn. Music ceases.*)

HARVEY: Two large gin and tonics, please, love.

(*HOSTESS exits.*)

The strange thing is, before I became mayor I think you used to like me.

BIRCH: Self-disgust demotes everything – especially one's equals.

HARVEY: Is that how you see me?

BIRCH: You are more of a fool than I am, Harvey, but less of a servant.

HARVEY: Being mayor is servanthood without the salary.

BIRCH: Come on, you don't have a bad life.

HARVEY: I instinctively need people like you to approve of me. I can't help it. That's the whole problem with the

Party. It can't bring itself to hate people like you. We want
you to like us when, in fact, you should fear us.

BIRCH: That is a comical concept.

HARVEY: Why?

BIRCH: Because everyone of talent or ability aspires to our
condition.

(*The HOSTESS returns with drinks.*)

HARVEY: Let me do this. You can get the next one.

HOSTESS: Perfume, cigars, cigarettes, spirits, wrist-watches?

HARVEY: Might as well use my allowance. Tell me, angel,
how much am I allowed to take through without paying
duty?

HOSTESS: In a future golden age, if you are flying in from
a Common Market country. (*To the tune of Twelve Days
of Christmas.*) Twelve Rolex Oysters, Eleven crates of
brandy, Ten quarts of Cointreau, Nine thousand Gaulloise,
Eight Schemellpenick, Seven pints of Chanel, Six cases
champagne, F-i-v-e ju-gs of gin, Four hundred Cuban cee-
gars, Three Boxes Beaune, Two bags of dope and a West
German colour TV.

HARVEY: I'll have two hundred Senior Service for the wife.

HOSTESS: I'll bring it in a moment, sir. We are just going to
start the free film show.

(*Lights down.*

*HARVEY and BIRCH tip their seats back as film music starts
for PRIVATE EYE.*

PRIVATE EYE enters in slouch hat and mac.)

PRIVATE EYE: Got this call to meet this dame. She was
worried about her husband.

(*BRENDA enters.*)

BRENDA: He's been acting very strangely since he was made
the mayor.

PRIVATE EYE: The mayor, huh? That's big-time. What
kinda strange?

BRENDA: He doesn't know which way to turn.

PRIVATE EYE: Is he having a homosexual affair?

BRENDA: He's capable of anything at the moment – lost all
sense of values. He's sold out.

PRIVATE EYE: At what kinda price? Was it worth it?

BRENDA: The town is dying on its feet. All the dreams are business dreams.

PRIVATE EYE: Leave the guy. He's as jerk.

HARVEY: No, Brenda! Don't – (*Wakes from a dream.*) Oh, thank God. I was dreaming.

(*Blackout.*

Lights up on BIRCH standing beside his desk.

The intercom buzzes. BIRCH answers it.)

BIRCH: Have him come in.

(*KILROY enters.*)

This is purely a courtesy, Kilroy.

KILROY: You know my rates have been doubled.

BIRCH: There is a rates appeal board. It's a free service.

KILROY: I've been there, as you know.

BIRCH: I don't follow the fortunes of every shopkeeper.

KILROY: You're trying to shut me down.

BIRCH: No local authority would use the rates that way.

KILROY: The shops on either side haven't had an increase.

BIRCH: Ah, but you occupy a site opposite the new shopping precinct, a big advantage.

KILROY: So do they.

BIRCH: You have had a new manhole cover. The pavement is scheduled to be re-laid. All this has to be paid for.

KILROY: I'm not getting anywhere, am I?

BIRCH: Don't despair. Wait. Better times are ahead.

KILROY: Look, this is my last bookshop. I've tried four times. I love books. All kinds of books. Books about everything. But people are reading less. You have to get them through the door, grab their interest. It was only a dozen copies I got done for…

BIRCH: That's all water under the bridge.

KILROY: How was your German trip?

BIRCH: (*Pause.*) Useful, I'd say.

KILROY: *Kennst du das Land wo die Zitronen bluhn?* (*Pause.*) Do you know the land where the lemon trees flower, Town Clerk?

(*Pause. BIRCH stares at him.*

KILROY leans over and shakes BIRCH's hand.)

A little pressure on the first joint. You should have been informed. I'm here on special duties, brother. Reassess those rates. And that's from the top. (*Exits.*)

(*SIR ALPHONSE is wheeled on by RODRIGUEZ.*)

SIR ALPHONSE: Penny for them, Birch.

BIRCH: Sir Alphonse, I think I must resign.

SIR ALPHONSE: You return in triumph from your travels, the Germans in tow, good deals in your pocket, and you talk of resigning?

BIRCH: Those Germans are hard men.

SIR ALPHONSE: After what they've been through, wouldn't you be? Think of the reconstruction of German. It's a heart-warming story.

RODRIGUEZ: The creation is merciless. It is a reproductive mania. If there is a god, he doesn't care what is made, as long as it is made.

BIRCH: I find intrigue increasingly distasteful.

SIR ALPHONSE: We need you. Who else will save this town? There's you, there's me, and a few others who in their half-cock ways can lend a hand. Don't worry, we'll win through.

BIRCH: Why does it have to be so shabby, so mundane? Why must life be like the News of the World?

RODRIGUEZ: The good parts belong to truth alone. We are not included. Would you like dinner now, sir?

BOURGE: Yes. We'll have it here.

(*RODRIGUEZ exits.*)

BIRCH: It's not a simple matter.

SIR ALPHONSE: Human affairs form patterns. Over the years I've had the more interesting ones I've detected reproduced on my products.

BIRCH: You can understand why I feel so soiled by commerce?

SIR ALPHONSE: There are only two kinds of commercial people; buy cheap and sell dear – and creatives. The first is ignoble, the second, so close to God it's dangerous.

(*RODRIGUEZ enters with fish and chips wrapped in newspaper.*)

RODRIGUEZ: Salt and vinegar are already on. I hope the *patatas fritas* haven't gone limp and the fish have not been over-battered.

(*SIR ALPHONSE unwraps his fish and chips and gives RODRIGUEZ the newspaper. He smooths the paper out and reads.*)

SIR ALPHONSE: Dig in. *Buon appetito.*

RODRIGUEZ: Advertisements in the paper reek of despair. Here we have the personal column saturated in salt and vinegar like the face of Christ on the cross. Listen to this: Widowed greyhound-trainer seeks fast-moving partner. Serial bankrupt needs backers. News item: Oyster-farm owner swept out to sea holding glass of champagne. It goes on and on every day...tragic... remorseless...

SIR ALPHONSE: Go on, Rodriguez. You're helping the Town Clerk no end.

BIRCH: Mmm. Oh, yes, he certainly is.

RODRIGUEZ: The passion for destruction is also a creative passion. What offends also enlivens. Disgust is a stimulant. To be appalled is to be made ready for great redeeming thoughts.

(*RODRIGUEZ crumples the newspaper into a ball, then clears up after the fish and chips.*)

SIR ALPHONSE: Are you interested in desserts? I usually have a Mars bar.

BIRCH: I must be going, thank you all the same. And thank you, señor.

RODRIGUEZ: The worst will always happen. Why be surprised? (*Exits.*)

BIRCH: You are very fortunate in your manservant, Sir Alphonse. I feel I can go on with renewed heart.

SIR ALPHONSE: I pay him handsomely. He then gives it all to ETA, the Basque Separatist Movement. It's a tonic to live in the same house as someone who really knows how to waste money.

BIRCH: I'll show myself out. (*Pause.*) Must we have the second-hand bookseller on board?

SIR ALPHONSE: Let draw aside the clouds for a moment. By now you will have cottoned on that we're operating at a deeper level. Petty porn disguises a man of international importance within the brotherhood.

BIRCH: But you fined him in court!

SIR ALPHONSE: Show trial.

BIRCH: You told me to put up his rates!

SIR ALPHONSE: No better camouflage than persecution.

BIRCH: Then I'll have to put up with my misgivings, I suppose.

SIR ALPHONSE: Revel in them, rather. Enjoy the tensions, the polarities. Creativity works this way. You will see to it that those Germans have the time of their lives over here, won't you?

BIRCH: They won't forget their visit, I promise. After our talk, I'm fired up and ready to go. But I have to say, the mayor is going to be an encumbrance.

SIR ALPHONSE: Leave Harvey to me.

BIRCH: I will, gladly. By the way, did you know German war-widows receive four times the pensions of our war-widows?

SIR ALPHONSE: Of course. And they have four times as many.

BIRCH: How did they do it? Kleine-Und-Seine was completely flattened during the war.

SIR ALPHONSE: It takes a mind of extraordinary muscle to grasp economic truth.

BIRCH: It certainly does!

SIR ALPHONSE: People see into spiritual and existential affairs with much greater ease. The way money works is a better kept secret than the truth behind the Trinity.

BIRCH: Yes, I think you're right. I did have a very bad moment with our German friends when I realised that I, a man with a first class honours in law, a Mason and a Christian, was sitting in a bordello selling vodka made from beetroot and paving the way for pornography.

SIR ALPHONSE: That is adventure! Oh, the wonderful rumpus room of trade! Part of the soul's great pilgrimage towards solvency. My dear Town Clerk, you're a man of conscience and intellect but don't let prissy reservations get in your way. Take yourself off to bed, now, there's a good fellow – and rise refreshed!

BIRCH: Yes, Sir Alphonse, I will. Thank you for putting me right.

(*Lights fade as they both exit.*

Lights up on BUNNY in a frontstage spot L making a speech in the Commons.)

BUNNY: It may surprise the House that I do not support the proposal to further subsidize the heavy textile industry. Government aid and protection is not what's needed. Even though my constituency has suffered more than most from the recession, with unemployment presently at ten per cent, and industrial expansion a virtual impossibility due to lack of capital and weak performance in overseas markets, I believe we must trust to the power of British ingenuity unfettered by industrial welfarism. Sacrifice is needed. Vision is needed. A return to those values that made us the greatest mercantile nation on earth is needed. Give British workers a goal to struggle towards and they won't let you down. But do not offer them charity.

(*BUNNY exits and NELLIE takes over her spot frontstage.*)

NELLIE: Brothers, sisters, comrades, good news from the management. An order has been received from Germany for two Maxi Mural-Makers, with plenty more orders starting to appear in the pipe-line! So Sir Alphonse thinks we can delay the anticipated redundancies in the dyeing department and the hessian cutters can breathe a little easier. Now, the agenda for this meeting was originally much more negative – overtime, canteen deficiencies, work study timings – same old grievances. Can I drag down the new hope we have today with that boring stuff? Sir Alphonse says this is a new time, a breakthrough. We're on the move, at last! It's up to you but as your convenor hope means more to me – to be able to detect a brightness in your eyes, a lightness in your step. Those are my feelings. What do you say? Is it to be hope – or nit-picking disharmony? (*Pause. She smiles.*) I agree. It's only common sense. And now we'll have the lads in the works silver band give us a few upbeat favourites during the rest of our fifteen-minute lunch-break.

(*Silver band music.*

NELLIE sits down with a pack of sandwiches. As she eats, she weeps. A dole queue shuffles on to the music, then livens up, dancing off in high style with NELLIE.

On an upper level BIRCH sits wearing headphones, listening to Mahler.

As the dole queue exits, the music takes over, sombre and magnificent.

BIRCH is left alone in the thrall of Mahler. The music ends, shaking him. He takes the headphones off and screams.

Blackout. Lights up on SIR ALPHONSE fly-fishing L and HARVEY fishing with a float and worm R.

RODRIGUEZ stands by with a tackle-box, looking through artificial flies.)

RODRIGUEZ: Pheasant Tail. Blue Charm. Black Heron. Red Upright. Bloody Butcher.

SIR ALPHONSE: It's all that was needed. A start.

HARVEY: We had a lot of pride to swallow. Swallow it, we did. They're coming over expecting a lot.

SIR ALPHONSE: I knew they'd jump at it.

HARVEY: More than these trout are doing. When I was a lad, this river was teeming with them. What have we done with the world since we've had it? (*Pause.*) The war was still there. You could smell it.

SIR ALPHONSE: (*Offering his fly-rod.*) Here, try this.

HARVEY: Me flog the water? Never!

SIR ALPHONSE: It's a knack. Come on. You should learn. It might be useful.

HARVEY: (*Accepting the rod.*) You have a go at worming then.

SIR ALPHONSE: Oh, I know how to worm.

(*HARVEY attempts a cast.*)

HARVEY: I'll never get the hang of this.

SIR ALPHONSE: Slowly back until vertical, elbow tucked in, wrist and forearm stiff. Bring it over. You're a natural.

HARVEY: (*Practising.*) It's fishing, that's all. If you can do it, I can do it.

SIR ALPHONSE: (*With HARVEY's rod.*) Very good. Get further and further out. Excellent. Put a fresh worm on my hook, Rodriguez. This one isn't trying.

RODRIGUEZ: In the beginning was the worm, and the worm was with God. The worm corrupted the woman and she brought down the man.
(*HARVEY increases the tempo of his casting.*
The German nite-club band strikes up over amplifiers. NELLIE
as stripper in her three red roses catches the line.)
SIR ALPHONSE: You're on! You're on! Bring it in!
(*HARVEY reels in NELLIE.*
RODRIGUEZ stands L putting a worm on the hook.
A CUSTOMS OFFICER appears on an upper level reading
a magazine.
Blackout.)

End of Act One.

ACT TWO

A Council meeting.

HARVEY in his chain of office, NELLIE, BIRCH, STURGEON and KILROY stand behind a battery of klaxons, bells, kazoos, cymbals, drums – playing anything that will make a noise. McALLISTER stands by, scribbling notes for the newspaper. SIR ALPHONSE and RODRIGUEZ are in shadow L. The din dies down. Pause.

BIRCH: The point I'm trying to make is –
> (*HARVEY softly presses the rubber ball on the klaxon so it makes a plaintive sound.*)
> The cost of the reception for the Kleine-Und-Zeine delegation will be only three thousand two hundred pounds.
> (*Cacophony again. HARVEY holds up a hand.*)

HARVEY: It may sound a lot, but in real terms, it's very little.
> (*Cacophony.*)
> Cheap at the price!

BIRCH: From Germany we expand into Switzerland – the strongest currency in the world. It's well known the Swiss have nothing on their walls but cuckoo-clocks. We can change all that.

HARVEY: We'll need some creative suggestions from the Entertainments Committee. There'll have to be a show of some sort.

STURGEON: Wine and dine them. Get them on our side. Give them a laugh. Works wonders.

BIRCH: It's our only chance. Things look very bleak out there. Two more firms closed down last month.
> (*Muted tinkles, peeps and taps on the percussion.*)
> All those in favour say aye.

HARVEY: We must do what we can. So, let's bite on the bullet and say, aye-aye, aye-aye, aye-aye!
> (*General exit with Council instruments.*
> *SIR ALPHONSE is pushed out of the shadows by RODRIGUEZ.*)

SIR ALPHONSE: Your thoughts?

RODRIGUEZ: General Franco maintains the economy at slump-level because he doesn't like too much going on. Inside the everyday depression is a worse one waiting, he says, a giant. Without him, it will get out.

SIR ALPHONSE: Business cannot be democratic. No exchange of views ever won an empire.

RODRIGUEZ: War defines peace, but peace defines nothing – which is why I'm content to serve you.

SIR ALPHONSE: That sounds either insulting or interesting...do go on.

(*RODRIGUEZ pushes SIR ALPHONSE off R.*)

RODRIGUEZ: (*As they go.*) All thought collides at the crossroads of nowhere.

(*Lights up on HARVEY and BRENDA watching television.*)

HARVEY: Mastermind. What a concept. Who thought that up, I wonder? A teacher, I bet.

BRENDA: You should apply.

HARVEY: Special subject – tight-rope walkers in the Persian Empire. Poor Birch...what a tortured man he is. You know, I quite like him these days. We're like brothers in crime.

BRENDA: He doesn't like himself.

HARVEY: Somewhere, he's a good man gone wrong. Education probably screwed him up. It usually does.

BRENDA: How can you be a Liberal and under someone's thumb? If Sir Alphonse is paying Bunny Legge six thousand a year to represent his interests in Parliament, how much is he paying the Town Clerk?

HARVEY: Never mind him. What about me?

BRENDA: You wouldn't take his money, would you?

HARVEY: He wouldn't bother to offer me any.

BRENDA: Your unsuitability for office is what saves you.

HARVEY: I'm a political animal, Brenda. A domesticated political animal.

BRENDA: I'm worried about you. You're drinking far too much.

HARVEY: Buddha could help. Born 563 BC – died 483 BC. Courtesy of Jesus, time was counted backwards in those

days. Buddha says: don't get too involved. Distil the spirit
of the universe and fill your glass.

(*As they continue to watch television, NELLIE enters, upset, with
SIR ALPHONSE and RODRIGUEZ to frontstage.*)

NELLIE: I've never been so insulted in my life!

SIR ALPHONSE: Nellie, dear, I could take you into the
basement of the National Gallery and show you far worse
pictures.

NELLIE: There you are! You agree it's bad!

SIR ALPHONSE: All the most exciting pictures are kept in
the dark.

NELLIE: I won't do it! I will not design a Mural-Maker from
that thing you showed me.

SIR ALPHONSE: That thing, as you call it, is from the
mosaic floor of a Roman villa which belonged to the
emperor Tiberius. It is considered to be of great artistic
value.

NELLIE: It's filthy and perverted and I won't do it!

SIR ALPHONSE: Nellie, you have to leave Sunday School at
some time. Come on, get wise to what's happening in the
world. All those old inhibitions are melting away.

RODRIGUEZ: What's so special about certain functions of
the human body? Why be uptight about what is doomed
to obsolescence? Day by day, technology eats away at our
uniqueness and we get closer to robothood. Will high-
intelligence computers have genitalia? I doubt it.

SIR ALPHONSE: You hear what Rodriguez is saying, Nellie?
You must liberate yourself – become truly cultured, before
it's too late. How many years have you been working for
me? Fifteen? Twenty? From girlhood! Have I ever tried to
corrupt you?

RODRIGUEZ: Employment is corruption. Only the dead
have good jobs.

SIR ALPHONSE: Silence! That's not what I meant!

(*General exit.*

'Deutschland Über Alles' played by a silver band.

*Enter from L HARVEY in his chain of office with BRENDA
and BIRCH, from R SLINGER and GROOT.*

*They advance, hands outstretched, and shake. McALLISTER
stands by making knots.)*

BRENDA: He's fresh. Gave me a little pressure there.

HARVEY: He thinks you're something you can't be. In his
enthusiasm he forgets you're not a man. You wouldn't
understand, love.

BIRCH: *(Aside.)* Time for your speech of welcome, Mr Mayor.

HARVEY: Old butties, aa'll keep this verra lile. You're in
forra reet gradely do. Worra piss-up this'll be.

GROOT: Excuse me? I thought my English was good but…

HARVEY: The international language of commerce and
trade, tha' knows! Aaa'll shurrup now and gi' thee floor.
Your turn, Herr Slinger!

SLINGER: *(From notes.)* My English friends, it gives me great
pleasure to be amongst you. Watching at your children
coming home from school, we were struck in an emotional
way by the common ancestry between us – those intrepid
men and women who sailed across the Narrow Seas in
cow-hide canoes to found the first colonies of the Germanic
peoples in these islands. Beneath where I stand today
you will find the imprint of the Angle, the Saxon and the
Jute. Now we, cousins in blood of this great heritage, are
friends again and working together. I declare this geriatrics
home open, compliment the economy-style architecture,
and admire the view overlooking the well-filled cemetery.
Thank you.

BIRCH: Shall we move on? You have a very full diary today.
Our Member of Parliament is waiting at the boardroom of
Bourge Floor-Coverings.

(GROOT and SLINGER exit with HARVEY and BRENDA.)

McALLISTER: Fancy bringing up the Dark Ages! What do
they think they're up to?

BIRCH: Why shouldn't they indulge in a little historical
whimsey? We live off replays of the Normandy Landings.
Without the last war cinema and television would run out
of stories long ago.

McALLISTER: Not everyone's pleased with this twinning
business, you know, Town Clerk. The British Legion has
shut its bar in a gesture of disapproval.

BIRCH: If you want to help your home town enter a period of prosperity, don't print news like that.

McALLISTER: Any plans to twin with the Japanese? That'll really get them going!

BIRCH: These few days must go smoothly. We must be perfect hosts.

McALLISTER: I'd better scoot along to the reception.

BIRCH: It will be a great success. Bear that it mind.

McALLISTER: Oh, I will. I know I will.

(*Blackout.*

Lights up on a cocktail party with background calypso music on the upper level.

BUNNY, HARVEY, BRENDA, McALLISTER, GROOT, SLINGER hold glasses of North Country Blunt full of bits and pieces.

STURGEON works a shaker.)

BUNNY: And what name have you given your new cocktail, Mr Sturgeon?

STURGEON: Morecambe Bay Sunset.

BUNNY: Jolly good.

GROOT: A brave sight!

HARVEY: Are we allowed to clear the undergrowth?

STURGEON: If you can bear to drink it through the dressing, the experience will be richer.

HARVEY: The whale, you know, and various sharks, are fitted with a strainer of baleen that sifts out the minute sea-life on which these monsters feed. Where is Sir Alphonse, by the way?

BUNNY: (*To McALLISTER.*) The Mayor's drunk already and we've barely started.

(*SIR ALPHONSE enters with RODRIGUEZ.*)

HARVEY: Ah, the Great White Shark swims through the shallows shouldering aside the sardines.

SIR ALPHONSE: Not bad. Out-alliterate him for me, Rodriguez.

RODRIGUEZ: The maudlin, emasculated mayor, chronically in his cups, imagines his wit to be wonderful.

HARVEY: Ouch! Oh, ouch-ouch-ouch!

SIR ALPHONSE: You're not letting yourself go with your customary Iberian verve, Rodriguez! How about the pent-up prattling of piss-artists is a pain in the posterior? (*To GROOT and SLINGER.*) Games we English play with our language, gentlemen. It keeps us on our toes. How are you? So glad to meet up. (*Shakes hands.*) I hope you are being well looked after?

HARVEY: It's the happiest day of their lives, isn't it lads?

BUNNY: (*To HARVEY.*) This is an official reception! Please behave! You're ruining everything!

STURGEON: Can't we get rid of him?

BUNNY: (*To BRENDA.*) You're his wife! Do something!

BRENDA: I'm the wife of the man, not the mayor.

BUNNY: Surely you have some influence.

HARVEY: Let's play Snakebite with North Country Blunt. I need salt and lemons. Any around? What kind of a party doesn't have salt and lemons?

BRENDA: Never mind the lemons. Give your speech, love. Back pocket.

HARVEY: Here we are. Thanks, Brenda. (*Reads.*) Not long ago I stood ruminating upon the Siegried Line, wondering why the German military engineers had based their design on the fortifications of the ancient Greek colony in Syracuse… (*Throws up into his mayoral hat.*)

BUNNY: This is sheer attention seeking!

BIRCH: (*Aside.*) Take over Bunny. We'll laugh it off.

BUNNY: I can assure our guests that without a stable society built upon a bedrock of shared values, such fooling as this would be neither possible nor tolerated. Readiness to appear more stupid than one is makes up part of our complex national humour, for which we are famous and in which we rejoice.

HARVEY: Winston Churchill often threw up into his bowler. Do we need nations any more, my brothers?

BUNNY: This is impossible. Sir Alphonse, I appeal to you…

SIR ALPHONSE: Oh, don't be so easily embarrassed. I don't think our guests are at all put out. A man may get drunk when he pleases, if the cause is right. Correct, gentlemen?

GROOT: But of course. If Hitler had taken a drink now and then like Winston Churchill, things might have turned out differently.

SIR ALPHONSE: The Mayor has his own genius. His heart is good.

HARVEY: Before you explain me away completely, Sir Alphonse, I do have a final paragraph in my carefully prepared speech alluding to the time I was shot down over Aachen and taken into the basement of the old post office. It makes me quirky to recall the SS man who dealt with me...very quirky... D'you mind me being quirky? It's my lack of toenails makes me walk this way.

SLINGER: The SS? My friend, if only I could undo your pain...

GROOT: Monsters! In my own family we suffered.

HARVEY: What can I do to please you?

SLINGER: How can we expect that terrible war to fade from memory in a mere thirty years? It will take a hundred! Maybe a thousand! It wouldn't surprise me if it was never forgotten at all.

SIR ALPHONSE: Nellie, this is a perfect moment to show the design.

(*A handclasp design is projected. A man being throttled has been roughly sketched in between the hands as a joke.*)

SIR ALPHONSE: This is sabotage.

NELLIE: Nothing to do with me.

GROOT: More buffoonery. Very good. This kind of expressionism suits us very well. We're very happy here.

(*HARVEY takes down his trousers and sings 'The Evening Star' from Tannhauser.*
Blackout.
Lights up on BIRCH and BUNNY in the aftermath of the party.
GROOT and SLINGER are nearby.)

BIRCH: Well, how did it go? Sorry I couldn't get here till now. I've been checking on the arrangements for the banquet tonight. The caterers got into a panic.

BUNNY: We needed your firm hand. Disaster.

BIRCH: Harvey?

BUNNY: He was drunk before he arrived, made a very
embarrassing speech and vandalized Sir Alphonse's
presentation.

GROOT: Madam, excuse me. I could not help overhearing.
We were not embarrassed. The Mayor is the kind of man
we understand. Lots of people in the ruins of post-war
Germany felt and drank like he does.

BIRCH: Herr Groot, I'm so sorry. I wanted this to be a happy
occasion.

GROOT: No need to be sorry. Maybe I'll ask the Mayor
to join my family at a spa town we visit every year…
somewhere he can purge himself.

BIRCH: Would you gentlemen like to return to your hotel for
a rest and a chance to clean up before this evening?

SLINGER: We are quite rested. We thought we might take
a stroll by the river to cast an eye over the very fine old
Customs House mentioned in the guidebook?

GROOT: We are both very charmed by old buildings of
character. May we take this liberty?

BIRCH: Of course. I'll call for you at the hotel at seven forty-
five. That should give you plenty of time.
(*GROOT and SLINGER bow and exit.*
Pause.)
Damn Harvey.

BUNNY: The man is completely unsuited for any kind of
public office.

BIRCH: He's not the only one. What must they think of us?

BUNNY: You handled that very well.

BIRCH: No, I must get out. He doesn't know it, but I
recognise Herr Slinger. I was with the Army legal
department. We prosecuted him and his father for black
marketeering. Not a great crime in Berlin at that time.

BUNNY: Oh. Well, I suppose many people did things in
the war they'd rather not reveal. I believe the present
American Secretary of State was the uncrowned king of the
Bavarian underworld.

BIRCH: Cloudy or Fair, Bunny?

BUNNY: Cloudy or Fair. This is the world we're in, Frank.

(*BIRCH and BUNNY exit R.*

GROOT and SLINGER in coats and hats enter L to the quayside.)

GROOT: (*Reading from a guidebook.*) Perhaps the most interesting and impressive edifice after the unvisitable castle, bracket it is still used as a grade B prison close bracket, is the Old Customs House on Saint Cuthbert's Quay, still in use after two hundred and fifty years.

SLINGER: A very nice old building. If I was a Customs Officer I'd be happy here.

(*KILROY enters.*)

KILROY: Welcome, brothers. Well met.

SLINGER: (*Shaking hands.*) Ah, Master Kilroy.

(*GROOT also shakes hands with KILROY.*)

KILROY: All set?

SLINGER: Tonight's tide, at about eight.

GROOT: We will be at the banquet in the Town Hall.

SLINGER: The consignment should be distributed tonight.

KILROY: That's all tied up.

GROOT: Maximum distribution throughout. Every outlet available. Keep your people working round the clock. We'd better get back to the hotel.

KILROY: Good luck, brothers.

GROOT: Good organisation is better. *Auf wiedersehen.*

(*They exit.*

Lights up on BRENDA and HARVEY getting ready for the banquet.)

BRENDA: Just remember when the indignation starts boiling up again – two more weeks and you're out. No more chains, no more silly hats, no more speeches.

HARVEY: But there's a job to do. I'm a walking cry for help, Brenda. There must be another way than the wearing of masks. D'you know why the actors in the old Greek drama wore masks?

BRENDA: Pass.

HARVEY: So the gods wouldn't know they were pretending to be something they weren't.

BRENDA: You'd think the gods would see through that one.

HARVEY: Be sure to sit next to me. I must have you near, Brenda.

BRENDA: I promise. Come on. You look fine. The come-back kid.

HARVEY: The way they look at me when I make an entrance after I've made another balls-up says it's all worthwhile. That mixture of pity, contempt and anticipation really gets through to me – matters more than respect or affection. How can that be?

BRENDA: Pass.

(*Blackout*

Lights up on the banquet set on the upper level.

GROOT and SLINGER are guests of honour. HARVEY and BRENDA sit on L side of them, BIRCH and BUNNY on the R. SIR ALPHONSE and RODRIGUEZ are at one end, STURGEON and McALLISTER on the other.

As the lights come up, a CLOG-DANCER enters with a 2' x 2' wooden board, puts it centre stage and performs on it.

Applause at the end.

The CLOG-DANCER exits.)

GROOT: Oh, those rhythms! Life itself!

SLINGER: So controlled, so full of verve!

RODRIGUEZ: Honoured guests, ladies and gentlemen...

(*He stands on the clog-dancer's board.*) As a migrant-worker, dependent on the hospitality of Britain, as our guests are, I have been appointed to make the speech of welcome in place of the Mayor who is indisposed.

HARVEY: What's this? Nobody told me.

SIR ALPHONSE: Be quiet, Harvey. You've had your say. Continue, Rodriguez.

RODRIGUEZ: Courtesy of the clog-dancer, Sam, whose minimalist artistry you have just enjoyed, we have been taken into the austere soul of the North. It is nothing fancy or overblown. Although tightly squeezed between class-barriers, it always manages to make its point. Rat-at-tat, rat-at-tat. As a democrat and a pilgrim I went to Speakers Corner in Hyde Park. This shrine of parliamentary freedom stands in the shadow of the Great War memorial to the Machine-Gun Corps. Rat-at-tat! Rat-at-tat! Rat-at-tat! On the plinth it says, 'Saul slew his thousands but David his tens of thousands.' How glorious! (*Does slow flamenco steps.*) Aha! Rat-at-tat, rat-at-tat! In my country machine-guns need no memorial. They are everywhere. (*Does Bavarian thigh-slapping dance.*) Your countryfolk in their famous leather gear! Rat-at-tat! Rat-at-tat! Everywhere you go in the world, there is smite, beat, clout, knock, hit, thump! (*Dances furiously.*) We are all knocking on the door, the same door, with our bangs and explosions and blasts and detonations –

GROOT: Friendships and co-operations!

RODRIGUEZ: Refusing to be overlooked! Insisting on our rights!

SIR ALPHONSE: Well said, Rodriguez!

RODRIGUEZ: Hammering on the doors of happiness!

BUNNY: Oh, how true! How true!

STURGEON: He makes you think, I'll say that for him.

HARVEY: The lad puts me to shame. I never noticed that memorial next to Speakers Corner. Says everything. Doesn't it? Those orators might as well shut up and go home.

RODRIGUEZ: I will leave you with this thought. While you embrace each other in a new spirit of brotherhood, hatred set aside, one old man in Madrid has been able, single-handed, to keep my people locked in war for forty years, a war on ice, a frozen war. Watch out for these old men. Starve them of power. When you find one – rat-at-tat! Rat-at-tat!

SIR ALPHONSE: Thank you, Rodriguez. You've given us a lot to think about. Now, a toast! Common humanity!

HARVEY: Can't argue with that. Common humanity! And, by God, it is common! Common as muck!
(*HARVEY slides under the table.*
Pause.
GROOT stands up.)

GROOT: This hiatus created by your English good humour is as good a time as any for a stranger to make his thanks, and, with your permission, add a few observations. In my country we do not waste these formal occasions on niceties but use them to make serious philosophical points. The heavy drinking of the English is legendary. It is good of the Mayor to be so honest about it. That is refreshing. I cannot remember any anthropological theory being put forward as to the cause of this national habit. However, I have my own opinion. A thousand years ago the Angles, Saxons and Jutes came here and were separated from their Germanic tribal rootstock. They became homesick and this created a special melancholy that even to this day can only be appeased by drink. I will now hand you over to my colleague, Herr Slinger, who has further remarks.

(*GROOT sits down to a smattering of applause.*
SLINGER stands up.)

SLINGER: Why should the English be left out in the cold when the fire in the Germanic hearth is still burning? If it's brotherhood you need and a simple political move can cure a thousand-year-old malady of the spirit, let's think what can be done. Re-unfication! Let's say it! Your monarchy is already German and can be easily absorbed… your favourite composer is Handel… The Welsh, the Irish and the Scots will be only too happy to go their own ways… This re-amalgamation of the English and Germans won't take much to achieve…

(*A CUSTOMS OFFICER enters with a parcel and waves at HARVEY.*)

CUSTOMS OFFICER: My uncle asked to see these the moment they arrived.

HARVEY: (*Rising from under the table.*) Hello, Rodney! Is that the pornography I asked you to look out for?

CUSTOMS OFFICER: Some might call it that, uncle. It's a pamphlet inciting British workers to destroy capitalism under lurid covers.

HARVEY: Oh, lie upon lie, Groot unt Slinger! You couldn't even keep a dirty deal!

BIRCH: Quiet, Harvey. This was arranged through the auspices of the order.

SLINGER: Yes, Town Clerk, but the order has changed.

GROOT: We have deceived you, but with a good heart. You came over to visit us by special plane, you went back by special plane. It's a long time since you were in Germany.

SLINGER: You see, comrades, there are two Hamburgs – one in the West, and on in the East, near Leipzig. By a fortuitous bureaucratic error in your Department of Overseas Trade and Industry, the town you're twinned with is the one in the East.

BUNNY: A communist country! (*Screams and faints.*)

BIRCH: Christ almighty, Sir Alphonse, what are we going to do?

SIR ALPHONSE: The pamphlets are being distributed to every household. One fact it hammers out. Tell them, Rodriguez.

RODRIGUEZ: Capitalism is dead. Long live the Republic! (*Crowd noises off.*)

SIR ALPHONSE: Ah, the electrifying prose is doing its work. Go and check for me, Rodriguez. See what's going on and report back.

(*RODRIGUEZ exits.*)

HARVEY: I'm trying to work out how many causes you're traitor to, Sir Alphonse. It must be a world record.

SIR ALPHONSE: Not to the cause of sincere conversion.

BUNNY: (*Coming round.*) I don't feel very well. Frank, darling, please take me home… I had this nightmare…

SIR ALPHONSE: Why resist the irresistible? Once I recognised my own corruption, it was easy to accept ten million deutschmarks at the present rate of exchange and become a good Marxist.

BIRCH: But we arranged this through the Freemasons!

SIR ALPHONSE: Any good Mason will feel perfectly at home in the Communist Party. The structure is identical. Secrets. Cells. Paranoia. Infiltration into the seats of power.

CUSTOMS OFFICER: I have to say, uncle, the pamphlet's persuaded me. It's got the forecast for the retail price index for 1977. I won't be able to pay my mortgage if things go on as they are. £11.50 for a pint of mild!

SLINGER: Litre.

CUSTOMS OFFICER: Alright, litre...two pints of mild! Even so, that's £5.25 for a pint!

SIR ALPHONSE: Don't worry. It's our intention to withdraw from the international money market for a while, until things settle down.

BUNNY: Oh, God, that this should happen in my constituency! You of all people, Sir Alphonse, my guide and mentor!

SIR ALPHONSE: Bunny, I advise you to declare for the rebels. There'll be plenty of work for bossy top-notch women like you.

STURGEON: I declare for the rebels! I'm on your side, Sir Alphonse. I've heard enough to convince me.

McALLISTER: I place my newspaper at your disposal. Give me the information and I'll get it out to the people. (*RODRIGUEZ enters.*)

RODRIGUEZ: The police have said yes. The fire-brigade have said yes. The vagrants in the square have said yes. The small shopkeepers have said yes. The prison warders have said yes. But all the traffic-wardens were shot before they could say yes.

CUSTOMS OFFICER: Don't forget H M Customs and Excise. They definitely say yes.

SIR ALPHONSE: Excellent. Don't bother to ask at the university. They'll say perhaps.

SHAND: Not necessarily. It's possible to argue that all political systems are mere surface rind. The British worker will be eating the same number of chips whatever happens.

SIR ALPHONSE: The banquet is cancelled. Everything is cancelled. What do you say, Birch? Are you one of us?

BIRCH: It's long been my dream to have a little shop selling nothing but barometers. I think the time has come, if you'll allow me.

GROOT: Time does not matter in the perfect state.

BIRCH: Of course. If time does not pass, the state does not wither. You'll never have to keep your promises.

BUNNY: Oh, Frank, how can you talk to them? We should attack them! Kick them! (*Lashes out.*) How dare you interfere in our affairs! This is a sovereign nation under God! (*She is restrained.*) I hate you! I do!

SIR ALPHONSE: Bunny, I fear that you and the Town Clerk and the Mayor will not be able to make the commitment the revolution requires. Take them away. We'll deal with them in the morning.

(*STURGEON and McALLISTER start to lead them off with the help of the CUSTOMS OFFICER and SHAND.*)

HARVEY: Brenda will join, won't you love? I'd like you to do that for me. Give the new system a chance.

SIR ALPHONSE: Well, Brenda? What is it to be? You're still an attractive woman. Another man will come along. It's not too late for children…one life ends, a new one begins…

(*A huge explosion.*)

My own factory. I ask you to witness the sacrifice. An end is always the cost of a new beginning.

(*Blackout.*)

The End.